THE VOICES OF RIVERS

THE

VOICES

OF

RIVERS

Reflections on Places Wild and Almost Wild

MATTHEW DICKERSON

WAYFARER BOOKS
WWW.WAYFARERBOOKS.ORG

Published in 2019 by Homebound Publications
Published in 2024 by Wayfarer Books
Cover & Interior Designed by Connor Wolfe
Interior Photos © by Matthew Dickerson.
Cover Photo © Robert Zunikoff
978-1-947003-41-5 First edition
978-1-965320-25-9 Second edition

PO Box 1601, Northampton, MA 01060

wayfarer@homeboundpublications.com

WAYFARERBOOKS.ORG

For Willard Dickerson, Jr. and Clara May Dickerson, who together instilled in me from my earliest years a love of both nature and literature: the flow of rivers and the flow of a well-told narrative: the stirring of my imagination when I come around a bend in a wooded stream and see a small cascade tumbling over a mossy ledge or when I turn a page in a story and am momentarily transported into the scene through the eyes of the narrator.

———————

ACKNOWLEDGMENTS

My deepest thanks are due to my wife Deborah, who for more than thirty years has supported my trips to wild places—often joining me, especially when a canoe is involved. Thanks also to: Thomas, Mark, Peter, and Israel for accompanying me on trips, and keeping me humble; Ted, Susie, Brad, and Michael for introducing me to some beautiful places in Alaska, and for years of adventures in Maine; Jody and Thanh for adventures together at the Allagash, Bryant Pond, and elsewhere; and my good friend Dave O'Hara for joining me on several excursions to Alaska and Maine, and for putting up with me co-writing three books, and to Christina O'Hara for sending her husband off into the wild with me.

Additional thanks to several individuals and organizations who helped make this book possible and enjoyable. I'm deeply grateful to Glen Alsworth Jr.—and the guides, pilots, and staff at the Farm Lodge and Lake Clark Air—for sharing knowledge and hospitality, for keeping me safe in the air, on the ground, and atop the water (and for teaching me the important hand signals for when I spot an elephant.) Thanks to Yuki Hu, Julia Kendrick, Andrew Ackerman, and Phil and Rob Brodersen for helping me tell stories about cutthroat trout in Wyoming.

Thanks to John Ceballos, Christopher Downs, Jessica Kusky, Daniel Lombardi, Ginger Rigdon, and the Glacier National Park staff and volunteers who worked with me during my artist residency and generously shared their time with me; also USGS biologists in Glacier National Park Clint Muhlfeld and Joe

Giersch; wrangler Rob and *Swan Mountain Outfitters*; guides Blake and Mark at *Glacier Anglers*. Thanks to Bruce Connery, Brian Henkel (with Wild Acadia), Alexa Pezzano, Kathie Petri, Katie Anton, Anastasia Roy, and all the staff at Acadia National Park and the Schoodic Institute for helping make my artist residency so fruitful; John Branson, Lucas Westcott, and Dan Young and all the Lake Clark NP&P staff for sharing valuable time during my visits in 2015 and 2017; the U.S. Forest Service, especially fisheries biologists Shawn Anderson (Shoshone NF) and Matt Anderson (Bridger-Teton NF), for helping me understand and appreciate the importance of native cutthroat trout in Wyoming and the Rocky Mountain west, and of work to restore and protect their habitat; the Appalachian Mountain Club and the staff at Little Lyford, Gorman Chairback, and Medawisla Lodges for hospitality and important conservation work.

And, last, but not least, I'm grateful to Middlebury College for generous support of my research, writing, and story-telling through faculty professional development and digital liberal arts initiative funds, for making it possible for me to teach in Alaska in the summer of 2015 in the innovative off-campus summer study, and for the use of equipment including cameras for the air, the ground, and under the water. Middlebury College is not just an institution, but a collection of great people. Thanks especially to Lynn Dunton, Suzanne Gurland, Bill Koulopoulos, Andi Lloyd, Jason Mittell, Ethan Murphy, Jim Ralph, Heather Stafford, and Catherine Wright.

CONTENTS

Acknowledgments

About the Author
About the Press

PROLOGUE
The Sound of a Bittern

Bridger-Teton National Forest
and the Allagash Wilderness Waterway

"Loot galoot."

I lifted my head and looked for the source of the sound. I was sitting on a hill overlooking La Barge Creek in Wyoming's Bridger-Teton National Forest, thinking and writing about the importance of native trout, clean water, and the preservation of public lands. From somewhere in the streamside meadow below I heard the familiar bird call again. "Loot galoot." To this day, that distinctive mysterious call propels me back to May of 1972 and a childhood visit to Maine's Allagash Wilderness Waterway when I first heard the American Bittern—and mistook the sound for a monstrous bullfrog hidden in the shoreline reeds. That moment forever shaped my imagination and love of wild places, especially rivers.

It was just a few weeks shy of my 9th birthday. My father had deemed me old enough for my first wilderness camping experience. He had already taken both my older brothers to the Allagash twice, leaving me at home to imagine all the fun they were having without me. A ten-hour drive north through the forested mountains of western Maine, across flat farmland of southern Quebec, and then back over the border across the St John River into the North Maine Woods heightened my anticipation. I still recall driving round the final bend, after creeping and bouncing the last forty miles on gravel lumber roads, and seeing the great Allagash River open up before me. Though I didn't tell my father, I felt a little disappointed by that first view. The narrows known as Thoroughfare between Umsaskis and Long Lakes did not look spectacular. It was not Alaska or Glacier National Park; no majestic peaks or thundering waterfalls decorated the background. The slow, lazy, current and bushy shoreline struck my eight-year-old imagination as nondescript. Yet I would come to love that big, quiet, beautiful, and wild place like no other on earth. For the next thirty-some years I would make an annual pilgrimage there with my father, sometimes my brothers or other friends, and later my own sons. Though wonderful fishing for wild native brook trout was part of the allure, my love and desire to keep returning was also fostered in large part by the bittern and other birds that provided a soundtrack for my childhood.

The soundtrack is still with me. The Allagash was the first place I ever heard loons. Their mournful eerie cries echoed across the water and filled the night, lulling me to sleep, or sometimes waking me up. I thought they were wolves until my father corrected me. Wilson's snipes added to the soundtrack. We usually heard the winnowing males before we saw them. I'd stop what I was doing and gaze into the sky until I spotted the male repeatedly climbing slowly in the sky and then plunging into his dive. A bird that made a mating call with its wings fascinated me almost as much as one that sounded like a bullfrog.

The Allagash also introduced me to osprey. Their shrill peep seemed small and undignified for such a majestic raptor, but their dramatic dives more than made up for it. I delighted when I saw one hover in imitation of an overgrown hummingbird, fold its wings, and plummet into the river—sometimes in water shallow enough for my eight-year-old self to have waded—exploding with a tremendous splash. If the bird was lucky and skillful, we'd watch it labor back up to a shoreline perch with a fish in its talons. I thought their fishing method was way cooler than mine.

We heard plenty of geese and ducks, too, their wingtips slapping the water in a hurried take-off if we came too close. The slapping often mingled with annoyed quacks or honks as they rocketed away just above the line of bushes, making me feel bad for disturbing their quiet afternoon. Still, it was the American bittern I most associated with those visits. "Loot galoot. Loot galoot". Every morning and evening when the lake was quiet, I'd hear them in the reeds nearby. "Loot galoot." I spent five years looking before I actually saw one. Over time, however, I learned to spot them standing perfectly still, neck and beak pointed skyward, camouflaged to match the lakeside grasses. Maybe that gift of hiding in plain sight was why their calls sparked a sense of wonder.

Many more years passed before I learned more about this river that had captured my imagination. In 1966, six years before my first visit, the state of Maine established the Allagash Wilderness Waterway to protect an important but increasingly threatened ecosystem. In 1970, the National Wild and Scenic River System provided additional federal protection. The importance of these acts may be best understood by a sharp contrast. In 1972, the year of my first visit to the Allagash, Maine's Androscoggin River was listed by *Time Magazine* as one of the ten filthiest rivers in the country. I was familiar with that river. A big oxbow in the ski town of Bethel where the Androscoggin turned briefly from east to north lay only a half-dozen miles from the village of Bryant Pond where I went to kindergarten. Lumber mills used the Androscoggin to flush out toxic chemicals, and several towns did the same with raw sewage. I wouldn't have put a canoe in that water, let along swam, waded or fished in it.

Though it may have been an extreme, the Androscoggin was far from unique. Two lumber mills sat on the shores of Bryant Pond, in the town of the same name where my family briefly lived. We looked out from our home across a small cove at one of the mills. Until a few years earlier, that mill had used the lake to store logs. Floating logs down rivers and storing them in lakes was common practice despite the damage it did to the lacustrine and fluvial ecosystems. I also read that lumberjacks in northern Maine used to pour oil into streams to kill black flies, apparently unconcerned that the action also killed most other creatures in and around the stream. When my family moved from Maine to Massachusetts, I discovered that rivers there—like the Nashua, which flowed through my new hometown—looked even more polluted as they passed through one industrial city after another. So my childhood was not filled with abundant memories of American bitterns, osprey, bald eagles, or most other birds I have more recently come to associate the rivers and lakes of New England. The now-iconic common loon was far from common. Even if loons and osprey populations hadn't already been decimated by habitat loss and widespread DDT use, they would not have come close to the sewage-laden paper-mill-refuse-filled Androscoggin.

The Allagash was an exception. State and federal designation protected the river and its shoreline. Lumbering was not allowed within two miles of the water. No paper mills, factories, or even private camps lined the waterfront. There were prohibitions on motorboats also, and on buildings and roads. People went there to camp, canoe, fish and enjoy wilderness. The preservation and resulting clean water provided habitat for creatures that had been driven out from nearly everywhere else I had ever visited.

+ + + + + +

Sitting by the banks of La Barge Creek in Wyoming many decades later, more than the sound of a bittern prompted my thinking about that first visit to the Allagash. The debate over control of public lands filled my news feed. Whether and to what extent should the federal government relinquish control over those lands? Of course, "public land" also means "public water"; both are serious concerns, and they are intimately interconnected. What is in the soil finds its way into the streams and lakes. To protect a river, you need to protect the land around it. If we give away public land or stop protecting it, we give away public water also.

It goes in the other direction as well: the health of land depends on the health of the water. To protect birds, terrestrial mammals, and even trees, we need to protect fish. Some of those dependencies are complex. The illegal introduction into Yellowstone Lake of lake trout, non-native voracious predators, caused a precipitous decline in the cutthroat trout population. Though the decline in cutthroat in the lakes and rivers may have been immediately obvious only to anglers, it had a visible result above the water: a reduction of nearly 95% in pairs of nesting osprey around the lake. I understood why from years of watching osprey on the Allagash. The raptors exist almost entirely on a fish diet. Replacing cutthroat trout, which swim close to the surface and spawn up shallow tributary rivers, with the deep-dwelling lake-spawning lake trout, removed the primary food source of osprey. And not only osprey. The population of American white pelicans around Yellowstone Lake is also dependent on the cutthroat, having co-adapted with them for at least 10,000 years.

The bittern I heard that day on that river in Wyoming dwelt there because of the rich habitat, protected by the Bridger-Teton National Forest. So did the bald eagle and osprey I saw flying over the river during my visit. Maybe they were there also because of recent collaborative efforts among the U.S. Forest Service and Wyoming Game and Fish to restore native cutthroat to the watershed, in part through restoring river habitat where those trout live.

The abundant native brook trout, along with its wilderness character, is what brought me to the famous Allagash River in 1972. More than four decades later, research and writing about native trout as a lens into broader questions of river ecology motivated my trip to La Barge Creek. The many trips described in this collection of essays also flowed out of, and connect back to, those experiences. My selection as June 2017 artist-in-residence at Glacier National Park resulted from a proposal to write about the past, present, and future of various waters where native westslope cutthroat and bull trout live or once lived. From 2015 through 2017, I took several trips to national and state parks and national forests in Alaska to learn about the threats to rivers in a changing climate amid increasing demands of research extraction—and to see what Dolly Varden trout could tell us about the ecologies of those waters. My May 2018 artist residency at Acadia National Park and my earlier visits to the AMC 100-Mile Wilderness conservation property was to learn and write about efforts to restore river habitats of native fish crucial to the aquatic and terrestrial ecologies of those places.

I suppose, therefore, that most of the essays in the book, exploring rivers in places wild or almost wild, connect back in one way or another to those early formative experiences at the Allagash with my family, listening to bitterns, loons, and osprey while fishing for native trout. So long as rivers like that remain protected, I have hope for the future of native fish and all the creatures that feed on them. I have hope for the numerous birds we saw and heard, and hope that my grandkids will one day hear the call of a bittern.

The Strength of the Hills
A Writer's Journal from Glacier National Park

"The music of the streams is the music of the shaping
of the earth, by which the rocks are pushed
and shifted downward toward the level of the sea."
–Wendell Berry

———

Introduction

In June of 2017, I had the privilege of serving as Artist-in-Residence at Glacier National Park. My primary responsibility was to write about rivers and native trout and make a small number of public presentations. The perk was use of a cabin on Lake McDonald for four weeks. The cabin had no Internet or cell service. To keep it from turning into a vacation, I was also not allowed guests except for a *short* visit by a family member. Undistracted time and place to write, and something worthwhile to write about, is a wonderful gift for a writer. Though being without Internet or cell service for even a few hours would be unappealing to many, for me it sounded wonderful—a great excuse not to reply to e-mail or text messages for an extended period of time.

If given a choice, I might have picked a July or August residency, when more of the high backcountry would be free of snow. I'm glad I wasn't given a choice. That summer turned out brutally hot. Fires erupted in the park, and across much of Idaho, Washington, and Oregon. The worst fires burned on the ridge above Lake McDonald destroying the historic Sperry Lodge. My news feed even had a photo of a fire truck in front of the iconic Lake McDonald Lodge just a few hundred yards down the road from my cabin.

June turned out to be a good month for many reasons. It is a month of transition when the changing of seasons is most evident in the park. This didn't reveal itself in anything as simple as a steady rise in temperature; my month-long stay started and ended with daytime temperatures in the eighties, while some days in between never rose above sixty. The progression toward summer was more evident in other ways: the blooming of the park's famous Bear Grass, the annual melting of the winter snowpack, a sharp rise and more gradual fall of river and lake levels, and the opening of the famous Going-to-the-Sun Road on my third-to-last day. Traffic gradually increased and then erupted with the road opening. Harlequin ducks arrived, and before my trip was half done the males departed. At the start of my trip, the cutthroat trout were spawning in the lower elevations. By the end, they were long done in the lower elevations, but just preparing to spawn in the high lakes still largely covered with ice.

On my first morning, as I sat beside a river engorged with snow runoff and full of silt and debris, I was reminded of a passage from Wendell Berry's essay "A Native Hill" about the constant call of sea-level. Water, Berry writes, is like a net flung over hills pulling those hills down bit by bit. This constant eroding work is at the center of the essay, even when it is only hinted at. It is the music of water, and the shaping of the earth. Whether in small streams, big rivers, or even beaver meadows and lakes, that notion remained in my thoughts through the month.

I went to Glacier National Park with plenty of ideas for writing. Yet time, place, and relationships have a way of changing us. Ultimately both the landscape and Berry's essay took my writing in unexpected directions. As a result, that essay weaves through much of my writing from my time there. This weaving was not intentional at first, but it became so as the month progressed. I thought of the book *Reading the Mountains of Home* by Vermont author John Elder. Elder blends his walk along a Vermont ridgeline with a walk through the Robert Frost poem "Directive". He offers a close reading of the poem hand-in-hand with a close reading of a landscape. Frost's poem becomes a guide to Elder, even as Elder aptly guides his readers through both the poem and a small stretch of the Green Mountain National Forest.

"A Native Hill" requires no guide or close reading from me; Berry's essay is itself already a close reading. Indeed, the essay helped me make sense of my experience in Glacier National Park and not vice versa. It became my own trail guide.

This collection of connected essays is my chronicle drawn from my daily journals of that four-week residency, but ultimately (I hope) more than mere chronicle, with the words of Wendell Berry woven throughout. Though the final versions are written with knowledge of (what was at the time I first wrote them) the future, I have left the essays in the present tense to reflect the immediacy I felt when writing them: a sense of both spatial and temporal presence and attentiveness I sought to practice.

And the Power of Rivers:
"Flung like a Net over the Hill"

Morning. June 7.

It is shortly after dawn on my first full day in Glacier National Park. I sit beside Upper McDonald Creek near the Avalanche Creek Trailhead, off the famous Going-to-the-Sun Road a few miles upstream of Lake McDonald where my cabin hides among cedars along the southeast shore. I'd like to have gone further up this road, further up the valley, closer to the sun, but the road is still closed to automobiles. Logan Pass remains buried from heavy winter snowfall. Though many more miles are open to bikers and hikers, there is no place to turn a car around beyond this point.

Yesterday afternoon, when I arrived at the park to start my four-week residence, the temperature was over 80F. Another warm afternoon is in the forecast. The snow is melting quickly. I should be able to drive over Logan Pass before my residence comes to a close. I'm anticipating an early morning trip to the top to sit and write. For now, however, I'm content where I am. The fast-melting snow means rivers are high and cold. The famous Flathead is a raging torrent where it races through nearby Columbia Falls. Judging from the submerged gravel bars and streamside trees, Upper McDonald Creek is also fuller and swifter than usual. When the midday summer sun shines down on the snow and ice, it will run even higher.

Lifting my eyes from the glacier-green tint of river, over darker greens of cedars and hemlocks lining the far shore, I see a pair of towering granite peaks etched by snow. Mount Vaught is due west. Heavens Peak is farther to my right, to the northwest. Both reach nearly 9000 feet above sea level. The spruce and pine creeping up their sides give way long before reaching the triangular spires. Only a few stray bushes, and patches of grass, moss, or lichen, bleed color into the otherwise bare rock. Morning sunlight provides an even sharper contrast to the varying shades of gray and green, the white of snow and the black shadows of narrow crevices.

I'm struck by the majesty of this park, as I was last night when I drove along Lake McDonald. The peaks radiate strength. They reflect the weight of glory. I am reminded of the words of the ancient Hebrew poet responsible for Psalm 95. In the familiar King James translation, the poem reads, "The strength of the hills is his also." I consider titling my essay "the Strength of the Hills." I hesitate. These words are used so often as an epigraph that they've become almost cliché. They are etched on the side of Mead Chapel at Middlebury College where I teach, some 2000 miles east of here. Yet "strength" seems such a wonderful word to describe these mountains. And the peak to my right *is* named Heavens Peak. I wonder if there is a missing apostrophe. Was it supposed to be Heaven's Peak? Bill Yenne's pictorial history, *Images of America: Glacier National Park*, mentions that Marias Pass used to be named Maria's Pass. So I will now think of this iconic mountain as "Heaven's Peak", both in reference to that ancient Hebrew poem, and because it makes more sense.

I think also about my friend Eugene Peterson who lives not far away on Flathead Lake. His back deck and office window look out over the lake toward this same range. An author and retired pastor, Peterson is most famous for his translation of the Bible known as *The Message*. Knowing how rooted he is in this part of Montana, I look up his translation of this psalm. It reads, "In one hand he holds deep caves and caverns, in the other hand grasps the high mountains." The high mountains. The strength of the mountains. The peaks of heaven. I imagine Peterson sitting in his office looking eastward toward these mountains as he translated.

My thoughts, however, soon turn from the strength of mountains to the power of rivers. Wendell Berry, in his beautiful essay "A Native Hill", speaks of the irresistible call of oceans that draw all waters across the earth.

> Underlying this country, nine hundred feet below the highest ridgetops, more than four hundred feet below the surface of the river, is sea level. We seldom think of it here; we are a long way from the coast, and the sea is alien to us. And yet the attraction of sea level dwells in this country as an ideal dwells in a man's mind. All our rains go in search of it, and, departing, they have carved the land in a shape that is fluent and falling…

All waters are one. This is a reach of the sea, flung like a net over the hill, and now drawn back to the sea. And as the sea is never raised in the earthly nets of fishermen, so the hill is never caught and pulled down by the watery net of the sea. But always a little of it is. Each of the gathering strands of the net carries back some of the hill melted in it. Sometimes, as now, it carries so little that the water flows clear; sometimes it carries a lot and is brown and heavy with it. Whenever greedy or thoughtless men have lived on it, the hill has literally flowed out of their tracks and into the bottom of the sea.[1]

Wendell Berry wrote this about Kentucky hills and rain-swollen rivers, but his words are also true of these rugged Montana mountains and the snow and ice melting off them to make the torrent rage at my feet. Not nine hundred, but nine thousand feet below the peaks, the Pacific calls. So do both the Hudson Bay and Gulf of Mexico. Glacier National Park holds the only point in North America from which water might flow to sea level in any of those three locations. The park is aptly known as the Crown of the Continent.

The waters of that melting snow—of myriad waterfalls tumbling down steep ridgelines above me into Upper McDonald Creek—obey the call as they must, always carrying with them some small bit of the mountains. So do the waters flowing down Saint Mary River on the other side of the Going-to-the-Sun Road, spilling over Saint Mary Falls on a long journey to Hudson Bay and the very edge of the Arctic. So also do the waters flowing out of Two Medicine Lake into Two Medicine River that will carry some of these mountains down the Mississippi into the Gulf of Mexico. Or, in the case of these June rivers swollen with spring melt, the waters carry a *large* amount of the mountains.

---

1 Wendell Berry, "A Native Hill", in *The Agrarian Essays of Wendell Berry*, ed. Norman Wirzba, (Berkeley: Counterpoint, 2003), pp. 15,18.

The melting mountains are visible in the green and white of the raging torrent. They are visible in that the bottom of the river is *invisible*. However much strength the mountains have, the one water that is all the waters of ice, snow, and rain, of waterfalls, creeks, and raging rivers, is stronger still. Ultimately the water will have its way and these mountains will melt away to the sea.

Thus always the mountains are being thrust up by invisible forces, and worn away by other forces as beautiful as the emerald tint of Upper McDonald Creek, or the less beautiful coffee brown that was the Middle Fork of the Flathead as I drove across it earlier. Thrust up. Worn down. The cycle continues.

✦   ✦   ✦   ✦   ✦   ✦

The sky has gone from dark blue to azure. As morning moves onward, I watch the sunlight creep down the hill. It is a steady crawl, and much faster than the opposite movement of trees climbing up the slope. In Vermont, whose eponymous Green Mountains are said to be among the oldest in the world, it took millennia for the trees to reach the summits. Their upward colonizing climb had to be matched and aided by the erosion and gradual descent of the mountains: the centuries-long melting of glaciers that once sprawled across New England, the annual melting of winter snow, and more regular summer rains. Eventually, however, the trees and the summits met on all but two of Vermont's peaks.

✦   ✦   ✦   ✦   ✦   ✦

A movement by the water draws my attention. I turn to look. I'm surprised to see a duck bobbing on the surface of this swollen river. It sits near the seam where slack water by the shore meets the swift current. His marking and coloration is striking. Two white bands circle his dark upper body like a pair of necklaces. He also has matching white slashes across each side of his head, and white rings where I imagine his ears. He turns to look at me, revealing a white face with a black stripe running up the middle of his forehead from beak to crest. The white of his face narrows to a pair of stripes, which change from white to reddish-brown where they straddle the crest. Hints of red-brown feathers peek up from below his wings, becoming more visible when he takes to flight. He looks built more for swimming than flying.

Despite all the time I have spent on rivers and lakes, I don't know ducks very well. I definitely don't know western duck species. I will only later learn that this is a male harlequin, a species that resides mostly in coastal Alaska and is a rare and prized sight in Glacier National Park. I will bump into hikers on an excursion to a remote pond in hopes of seeing a harlequin, and I will feel guilty—and slightly smug—for having seen one so easily on my first morning without even trying. Though the females will stay for a few weeks until their ducklings can fly, the males are here only to mate, and will leave before my four weeks are over.

Seconds after I see Mr. Harlequin, he disappears under the water. So he, at least, is undisturbed by the cold or swiftness of this melting snow. Those strikingly handsome feathers are well-oiled, and like his stubby wings are as qualified for a swim in icy water as for a long flight to Alaska. A minute later he reappears, bobbing to the surface to swim along for a while before disappearing again in search of more food. Up again, then down again. For thirty minutes in the quiet of the morning I watch him work. I think in geologic time of mountains popping up—perhaps from sea level, or even below the ocean—in a dramatic geologic event: a volcanic eruption, or the slower upheaval from the collision of continental plates. Then the mountains fall back down again, drawn by the pull of the sea as this duck is drawn down by a waiting meal.

Sometime later I'm even more surprised to see a beaver plodding its way upstream in the sluggish water along the near shore. Its progress is slow against the heavy current. I take several photos—all of which will look much the same, but I have a DSLR and photos are cheap. As I click off shot after shot hoping the beaver will do something picture-worthy, I wonder where it is going and where it lives. The main channel of the river appears too large and swift for even the most ambitious of nature's dam-makers. There must be a quieter braid or tributary flowing in off a meadow nearby. If I wander the shoreline, maybe I'll find it.

✦　✦　✦　✦　✦　✦

A mosquito lands on my computer, drawn by the glow of the screen, or my exhaling of CO_2. June is mosquito season. I've come attired in clothing manufacturer-treated with insect-repellent permethrin. That lone mosquito, however, is the only one I see in two hours. My cold and sluggish fingers suggest the reason. As I ate dinner last night, the thermostat in full afternoon sunlight read ninety. When I awoke this morning, it read forty-something. I suspect the mosquitoes will be out in another hour or two, swelling in numbers as the river swells with the warming sun. So despite the cold in my fingers as I hammer characters on my laptop, I stay longer, enjoying the quiet beauty of morning light, and the lack of people and insects beside the creek.

By the time I am ready to leave, sunlight shines full on the east-facing slope in front of me. Though I still sit in the shadow of a ridgeline to my east, a few hundred yards downstream the sun has reached the water. I've seen no more sign of beaver or harlequin, but I hear melodies of songbirds falling from the thick riparian canopy above: robins, hermit thrushes, and a strangely unnatural whistle I will only later learn is a varied thrush. I look, but I see only a sandpiper running along the wet sand at the creek's edge. Despite my lack of duck-knowledge, I'm proud that I recognize it from my days on the Allagash River. Then I learn that seven varieties of sandpipers roam the western side of the park. My pride falls. I don't know which this is.

I take a final look at the creek rushing past. Right now, I think I could fish it, working clear slack water near the gravelly shorelines, and eddies behind boulders and fallen trees. Upper McDonald Creek is a poor trout stream. Still, I'm eager to stand in a river with the strength of these hills towering over me and the power of water tugging persistently on my legs. We humans seem particularly given to pride. Our growing technological power makes that even easier. Standing in a river, looking up at mountains and feeling them flow past me, helps me remember how illusory are the bases for that pride. I pack my camera and walk back to my car. Lacking Internet, I'm going to have to buy an illustrated guide to birds in the park.

Of Beavers, Mosquitoes and Cutthroat: "Blessed Beyond My Understanding"

Evening. June 7.

My late night begins at 5:15pm. I meet up with park employees Daniel and Whitney as they get out of work. I met Daniel only a few hours earlier, but he generously invited me to hike with him and his wife to a nearby lake where he had spotted cutthroat trout stacked up below a beaver dam. Both of us are interested in videoing the beautiful wild fish. Knowing it will be a couple weeks before the major rivers have dropped enough for good fishing, I am also interested in casting some flies.

The drive to the trailhead takes thirty minutes, some of it along the edge of a steep valley. The hundred-foot drop from the one lane road is steep with no guard rail to keep an inattentive driver from a precipitous fall. A small river runs below us. Beaver dam follows beaver dam all the way up. We drive past at least five, as well as two beaver houses. I cannot give them much attention, however; I do not want to be that inattentive driver. When we meet a car coming in the opposite direction, I pull as close as I can get to the steep wall towering over us. The other driver inches past. I'm glad I'm on the inside and not the outside. We continue on. Coming around a bend, we reach the end of the steep valley. The land levels out. We drive past luscious green meadows that I guess had been beaver meadows at one time. I want to look for moose, but the road is still too winding and narrow to take my eyes off it.

At the trailhead, we load up with photography and fishing gear. Daniel has warned me about mosquitoes. I armor myself from feet to waist in mosquito-repellent clothing, and stash in my pack more armor to cover my head and torso when we arrive. The two-mile hike takes thirty minutes through the skeletons of trees left from the 2003 Roberts Fire, which burned 57,570 acres.[2] That was one of six major wildfires that summer whose combined dramatic effect on the landscape will be visible for a few decades to the casual eye and for a century or more to trained eyes. Yet a new forest already grows amidst the old bones. The young trees are shorter than I am, and the ground is relatively open. With so much available sunlight, the hillside is strewn with a variety of wildflowers including wild roses, chartreuse paintbrushes, and the park's famous and ubiquitous white bear grass. The bear grass—which, it turns out, bears don't really like to eat—is in the midst of a banner year, thanks to a wet spring. Some blossoms are just starting to pop out, but others are already fully bloomed. Within a few days it will blanket forests everywhere I look.

Several times during my stay at Glacier National Park, I will come upon a particularly beautiful stretch of wildflowers, and think of another passage from "A Native Hill".

One early morning last spring, I came and found the woods floor strewn with bluebells. In the cool sunlight and the lacy shadows of the spring woods the blueness of those flowers, their elegant shape, their delicate fresh scent kept

---

2 "A History of Fire in Glacier National Park", Flathead Beacon, July 22, 2015, https://flatheadbeacon.com/2015/07/22/a-history-of-fire-in-glacier-park/. Date retrieved; July 19, 2018.

me standing and looking. I found a delight in them that I cannot describe and that I will never forget. Though I had been familiar for years with most of the spring woods flowers, I had never seen these and had not known they were here. Looking at them, I felt a strange loss and sorrow that I had never seen them before. But I was also exultant that I saw them now—that they were here.

For me, in the thought of them will always be the sense of the joyful surprise with which I found them—the sense that came suddenly to me then that the world is blessed beyond my understanding, more abundantly than I will ever know... Though as a man I inherit great evils and the possibility of great loss and suffering, I know that my life is blessed and graced by the yearly flowering of the bluebells. How perfect they are! In their presence I am humble and joyful. If I were given all the learning and all the methods off my race I could not make one of them, or even imagine one. Solomon in all his glory was not arrayed like one of these. It is the privilege and the labor of the apprentice of creation to come with his imagination into the unimaginable, and with his speech into the unspeakable.[3]

Wendell Berry wrote out of deep familiarity with a part of Kentucky he had known and loved for years, where many generations of his family had lived. By contrast I am visiting a hillside in Montana for the first time. Yet Berry's words pop into my thoughts often when I walk past a patch of wildflowers on a stroll in the woods, whether the familiar woods of my Vermont home where I have lived for twenty years, or an unfamiliar wood I am seeing for the first time. As I stroll through woods and meadows of Glacier National Park and stop to admire wildflowers, that sense of "loss and sorrow" comes from the realization that I might never pass this way again. Yet I certainly exult as well that I

---

3 Berry, p.24.

get to see this place even once. I think of the challenge of writing about all of this. I must indeed come with my imagination into the unimaginable as I seek to put into written words that which is too deep to be captured in writing. I am a mere apprentice.

◆　　　◆　　　◆　　　◆　　　◆　　　◆

A few mosquitoes buzz us as we walk, but despite Daniel's warnings they aren't thick. When we arrive at the lake, yet another stunning view takes my breath away. The water—with the help of beavers—has created a nearly perfect mirror in which to enjoy the views of the peaks lining the horizon on the far side. I am looking at the south sides of Stanton Mountain, and farther away to the left, the taller Longfellow Peak. Eager though I am to find cutthroat, I can't take my eyes away from the view.

As I cool down from the hike, I wait for the notorious mosquitoes to find me before I put extra layers on my sweaty torso. To my delight, they never come. I stay in my t-shirt. By the time I finish another batch of clichéd photos of jagged mountains, change into my sandals, and have my underwater camera ready, Daniel has donned his wet suit. He passes on the good news: the trout are still here, spread out over four pools below the beaver dam, finning in the slow current around submerged logs and flooded grass. While I prepare to catch some photos with a GoPro on a stick, he is going underwater with a high quality DSLR to get photos by swimming *with* the fish.

Wading ankle deep through the flooded grass and sneaking up to the uppermost pool just below the near side of the dam, I spot some cutthroat almost at once. A dozen or more cruise the pool. Most are six to ten inches long, but at least three are over a foot long. The largest ones hang in the shelter of a fallen log, which bisects the pool. I adjust the angle of the GoPro, start a video recording, and slip it into the water hoping not to spook the wild trout.

A few fish move out of the way, but they appear unperturbed. Soon their curiosity overcomes their natural caution. Two of the biggest fish swim up to the lens and peer into it, perhaps wondering whether it might be something to eat. For the next ten minutes, I delight at videoing and photographing this pod of brightly colored native westslope cutthroat, *Oncorhynchus clarki lewisi*. These native fish and their history, current place, and future in the greater eco-system of Glacier National Park, is one of the central topics I am here to write about. I rejoice to see so many of these beautiful fish in a wild natural environment.

Then I can't resist any more. I put my camera away and unpack my fly rod. Though a few fish have risen to hit something on the surface, the only insects I see above the water are cruising darting dragonflies. I know the dragonflies and trout must be hunting something, but I can't see what it is. Most of a trout's feeding is below the surface. For every time a trout grabs a mayfly or caddisfly that lands on the water to lay eggs, or is lucky enough to snack on a grasshopper or ant that blows onto the water, it will munch on ten to twenty aquatic insects underwater. Looking at this pool, however, I think if I drop a nymph below the surface it will likely end up wrapped around the log—if not before a trout bites it, then certainly after. In any case, even if it is often less effective, fishing dry flies on the surface is more thrilling than drifting nymphs along the bottom. So I tie on one of my favorite dry fly attractor patterns for alpine ponds: a size #14 Royal Wulff I had inexpertly tied myself. On three successive casts, the fly draws swirls and strikes from trout. I miss all the strikes. Then the fly manages to find a branch on the lone tree behind me. Before I notice the snag, my line snaps and the fly is gone.

I tie on another Royal Wulff, smaller than the first. This one draws more aggressive strikes. Over the next hour I work through three different pockets and land and release a dozen cutthroat. The largest ones are fourteen inches long. As I stand casting with my shoulders just above the level of the top of the dam, one of the dam's builders swims over on the upper side. Maybe it doesn't see me. Or maybe it does, and is coming to check me out. I hold still and watch it putter around only twenty-five feet away. Then it seems to notice me. I expect the loud tail slap, but I don't get one. It looks me over, then turns and swims away.

If the evening hadn't already been perfect, it had just become so. I love watching beavers. Before their pelts helped pay the way for European settlement of North America, beavers were ubiquitous. They were common even in relatively arid landscapes like the mountains of Arizona. Bison may get more attention for having roamed much of the country. Estimates of the vast herds scattered across the Great Plains are hard for me to fathom. Their wholesale slaughter is one of the sad stories of European settlement of this continent. Now they thrive only in a few protected areas, like Yellowstone National Park and some state and federal lands in western South Dakota.

The story of beavers is similar. One factory in York processed an average of 35,000 pelts per year from 1716 to 1770, and peaked at 55,000 a year in 1730 and 1731. The Fort Albany factory added another 50% to that total.[4] Within a few decades, beavers were extirpated from much of their native range. As the west was settled—again funded in part by the pelt trade—the process continued. The ecological results of that slaughter have been devastating. Greg McNamee writes in his book *Gila: the Life and Death of an American River*: "The wholesale destruction of the beaver [in the 19th century] disrupted ... ecological relationships, and for the first time erosion became a major problem as the [Gila] river flooded unchecked. Animal populations fluctuated wildly as their habitats began to disappear."[5]

---

4 Amy M. Carols and Frank D. Lewis, "The Economic History of the Fur Trade: 1670 to 1870", Economic History Association, https://eh.net/encyclopedia/the-economic-history-of-the-fur-trade-1670-to-1870/. Date retrieved; July 19, 2018.

5 Gregory McNamee, *Gila: The Life and Death of an American River*, (Albuquerque: University of New Mexico Press, 1998), p.82.

Beavers are a keystone species. A few beavers can change a landscape as dramatically as a wildfire, and though the change might not happen as quickly it can be even more permanent. I am tempted to write that beavers alter a whole ecosystem. Yet it is more accurate to say that they are an important *part* of the ecosystem: a vital native part like the cutthroat trout I have come to observe. Other creatures have co-evolved or co-adapted with the beaver and depend upon the habitat beavers create. Beaver ponds and wetlands are only the first stage. Over several decades, beaver ponds turn into meadows, then trees colonize the meadow, and in a few centuries they become climax forests, until another forest fire roars through and a new cycle begins.

Of equal importance is the impact on erosion and water quality. Beavers not only create important wetland habitat—for everything from waterfowl to large mammals—but those wetlands actually clean water. In the year before my visit to Glacier National Park, the phrase "draining the swamp" became an unfortunate metaphor for removing the political equivalent of pollution. However beaver dams, along with swamps and other examples of nature's wetlands, are not places that breed pollution. Quite the opposite, they are places of purifying, cleansing, and filtering. By slowing the flow of streams, for example, beaver ponds provide an important check against erosion. Thinking back to Wendell Berry's essay, a beaver pond can slow the melting of mountains. If rivers are part of the net of the sea cast upon land, catching mountains and pulling them down, then beaver dams are a different sort of net: they are a seine that trap the mountains as they try to slip away, and hold at least some of them back. That is how beaver ponds, over decades, become beaver meadows: they slowly fill in with all the silt settling out of the water. The silt remains on the bottom of the pond *in* the mountain instead of flowing down to the sea.

Now in many places—often thanks to the protection of national parks and forests—beavers have returned to the landscape. I have delighted to see so many signs of them at Glacier National Park creating the vital habitats they are so good at creating. Their work isn't always appreciated by all creatures, of course. Some trees suffer at the paws and jaws of beavers. Many species of stoneflies, mayflies and other aquatic macro-invertebrates need moving water for their habitat. I even think about the cutthroat stacked up below the dam in front of me. They seem to be looking for a way upstream, but are blocked by the beavers' work. The pools where they are stuck don't appear to have enough food or cold water for so many fish. Even in early June, the water feels warm on my feet as I stand casting in it. By July or August, it will be intolerable for a trout. If these fish haven't found a way over the dam, or dropped back downstream to colder water, they will most likely die.

Daniel had earlier suggested the trout might have come upriver to spawn, but the silty slow water below the dam where they now congregate is not spawning habitat. I come up with an alternate conjecture. In many mountain lakes fed by snow melt, cutthroat spawn in the *outlet* instead of, or in addition to, the inlets. Even the famous Yellowstone Lake, which holds the largest cutthroat population in the world and has plenty of tributaries where cutthroat spawn, also has a subpopulation of cutthroat that spawn in the outlet: the upper portion of the Yellowstone River below Fishing Bridge. Hidden Lake, within Glacier National Park, also has outlet-spawning cutthroat. Was it possible these cutthroat in front of me had gone *downstream* to spawn, passing over the beaver dam a few weeks earlier in higher water? That now, in lower water after spawning, they struggled to find a way back up? Or maybe they did come up the tiny stream from far below, seeking some higher habitat in which to reproduce, following the same instinct to colonize that had brought their kind up the Columbia River several millennia earlier.

✦　　✦　　✦　　✦　　✦　　✦

The sun approaches the western horizon as we pack our gear to leave. Just as I get my pack on, the beaver returns. I can't resist getting my camera out again and putting on a telephoto lens. The beaver zigzags across the pond starting a hundred feet away, slapping its tail and diving every time it turns, while slowly drawing closer to us. I take photos by the dozens, trying to capture the exact moment of the tail-slap, or the perfect location in the reflection of a distant mountain. About the time I finally put my camera away again, the beaver's mate appears. Had the first beaver's tail-slapping had been intended to call its mate, or warn it to stay away? If the latter, then as so often happens with mates of my own species, the instructions were ignored. The pair paddles around the quiet water as we turn and walk away.

Mosquitoes finally come out thick and heavy at dusk. They dive-bomb us on our hike out, making it less pleasant to snap photos of a spectacularly colored skyline ahead. Maybe some hatched in the slack-water pools below the dam, or went back there to lay eggs after sucking our blood. Maybe they will feed hungry overcrowded trout in their refugee camp. By the time I get back to my cabin, cook dinner, shower, and climb into bed, it is nearly midnight. I give up my plans for another 5:00am wake up, but without any regrets.

OF WILD DUCKS AND TAME DEER: "HOW THIS COUNTRY LOOKED IN THE BEGINNING"

MORNING. JUNE 9.

I wake with a tentative plan of hiking to Fish Lake. The trailhead is only a half-mile from my cabin, and from there it's less than three miles each way, with a vertical gain of 1000 feet. I also have another option in the back of my mind, more appealing though also more ambitious. A trail junction part way to Fish Lake breaks off to Snyder Lake. That hike would be closer to four and a half miles each way with more than 2000 feet gain in elevation, but would lead to more spectacular views as well as the possibility of finding wild cutthroat trout. Either would bring me to a higher elevation than I've yet attained in my first couple days in the park.

Both options, however, are dependent on luck. Hiking alone into the backcountry of Glacier National Park is not wise. There are too many risks, not the least of which is an unpleasant encounter with a grizzly. My hope is to bump into other hikers I can tag along with. I pack my fly rod, flies, sandals for wading, and camera. At the Sperry Trailhead I read the standard warning signs. *This is grizzly country. Don't hike at night. Don't hike alone.* I see no signs of other hikers. It must be too early in the day. I make a safer choice and turn instead down the horse trail toward Johns Lake—a loop that stays within a few hundred yards of the Going-to-the-Sun Road, has no real elevation gain, and is frequented by trail riders and day hikers—for a six and half mile trek. The trail is puddled with mud from the previous night's thunderstorm, and decorated with paddies from passing horses.

✦　　✦　　✦　　✦　　✦　　✦

I arrive at Johns Lake an hour later. Coming over a rise, I catch sight of the reflection of water nestled in a depression. I scout it as I follow the trail along the southern shoreline. The lake is just a few acres in size. It is shallow, muddy on the bottom, and dotted with lily pads. Trees grow thick down to a boggy shoreline that offers no promise of solid footing. The water looks warm. If it isn't warm yet, with its shallow dark bottom and still water it will become so in the afternoon sun.

In New England this would be too small to be named a lake. It might be considered a pond, though in Maine it might be too small even to warrant a name. This is definitely *not* trout water. It looks like a mosquito haven. There should be a moose here. My fly-fishing gear and sandals were unnecessary weight. Yet I have no regrets. The pond is beautiful and peaceful. Two pairs of ducks paddle around. The two on the far side are white, and when I first catch a glimpse of them through the trees I think they might be snow geese like those that migrate through Vermont every fall. When I get closer, I see they are too small to be geese. The other two ducks are closer to my side of the pond, diving for something.

This is not the sort of place most visitors to Glacier National Park have in mind. It lacks the majesty of high peaks, glaciers, flood-swollen rivers pouring down waterfalls and through narrow gorges. The only mountain I can see reflecting in the surface of the pond is Stanton, a mere 7750 feet in elevation, though still sporting patches of snow. A breeze is up. The trees—cedar, hemlock, and larch—creak and groan. If I had hiked to Snyder Lake, these species would have given way at higher elevations to spruce, pine, and fir. This looks like a pond in the rugged granite peaks of New Hampshire's White Mountains along the Appalachian Trail. I suspect, however, that the species of hemlocks and cedar here are different. Maybe even the texture of their creaking is unique. I suspect also that most of the ducks found here are not native in the east. Speaking of which, what are these? Not harlequins, which I learned to identify on my first full day in the park. The near one has a brown head, yellowish bill, and black and white striated wings. Songbirds sing in these woods also. They sound like thrushes of some variety. With the exception of barred owls, black-capped chickadees, cardinals, and a few other distinctive New England species, I am as bad at identifying birds by their calls as I am at identifying ducks. In fact, I'm not great at identifying any birds by sight, especially the little ones. "Little brown bird" is my description of at least twenty birds on the Glacier Bird Checklist.

As a nature writer, I feel guilty about my lack of knowledge. Yesterday I talked to a park employee who could immediately identify ducks by photo or description. Then again, that same person couldn't tell the difference between a cutthroat trout and brook trout—the latter of which isn't even a trout, but a char of the genus *Salvelinus*. I wanted to tell her I could not only distinguish between a brook trout and a cutthroat, but between a brook trout, bull trout, and lake trout, all of which are members of the same genus, but only one of which is native to the west slope of the Rockies.

I can identify an American robin, also, by sound as well as sight. Large members of the thrush family, their song is pretty and melodious, though not especially elaborate. I have seen and heard them regularly since arriving at Glacier National Park. Two days before I departed for Montana, my wife and I were walking along the street in front of our home talking about robins—whose delightful song can be heard even along tree-lined streets of suburban and urban areas—and about their stereotypical food: earthworms. She had heard that both robins and earthworms were invasive to North America. Though I know it is not a definitive source, I looked this up quickly on Wikipedia and read that she was only partly correct. There is an unrelated but similar-looking European robin after which the American robin gets its name. (The European robin is more closely related to the flycatcher than to the thrush family.) The American robin is not only a native species, but is believed to be the second most abundant and widely distributed land bird on the continent.[6]

Earthworms are another story. Roughly one third of the 182 species of earthworms found in the United States and Canada are introduced from Europe and Asia. These invasives "have spread to areas without any native species" causing a significant shift in

6 Wikipedia contributors, "American robin", *Wikipedia, The Free Encyclopedia*. Date of last revision: 2 June, 2018. Date retrieved; 4 June, 2018. Permanent link: https://en.wikipedia.org/w/index.php?title=American_robin&oldid=844107964

ecosystems.[7] In particular, earthworms have slowly made their way north above the 45-degree latitude. This is significant because, like beavers, they are a keystone species. They have a dramatic impact on the ecosystems they inhabit—though in the case of earthworms it takes an entire population, and not just a single dam-building family. Though their work is invisible, the ecological results are evident. They are detritivores; they redistribute nutrients, mix soil layers, and change the very nature of the earth. This changes the fundamental makeup of trees and plants, which in turn impacts everything else. An invasion of earthworms can change a landscape as dramatically as a beaver or wildfire.

I wonder how many species of earthworms were intentionally brought to this continent, and how many hitchhiked in the soil of plants and found their way by accident, yet still thanks to human behavior. I think about how human-introduced exotic and invasive species have had such a dramatic—and at times devastating—impact on ecological systems. It's true even here, in this comparatively wild Glacier National Park landscape, one of the rare places left in the continent where all the big mammals that roamed when European settlers first came west *still* roam. I will learn, over the course of the summer, about the direct impact of invasive lake trout, brook trout, and rainbow trout on native fish and the local ecosystem, and the indirect impact of other introduced species such as shrimp.

That's one reason it's important to be able to distinguish between a brook trout and bull trout. Invasive brook trout tend to overpopulate Rocky Mountain waters, driving out the native cutthroat. Lake trout are also a threat, except rather than outcompeting cutthroat trout, they eat them. Once they invade, Lake trout usually extirpate their char cousins, the bull trout. It's one of the population dynamics I came to observe and write

---

7 Wikipedia contributors, "Earthworms as invasive species", *Wikipedia, The Free Encyclopedia*. Date of last revision: 16 March 2018. Date retrieved; 4 June, 2018. Permanent link: https://en.wikipedia.org/w/index. php?title=Earthworms_as_invasive_species&oldid=830700127.

about. I wouldn't hesitate to keep a brook trout—or even several brook trout—if I caught them in the park. Bull trout, by contrast, are endangered and should not be kept or even targeted in fishing.

I think of the cutthroat species that spent thousands of years moving up the Columbia River along the Oregon-Washington border, then across Washington and Idaho, and eventually into Montana. I think of them colonizing these headwaters, and maybe as recently as ten thousand years ago managing to get over the divide and onto the East Slope to populate all three watersheds that come together in Glacier National Park. I think of the whole local ecosystem adapting and co-evolving with cutthroat, which were once the most widely distributed species of salmonids in the continent. When the cutthroat spawn out of higher mountain lakes, grizzlies line the shores to feed on them. Pelicans, osprey, and mink do the same. Massive quantities of nutrients from consumed fish, preprocessed by bears and birds, find its way into the forest soil promoting the health of trees and other plants. Then I think of fish species like rainbow trout, brook trout, and the monsters of the deep known as lake trout, that have been introduced and often sustained through stocking for the sake of anglers. When lake trout consume cutthroat trout, the grizzlies, pelicans, and osprey go hungry and disappear.

Again I think of a passage from "A Native Hill", and the observations of Wendell Berry as he walked from his home down toward the Kentucky River, following the path of water drawn irresistibly toward the sea.

> It occurs to me that it is no longer possible to imagine how this country looked in the beginning, before the white people drove their plows into it... The original surface of the hill is as extinct as the passenger pigeon. The pristine America that the first white man saw is a lost continent, sunk like Atlantis in the sea. The thought of what was here once and is gone forever will not leave me as long as I live. It is as though I walk knee-deep in its absence.[8]

---

8 Berry, pp. 15-16.

I may later reflect on the human impact of unhealthy practices of industrialized agriculture, road-building, massive deforestation, mountain-top removal, strip-mining, and dam-building. Or I may think of how the landscape is different because we nearly wiped out beavers, bison, and wolves. It is indeed impossible to imagine this country before any of that. For now, however, I think of the seemingly more benign impact of all the invasive species we have brought with us, intentionally or unintentionally, and set loose on the land and water.

For decades, not knowing any better, state fisheries programs as well as national parks—and many private individuals—stocked invasive fish for the sake of recreation. Now that the impact of these invasive species is better understood, fisheries management in places like Glacier National Park have shifted to emphasize native species: particularly cutthroat trout, and the endangered bull trout. Unfortunately, the damage already done is irreversible, and we are only beginning to fathom how deep and far-reaching it is. Yet I'm glad at least for the management shift, and glad for the vast tracts of land and miles of river under the control of the National Park Service and U.S. Forest Service, where such conservation efforts are possible. I'm glad for the efforts to restore something of what has been lost.

＊　　＊　　＊　　＊　　＊　　＊

I'm also glad for the wind that makes these trees creak. It ranges from a soft sough to a loud roar. The wind, and maybe the thirty-degree temperature drop, keeps off the mosquitoes. I think wishfully: maybe the cooler air will result in slower snow melt and lower, less silty rivers today; maybe I'll find some little eddy where a clear creek flows into Upper McDonald from a beaver pond, and I'll make use of my fly rod to find one of those native cutthroat trout that still inhabit these waters as they have for thousands of years. Maybe I won't find any place that looks even remotely fishable, but I'll make use of my rod anyway just so I won't feel like I carried it in vain.

I unfold my camping chair and settle in to watch, listen, and write. Even a third of a mile away from Upper McDonald Creek, over a thickly wooded ridge, I hear the roar of river mixed with the rustling of leaves in the wind. It takes me several moments to distinguish between them. Hopes of casting dissipate further as I imagine the state of the river that would produce such volume. I watch the pond instead. The duck with the yellow-brown beak swims closer and I take photos. Then I sit down again.

Sitting quietly has advantages. A deer, startled by a shift in the wind, or by other hikers, bolts down the trail toward me. It stops almost close enough to touch, and peers into my eyes. I want to reach for my camera, but I hold still. Slowly the deer backs up, turns, and lopes into the woods. Two hikers come by three minutes later. Though they disturb my quiet, I'm glad to see them. Many who come to the park never see the quiet beauty of this place. The park is so spectacular; it is easy to get so wrapped up in majestic mountains, glacier-carved ridges, powerful rivers, and waterfalls, that we never lower our eyes. I came to Glacier National Park most excited about the cold rivers and streams, and the inlets and outlets of alpine lakes, where I hoped to find cutthroat trout sipping insects. Yet I am quickly falling in love with the quieter, flatter waters of the park which often aren't trout habitat at all but little murky duck ponds, beaver ponds, or moose buffets, away from the loud roar of mountain-melting rivers. Even with a tree-creaking breeze overhead, the surface of Johns Lake, nestled in this little dell, is textured only by corduroy ripples.

I find these peaceful surfaces reflective—in both a literal and metaphorical sense. It is a wonderful place to sit and think about the day past, the days ahead, and especially this morning and place in which I can be fully present. I think about viewing this park indirectly, only through these reflections. I gaze at the reflection of

Stanton Mountain. If I step into the muck for a different angle, I might see the taller Mount Vaught again. After a time, I walk down the eastern shoreline for a closer look at the ducks and different angle of reflection. I see a gap in the trees that might offer a good photo. The ground looks unusually solid compared with the bog I've been trying to navigate. Just two steps will bring me to a nice high clump of grass. I step onto a bare patch of what looks like dry dirt, and plunge immediately down to my left knee in water. I lurch back up and lunge to solid ground. My pant leg is soaked. My boot is full of water; their waterproof exterior doesn't help much when the water goes over the top. I resist the urge to race home and change into dry clothing. I've put up with much worse on camping and fishing trips. I stay another half hour to sit and write, and make a point to remember my wading staff next time and test the ground before stepping near the edge of the pond.

* * * * * *

Packing up my chair, I leave Johns Lake around the opposite side I came from, strolling a third of a mile down to the edge of Upper McDonald Creek to a little footbridge. The volume of the roar was not deceptive. It is, indeed, raging. The transformation is even more dramatic from two mornings ago. Trapped in this steep valley with little to absorb the water, last night's heavy thunderstorm has more than compensated for any slowing of the snowmelt. The river flows an even frothier opaque white and green without a hint of fishable water. I don't think the beaver or Harlequin is swimming here now.

I head back into the woods to walk home by the trail, choosing to risk horse mines rather than three miles of roadside walking. I'm only fifty yards in when a deer appears. It looks at me, and ambles off into the trees. I walk on, and two minutes later the deer ambles back to the trail right in front of me. For the next mile it walks along just fifteen feet in front of me, pausing now and then to nibble on trailside browse. For the most part, it acts unafraid. Three or four times I stumble on a rock and make a sudden lurch, and the deer retreats a few quick steps into the woods. Yet each time it only keeps pace with me, and then returns to the trail, always in front of me. Maybe it knows I'm carrying bear spray.

✦   ✦   ✦   ✦   ✦   ✦

I spend the rest of the day writing at my cabin. Jessica, the volunteer coordinator for Glacier who has been my liaison to the park, is leaving to take a position back east at Shenandoah National Park. Today is her last day. She comes to check on how I'm doing, and to say goodbye. I ask her about her next job, and what she is looking forward to. She reflects on the importance of volunteers and the tremendous potential at Shenandoah because of its proximity to major population areas, and also the popularity of the Appalachian Trail, which runs through the park. We discuss not only the importance of volunteers for getting work done, but also for becoming engaged people who will be more passionate and more knowledgeable about the important work of the national parks, and the lands, rivers, and ecosystems within them.

Our conversation turns to the strange dichotomy or paradox of "managing wilderness". Nearly all of Glacier National Park is managed as wilderness. It is certainly more pristine and wild than it would otherwise be, thanks to the protection afforded as part of our system of national parks, forests, and preserves. It is not the site of a heavy metal mine, mountaintop removal, or clearcut. Yet the park still bears the unmistakable marks of human presence. We also are a keystone species whose impact dwarfs even the industrious beaver or the earthworm. Even here, Wendell Berry's words ring true: "it is no longer possible to imagine how this country looked in the beginning."

I think of the tame animals, like that deer that followed me, or another that showed up outside the lodge by Snyder Creek and posed for a dozen tourists. I think of changes to landscapes: the roads, trails, and lodges. I think of fish species introduced for recreational purposes. Jessica and I agree that the work of Glacier National Park is really important, and we think of what might have happened were the park not here. We think and hope that most of these human-wrought changes will be like the work of a beaver that creates new beauty. We reflect on how the parks have enabled enjoyment, and thus in turn prompted commitment and engagement not only from backcountry hikers and alpine-lake-seeking anglers, but also tourists with cameras who never get more than fifty yards from a parking spot—and are still awed and inspired by the breathtaking landscapes around them. Or by the quiet reflections of a little wooded pond.

Settling Into Place:
"The Part Representing the Whole"

Morning. June 10.

The year I graduated from college my family took a two-week trip around British Columbia, across to Alberta, and down the Rockies to Colorado. My parents orchestrated the trip. I, my younger foster brother Thanh, and my oldest brother Jody along with his wife Diane and two-year-old daughter Abby went along. I met up with my brothers in western Washington where we rented a van, drove to Vancouver, ferried to Vancouver Island, drove north from Nanaimo to Port Hardy, got on a larger ferry to Prince Rupert, drove inland up the Skeena River two hours, and picked up my parents at the little airport in the city of Terrace. Among my impressions of the drive were the thousands of acres of clear-cut hillsides on Vancouver Island. I'd never seen anything like it. I would later learn about the devastation those clear-cuts caused to the salmon and steelhead runs.

From Terrace it was less than an hour drive to the village of Usk where my uncle had homesteaded years before. Usk was a small

community on the Skeena River accessible in the summer only by
a cable-operated pontoon-style two-car river-ferry. In the winter,
the ferry didn't operate at all; residents left cars on the south bank
and crossed the river on an aerial trolley. With young kids growing
up, my uncle was moving back into civilization. His last summer
in his homestead, he wanted to host a family reunion. For most
of my relatives, there wasn't much to do in the little community
except sit around and eat and talk. I, however, was excited about
the fishing. I tried casting for salmon in the Skeena, but I didn't
know what I was doing. Most of my fishing was for smaller trout.
Before I knew anything about the cutthroat species or their
history, I caught several ten- to twelve-inch cutthroat with a fly
rod in a long beaver pond in front of my uncle's house. I hooked
a few slightly larger trout in the eddies of the Skeena. I think
the cutthroat in both the river and stream-fed beaver pond were
of wild native stock, in which case they would have been of the
Pacific coastal subspecies (*Oncorhynchus clarkii clarkii*), distinct
from the native cutthroat I would later spend time catching in the
national parks and forests of Wyoming and Montana: Colorado
River (*O.c.pleuriticus*), Yellowstone (*O.c.bouvierii*), Snake River
fine-spotted (*O.c.behnkei*), and westslope cutthroat (*O.c.lewisi*).
At the time, however, more than thirty years ago, they were just
"trout" to me.

After three days with aunts, uncles, cousins, and grandparents,
we had a little over a week to make it across British Columbia
to Alberta and down to Boulder for the wedding of my middle
brother who had not joined us on the trip. Along the way we
spent a day in Jasper National Park and a day and a half in Banff
National Park. My father hired a fishing guide in Jasper to take
us trolling on Maligne Lake for introduced rainbow and brook
trout. We got a rare summer snow squall, spent the day shivering
in canoes, and between four of us landed only a single fourteen-
inch brook trout. On a day hike in Banff I did a little better,
managing to catch a couple wild cutthroat from the shore in a

high mountain lake, and another couple fishing a roadside river where we stopped for a picnic lunch. Then we were moving on again, continuing south down the Rockies. We spent a couple hours visiting the Athabasca Glacier in southern Alberta. We'd planned to visit the east side of Glacier National Park, but got too pressed for time and only got to gaze at the peaks from what seemed like a hundred miles away. We enjoyed only one evening, one morning, and an afternoon drive in Yellowstone.

That summer provided my first experience with cutthroat. At the time, I had no knowledge of different strains or subspecies, or even different life histories within the same subspecies. The trip was both wonderful and frustrating. The wild beauty inspired and enchanted me, and filled me with longing to experience more. Though my father and brother Jody enjoyed picking up a rod and trolling for trout in rivers or lakes of Maine, and Thanh would later take up fly fishing, I was the only one at the time with a real passion for fly fishing. As a result, not much time got devoted to that pursuit. I was also relatively new to the sport and completely new to the waters we visited, yet I still had success almost everywhere I went. I was also frustrated. We had so many miles to drive, and so little time to do so. We would just arrive some place, begin to experience the landscape, find the locations I *wanted* to visit, and then we left. I wanted to settle in and get a sense for local landscapes and ecosystems. Where did the bear and elk hang out? What were the insect hatches? I knew I had to come back and spend more time in these areas.

It took me only two years to get back to Banff National Park for a five-day backpacking trip, including two nights at one of the alpine lakes I had visited briefly on my first trip. It took me more than twenty years to get back to Yellowstone National Park, and when I did it was as a father of three sons. I made sure to spend a full week in the park, and another four days in the Shoshone National Forest outside the park. I could have spent a month there.

Glacier National Park remained on my wish list, and my wife's, until this year.

+ + + + + +

The memory of that trip more than three decades ago comes back to me now. I've finally made it to Glacier National Park, and with more time than just a day to snap a few photos from the Going-to-the-Sun Road. I have time to settle in and begin to experience *place*. I will never know this land like Wendell Berry knows his Kentucky Farm. Nobody could know much more than a fraction of Glacier National Park with that intimacy, though I could imagine spending a decade or two getting to know one valley or one of the smaller lakes. Still, I try to make myself present here.

Berry writes in that essay, "When I have thought of the welfare of the earth, the problems of its health and preservation, the care of its life, I have had this place before me, the part representing the whole more vividly and accurately, making clearer and more pressing demands, than any *idea* of the whole."[9] That principle holds true for me also. I'm not interested in the principle as mere abstraction, but in the particulars to which it applies. To care for the welfare, health, and preservation of the life of *the earth*, we must care for specific places. And on the flip side, it is also the specific places that motivate us to care for the whole. I think one of many benefits of our national parks and their stunning landscapes is the motivation they may give to people to care. Or maybe I only hope that because I know it has been true of me. Coming into the unimaginable shapes my imagination powerfully, and somehow coming into the unspeakable helps give word to my writing, however inadequate it may be.

So I sit at the table in my cabin several times a day looking out across Lake McDonald at the constantly changing cloudscapes over and along Howe Ridge. I experience crisp mornings not

---

9 Berry, p. 5.

much above freezing, and hot afternoons when an occasional fish makes a ring on the flat water in front of me. I watch white caps one afternoon and near-perfect reflections another, soft rains like this morning, and ripping thunderstorms like last Thursday. One evening, when my wife is in the park for a short visit, we see a bald eagle and an osprey duel over the lake just two hundred yards in front of my cabin. Whether they are arguing over a piece of prey, or more generally over territorial hunting rights, I don't know, but the osprey appears to win. The eagle folds its wings and drops into the water away from the harassment of its smaller cousin. The osprey flies away. I stare at the bird in the water. Can it really be an eagle? I peer through my camera zoom lens and double-check. It is. I grab my video camera and try to film it, but the tripod isn't set up and I can't hold the camera steady enough at full zoom. The eagle begins to cry: a repeated frantic scree-scree-scree in its distinctive loud shrill peep. I wonder if it is drowning. Surely a bird that makes a living grabbing fish from the water can take off if it isn't wounded. With the osprey gone, two crows fly out from shore and start squawking at the eagle. The eagle spreads its powerful wings and with two flaps lifts off the water. My wife says the crows went out to encourage the eagle. I think they flew out to make sure it left. Such drama!

Unlike most of the native species we find at Glacier National Park, eagles and osprey are again common in the northeast and I have watched them for the past few decades. I've seen osprey drive off bald eagles once or twice, but never have I seen an eagle escape by going for a swim. I could be here twenty years and never see such a sight again. It's like stumbling on a patch of never-before-noticed wildflowers on a familiar wooded path. I could easily spend two or three years here and not exhaust the inspiration to write. I'm already regretting all the places I won't get to visit at all or will get to visit only once. Each day I must choose between revisiting some pond or stream and becoming more familiar with its moods and characteristics perhaps in different light, or exploring a new lake, river, or ridgeline.

◆ ◆ ◆ ◆ ◆ ◆

I wake on Saturday morning shortly after dawn. The temperature is only a nose above 40°F. It takes me a while to eat and prepare for the day. I want to do my first morning video session. I double and triple-check that I have what I need. At 7:00am I drive a short distance down the road. I am thinking of that tradeoff between familiarity and exploration, between intimacy and discovery. This morning I choose the former. I return to Johns Lake. I can't quite call it early morning, but I am a couple hours earlier than yesterday. I hope to see a moose, or get a better look at the ducks, or even just see Johns Lake in different light—maybe catch the reflection as the sun slides down the mountain.

The lake is quiet. Having been told it is frequented by moose, I'm disappointed not to see one. Am I too late? Are the woods in shock because of the temperature drop? Even the ducks are quiet. The same two pairs are here, but they stay far away and don't move around much. I think again that I need a bird guide. I stay three hours, listening quietly. One of the ducks eventually comes closer and I take video. I do a lot more sitting, watching, and waiting. I feel fidgety for some reason, but slowly I let the quiet work on me. After a while, the view feels familiar. I can close my eyes and imagine the angle of reflection of the mountain, or the location of the fallen tree, or the patches of lily pads. The trees above me are becoming familiar also. If I come here again for an hour tomorrow, and the next day, and repeat that every few weeks for a couple more years, I might know this one small spot.

I leave at 10:30am and revisit another place I have already been to: the beaver dam on the little inlet across the river. I feel foolish carrying my heavy gear—my DSLR, the video camera on its tripod, my camping chair, water, and of course bear spray—down across the bridge and upstream along the river on the other side. The water is still high and whitish green with little visibility, but it has come down from yesterday. On the trail I meet a couple from

Massachusetts. They had gone in search of the beaver pond, but turned around too soon. They turn once more and follow me, and we talk as I lead them there. I grew up in eastern Massachusetts. We are familiar with the same places around Boston. That shared familiarity creates an instant connection of trust. Can familiarity with a landscape do the same thing?

I take more video at the beaver pond. I don't see ducks or beaver. I watch several pairs of Canada geese making good use of the beaver pond habitat, but they are not positioned well for a video. The truck thermometer reads an outside temperature of 54°F as I drive back to the cabin. It does not rise much above that as I spend the rest of the day indoors writing. Whitecaps roil the lake as they did during the thunderstorm. Lake McDonald is deeper than yesterday. The gravel beach in front of the cabin is now under two feet of water. The lake rises up the trunks of trees, both young and old. But they have grown here. This lake rises annually. They have adapted to the fluctuations.

FLATHEAD NATIONAL FOREST: "AT THE JOININGS OF STREAMS"

AFTERNOON. JUNE 11.

Sunday morning after breakfast I head out of the park and down to Columbia Falls for mocha and pastry, followed by a worship service at a local church, then a trip to the grocery store to replenish supplies, and finally to a nearby restaurant for lunch. My post-lunch plan is to head into the Flathead National Forest. I'm hesitant to spend time outside of Glacier National Park because there is so much to see within it. Yet I want to make at least a couple visits to Flathead while I am in northern Montana so close to its boundaries.

One thing (of many) that makes Glacier National Park such an important ecological treasure is its proximity to the Flathead National Forest, which adjoins it on both the south and west.

Nearly all of Glacier National Park's million acres is managed as wilderness, and among the two-and-a-half million acres of Flathead National Forest are three large designated wilderness areas: the Bob Marshall Wilderness, Great Bear Wilderness, and Mission Mountains Wilderness. The Bob Marshall Wilderness Complex alone spans three national forests and has a million and a half acres, making it the third largest wilderness complex in the lower forty-eight. Together the park and forests provide a much larger contiguous area of protected lands. This is a vital wildlife corridor for migrating birds as well as large mammals like grizzly bears, cougars, and elk, which need a large land area for individual members as well as population dynamics.

Then there are the microscopic beetle mites, weevils, and springtails. They may not have the celebrity of bear and elk, and they are a lot smaller, but they are very important to the soil and thus to the entire ecosystem. They also need a lot of protected forest. Before I left for my month in Glacier, my wife gave me *The Hidden Life of Trees* by Peter Wohlleben. I brought it with me and began reading it in the evenings. Wohlleben's research suggests how vital these microscopic creatures are. "In the forest," he writes, "these little guys are the first link in the food chain and can, therefore, be considered terrestrial plankton." Speaking specifically about beetle mites, he adds, "they appear everywhere at the intersection of birth and decay, and so they must be considered essential components of the ecosystem."[10] Some species of weevil, however, are capable of traveling only thirty feet in a year, while beetle mites can barely travel three feet in a lifetime. This has serious implications for the impact of deforestation. Writing about European forests, Wohlleben notes:

If the environment around a tree changes because the tree dies, all a weevil has to do is make it to the next tree

10 Peter Wohlleben, *The Hidden Life of Trees: What They Feel, How They Communicate*, (Vancouver: Greystone Books, 2015), pp. 87-88.

and continue nibbling around there in the rotting leaf litter. If you find weevils, you can be sure the forest has a long uninterrupted history. If the forest was cleared in the Middle Ages and later replanted, you won't find these insects, because it would simply have been too far for them to walk to the next old forest.[11]

And so the importance of contiguous forests and unbroken wilderness and protected areas may be far greater than imagined. What happens when these microscopic creatures are gone from the forest soil? Wohlleben addresses that troubling question.

We don't know how long it will take until true forest soil is created once again, but we do know that a hundred years is not enough.

To make it possible for this regeneration to happen at all, you need preserves with ancient forests free from any human interference. These are places where the diversity of soil life can survive, and these refuges can be the nucleuses for recovery in surrounding areas.[12]

So I keep looking at a map, and even when I stay within Glacier National Park I am aware of the contiguous national forest and especially its wilderness areas.

I'm also interested in the Flathead National Forest for its own sake. I spent a month the previous summer in two national forests in Wyoming: the Bridger-Teton and both the northern and southern parts of the Shoshone. Now I want to spend some time visiting one of Montana's most important national forests. Then, too, there are the cutthroat and the chance to cast for some. The rivers in Glacier are too high with runoff to be fishable. I'd like to find some small stream in Flathead where I can spend an

11 Wohlleben, p. 89.
12 Wohlleben, p. 91.

hour or two casting. My month is too short to spend a lot of it commuting from one spot to another, but my trip to Columbia Falls for groceries is a convenient opportunity for an excursion into the forest.

So after lunch I follow a hint of a local fishing guide and head down into the Flathead to find some trout in streams not flooded with spring melt. The guide had given me a few general ideas, but was either intentionally vague on the details, or just assumed I knew the area better than I do. One of his suggestions, if I understood correctly, was to follow a reservoir tributary upriver and look for small feeder creeks coming in from the side. He said there would be several and I couldn't miss them. So I meander down a gravel forest road along the east shoreline of Hungry Horse Reservoir looking for any running water that looks fishable and not so swollen. The first creek mouth, at the upper end of a cove full of green water, would be a beautiful place to fish and photograph, but a camper has already set up there.

I pass two more coves and then the road turns east. Though I can't see Hungry Horse Creek, my memory of the map tells me it is not far off to my right in the woods. My uncertainty leaves me nervous. I cross a wooden bridge over a swift tumbling creek flowing in from the left. The creek is about eight feet wide. I stop the truck on the bridge and look downstream as it passes through a thick evergreen forest tangled with underbrush. The only way to follow this creek will be in the water. I can't see any sign of a confluence with Hungry Horse Creek. I drive on. I cross over another smaller creek, this one passing through a culvert. I expect a few more creek crossings, but I see none. The road winds up a hill. I get glimpses of spectacular views through the gap between the trees. However, the downward slope on my right is steepening as I climb, and I soon realize that if I'm still following a creek it is far below me in deep and narrow valley. After a few miles, the road crests a hill and begins a long descent. I'm quite sure now that I have left the basin of Hungry Horse Creek, though I never even saw the water. I turn around and wind back down along the valley until I am again level with the woods beside me.

Returning to the wooden bridge where I briefly stopped earlier, I park on a pull-off. The last half hour has given me a better sense of the landscape. I now have confidence that if I follow this stream down I will find myself on Hungry Horse Creek. I note again, however, that the woods are a tangle of tightly packed trees and underbrush crowding right up to the creek's edge. It's a great canopy to keep the water cool, plus a wonderful root system to protect against erosion. It's not so great for me, though. This is grizzly country. I am alone. Bear spray won't do much good if I startle a bear in thick brush at close range. Wading down this swift stream won't be easy. Wading back up will be even harder. Before I try, I want to know how far it is to the confluence. I take out the borrowed drone I have been eager to fly. I can't fly it in the national park, but while it is excluded in the wilderness area of Flathead, it is allowed in most other parts. I send it up over the trees, point its camera down, and fly it down the little creek to see if I can spot the confluence.

I am always looking for places where streams flow together. My intuition tells me there should be double the chance of finding a trout at a confluence where it has two sources of food. And when we expect to find something, we are more likely to find it. Some call that confirmation bias. More even than the desire to catch fish influences me, however. The meeting of streams feels enchanted. Coming upon a confluence from any direction is like making an exciting discovery. It opens up choices. Again I think of one of Wendell Berry's reflections in "A Native Hill":

> My mind is never empty or idle at the joinings of streams. Here is the work of the world going on. The creation is felt, alive and intent on its materials, in such

places… Its becoming is only incidental to its being. It will be because it is. It has no aim or end except to be. By being, it is growing and wearing into what it will be. The fork of the stream lies at the foot of the slope like hammer and chisel laid down at the foot of a finished sculpture. But the stream is no dead tool; it is alive, it is still at its work. Put your hand to it to learn the health of this part of the world.[13]

So despite the names on maps, one stream doesn't end when it flows into another. The two become one—something different than either of them individually. Is that mystical? Relational? Is it like a marriage?

Unfortunately, I never find this joining. My cell phone screen is too small to see much of the video. I will download it onto my laptop later and look on a larger monitor. For now, I need to explore on foot or give up. I don't want to give up, so I walk up the road until I find a break in the woods. It's too small to be called a "meadow", but compared to the other places that separate me from the creek of my desire, it is relatively open. I pull out my bear spray and begin to sing and whistle as I step into the trees. I walk seventy-five yards off the road, veering slightly to the right along the edge of an old creek bed to avoid denser woods. Finally, I stumble upon Hungry Horse Creek. It looks only slightly larger than the tributary I had just been gazing down, and the shore is almost as tangled with forest understory.

Yet the place of my own confluence with this creek couldn't have been more fortunate. Directly below me is a shallow gravelly riff. I gaze into the water and see no shadows of fish. Only ten yards downstream, however, a log jam has formed a wide pool on the back side. It looks promising. I creep along the bank, cautiously peer down, and spot a pair of trout finning in the current. They look large for this creek—thirteen or fourteen inches long. I'm not

13 Berry, p. 19.

at a confluence, but this is certainly what I had been hoping for. I return to the car, don my waders, rig my fly rod, and head back into the woods with excitement—but still singing and whistling loudly, and with my bear spray at my hip.

Bowman Lake:
"Loitered By and Imagined"

June 12.

My alarm wakes me at 4:45am. Other than turning off the alarm and lying in bed an extra ten minutes, the day starts as I intend. I'm up, dressed, and out the door in twenty minutes with a thermos of coffee for some early morning photography followed by writing in my backpacking chair. I again hope to see beavers and moose, and maybe a bear. It is the coldest morning yet. Though the temperature on the truck's thermometer starts at 44°F, by the time I get partway up the hill on the other side of the lake the gauge reads 39°F. It must be below freezing on the peaks. This will slow the melting of snow and delay my trip up the Going-to-the-Sun Road. It also slows the working of my fingers.

The extra ten minutes in bed turns out to have been a mistake. I had done a good job estimating my wakeup time when I set my alarm. As I crest the hill and turn toward the Fish Creek Campground, stunning panoramic views open to my right. The last vestiges of pink are just disappearing. Still, I get to see the mountains backlit by a bright yellow halo. Is this what they call alpenglow? I snap shots of the valley patched with morning fog as the sunlight touches the peak behind them.

After a foray up the Inner North Fork Road, with stops to photograph beaver dams on Fish Creek, and mist along Camas Creek where the road ends, I head back down Inner North Fork Road and up Outer North Fork Road for my first visit to the northwestern part of the park. The morning is still early. I have the road to myself and the drive is beautiful. As I temporarily leave

Glacier National Park and cross the North Fork of the Flathead into national forest, I am blessed by yet more stunning panoramas. Standing on the bridge and looking upriver, I see across the whole river valley to an unending line of peaks bathed in morning light while river fog meanders along the low-lying areas.

After cutting through the national forest on the west side of the river, I reach Polebridge and cross back into the park. From there I wind up a narrow, rutted gravel road toward Bowman Lake. For a short while I am looking down on my right into Bowman Creek and a small valley cleared by fire and now filled with wildflowers. Then the roads turns into the woods and winds over a hill. When I arrive at the lake, I find two guys from a trail crew who have just finished loading a canoe with gear to haul to their cabin. They assure me they have just finished a lot of work on the trail to Quartz Lake and that it's in great shape. One of them is also an avid fly fisher. He shares a few local places where he has been successful the past year. I contemplate a hike to Quartz Lake. However, when I see the outlet of Bowman Lake and how beautiful it is, I decide to stay there and maybe hike to Quartz Creek when my wife comes to visit for a long weekend. Bowman Creek is running clear and looks very fishable. Within a few minutes, I see rises on the lake close enough to shore that I could possible cast to them if I wade out. I set up my chair in the shade beside the bridge and write.

Only when I put down the date in my journal do I realize that today is my birthday. Though I have nobody to celebrate it with, and no cake, I can't think of a more beautiful place to spend it. I love sitting beside flowing water, or setting up a tent by a river and going to bed to its beautiful music. Mountain streams are my favorite. In "A Native Hill", Berry suggests:

> Perhaps it is to prepare to hear someday the music of the spheres that I am always turning my ears to the music of streams. There is indeed a music in streams but it is not

for the hurried. It has to be loitered by and imagined. Or imagined *toward*, for it is hardly for men at all. Nature has a patient ear.[14]

I think Berry is right. I am happy to be here for the day, with no place I need to go. I am happy to sit and listen and watch whatever stories unfold around me at whatever pace they unfold. Once again, I have several songbirds and the rush of the creek as my soundtrack. And what a soundtrack. "The music of the streams is the music of the shaping of the earth, by which the rocks are pushed and shifted downward toward the level of the sea."[15]

Unlike Upper McDonald Creek, Bowman Creek is not laden with the silt of melted mountains. Yet I know this creek is still shaping the earth. I saw the result of that shaping in the valley I just drove along. Now and then I hear the sharp pop or crack of rock rolling or shifting in the creek. This is the part of the music, and part of their constant shaping and shifting.

Northeast across the lake, Numa Ridge stands guard over the water, and behind that Kintla Peak towers at 10,000 feet. Around to the right, Mount Carter is only slightly lower at 9,843 feet, and Square Peak at 8777 feet. Seeing these mountains, and their reflections in the calm surface of Bowman Lake, I think again how I might have written Psalm 95, sitting near the crown of the continent at an elevation of 4000 feet gazing at snow-covered peaks rising some 6,000 feet above me, instead of in the hill country of Jerusalem not far from the Sea of Galilee where the ancient Hebrew poet wrote. Jerusalem sits at 2500 feet, but the Sea of Galilee is almost 700 feet below sea level where it is much more difficult to imagine glaciation and melting snow shaping that landscape. Sitting here, I might instead write:

The majesty of the lofty mountains,
The weight of carving glaciers,
And the power of mighty rivers

---

14 Berry, p.19.
15 Ibid.

That carry them both away
inexorably to the sea.

✦   ✦   ✦   ✦   ✦   ✦

I write for a while in my chair, and then decide to wade out and cast flies. I'm at the mouth of the creek where the current draining the lake visibly picks up. It doesn't look too swift for wading, however, and I see plenty of shallow spots where I can cast to good-looking water. I check the water temperature. It's 49F. This is warmer than I expected for a lake that gets its water from melting snow and ice, yet still chilly enough to numb my feet quickly. Nonetheless, I take off my pant legs, slip into sandals, and wade out. I tie on a streamer fly imitating a small trout and swing it across the current downstream of the bridge, looking for any flash or movement below the surface. I cover a lot of river from one side to the other, and an equal distance downstream. I don't see any movement of fish, but I am refreshed by the movement of water across my legs and its music across my ears. I move upstream of the bridge and cast out into the lake where I'd seen fish rising earlier. I don't see anything there either.

When my legs grow too cold to continue, I return to the bridge, set my fly rod down, and slip back into my wool socks and hiking boots to warm my feet. A man and woman cross the bridge. The man sees my fly rod and we talk fishing. He notes that he has caught some trout in the lake. He tells me he does best from his canoe. Last night he landed an 18-inch cutthroat on a dry fly. But he does catch them in the river also, he says, and has landed some near the mouth where I'd just been fishing. I need to come back to Bowman Lake with a canoe. Meanwhile I cast some more streamers from the dry bridge in my socks and boots.

Lunch time has come and gone. I eat my orange and granola bar.

✦   ✦   ✦   ✦   ✦   ✦

On my drive back south I stop at Home Ranch Bottoms, a little tavern and store in the small North Fork community between Polebridge and Fish Creek on private land within the Flathead National Forest. The sign advertises huckleberry ice cream and huckleberry pie. Every place around advertises huckleberry something. This time I'm finally enticed, particularly when I see the sign advertising Internet also. It's mid-afternoon—too late for lunch and too early for supper. I get a huckleberry milkshake to celebrate my birthday. It is thick and delicious, and it takes me a while to finish. I'm in no rush. I'm making use of the Internet to check my mail when I learn from the owner that the whole place is off the grid. They get their electricity from solar and diesel. I get caught up on a couple days of e-mail and post some photos to Instagram.

Another customer enters. He starts talking with the owner about the beers on tap. One catches my interest. Not ready to depart, I chase the milkshake with Moose Drool, a local dark brown ale. The menu looks enticing. Another customer mentions that this place was named the seventh best restaurant in an out-of-the-way place in the United States. It's definitely out of the way. The milkshake was good, though. And I'm longing for some huckleberry pie. I add this to my list of places to bring my wife when she comes for her short visit.

I end the day having done much less writing than usual. That was my birthday celebration, I guess. Tomorrow is set aside for writing. I need to get caught up trying to put into words more of my experiences that are beyond words, and to piece together more that I've been learning. Whether I had made that plan or not, it would have become my plan for I wake the next morning to an overcast sky. Before I've finished breakfast the clouds let loose.

Rain falls steadily all day. I'm able to write without thinking of all the things I'm missing by being inside.

Avalanche Lake and Lower Quartz: "A Lifetime will not be Enough"

June 14.

On Wednesday, I am scheduled to make my first public presentation. I also have a week's worth of dirty laundry, and I'm running low on food. In the morning, I drive to the village of Coram fifteen miles outside the park to find the nearest coin-operated laundry facility. While my clothes are washing, I head into the diner. To pay for the seat and WIFI, I ask the waitress if they have huckleberry pie because huckleberries are what everybody around here has, and because diners should have pie. They don't have any. They do, however have huckleberry bread pudding. I order one hot with ice cream. It's well-worth the calories. I let it melt in my mouth while I check my e-mail and prepare my presentation.

I arrive at noon at the Community Center near park headquarters in West Glacier to find two dozen park staff gathered to hear me. I introduce myself and my goals for my month-long residency, and I read one of my essays about ecology and cutthroat trout. After I finish, somebody in a ranger uniform stands up and introduces himself as John. To my amazement, he tells me he used to live in Middlebury and that his dad read my columns. I discover that he not only lived in the same town where I now live, but on the same street just a couple blocks away. My motto for the month now becomes, "It's a big park but a small world." What's really exciting—even more than discovering that somebody actually reads my columns—is that John asks if I would be interested in going fishing with him some time. No arm-twisting is required. We exchange contact information as folks filter out. Then I head back out of the park and down to Columbia Falls.

My trip is productive. In addition to another week's worth of groceries, I head to the airport and pick up my wife who has come for a short visit. I have been looking forward to sharing a few of my favorite discoveries. I'm also excited to explore some backcountry locations I've been hesitant to visit alone. Having a hiking partner will offer new freedom. As if to emphasize that point, after dropping her luggage off at the cabin, we head immediately to the Avalanche Lake trailhead. A published hiking guide describes it as one of the most popular hikes in the park: a modest trek of not much more than two miles with only a thousand feet of elevation gain to a stunningly beautiful lake surrounded by steep walls and fed by half a dozen waterfalls pouring off melting snow.

We manage to find parking at the popular trailhead and start up the boardwalk. We pause at a footbridge on the lower loop and enjoy a cascade tumbling out of a little gorge. Then the trail leaves the boardwalk and starts its climb along Avalanche Creek through a stand of tall cedars and larch. "The streams are great collectors of comings and goings," Wendell Berry writes. "The streams go down, and paths always go down beside the streams."[16] It's true. Part of the reason is the limitation imposed by terrains. I think there is another good reason, or a fortunate side benefit. Mountain streams are beautiful, cascading and tumbling from pool to pool. The views of the water are as beautiful as those of the peaks. They also provide soundtracks nearly as beautiful, though not quite as melodic, as thrushes and warblers. I love walking alongside streams. We stop several times, not out of fatigue, but to admire the water or some particularly inspiring tree.

We are not alone. Though it is late afternoon, numerous hikers ascend ahead and behind us, and more pass by in the opposite direction. I am reminded of my most recent trip to Banff National Park in late September when larches were attired in yellow fall foliage. For the first two miles of my hike that day, a continuous line of other hikers separated by an arm's length stretched out of

16 Berry, p.17.

sight in both directions. Banff's fall foliage was notorious, and deservedly so. I had to hike over an hour to get past the crowds. I wonder what the slopes of Glacier National Park look like when the larches are yellow.

It's not as crowded here as that day in Banff. And though we are not alone, nature drowns out any noise of other hikers. We have both the stream and birds for our soundtrack. The varied thrush is hard to miss; I keep looking for somebody with a bear whistle. I remember how on my very first morning in the park, I had come to the trailhead at 6:00am. I was alone then and the trail was empty. As I did on several other occasions, I chose that morning not to hike alone in backcountry. Now I have my chance. An hour after we start, we arrive at Avalanche Lake warm and damp from the hike. It is as beautiful as the guidebooks say. A sequence of tall waterfalls line the cliff face across the lake, pouring down from the winter snowpack visible above. A chill wind also pours off that snow, across the lake, and into our faces. What heat we had from the hike disappears. I slip my long-sleeve merino wool tee-shirt over my head. I have my pack fly rod with me, but I don't bother setting it up. We stay only fifteen minutes, huddled together on a log by the western shoreline, and then head back down the trail where the thick trees shelter us from the wind.

Deborah has had a long day of travel. We head to the cabin where she gets ready for bed and I spend some time writing. A day later, I will hear that Avalanche Lake has been closed because a sow grizzly and cub are hanging out on the trail. Though none of the encounters with hikers ended in disaster, it will remain closed for several more days. I think first of how glad I am that we made the hike when we did. Then I think that maybe my choice not to hike up there alone, especially in the morning when the trail was empty, wasn't such a bad or timid choice after all.

✦   ✦   ✦   ✦   ✦   ✦

Thursday morning. It's my wife's first full day in the park, and the forecast is for beautiful weather. We eat a hearty breakfast, and then drive up the Outer North Fork Road toward Polebridge and Bowman Lake for a hike into Lower Quartz. The drive takes longer than I expect. We encounter two delightful delays in Flathead National Forest between Camas gate and the Polebridge entrance. The first comes when we see a cow elk with twin calves in a wide meadow a hundred yards from the road. We pull over and watch for a while. The cow checks us out, but we stay beside the car by the road on the other side of a wooden fence. When she decides we aren't a threat, she continues grazing. As the trio eats its way across the meadow, the calves stop from time to time to dance and play. When a flock of black birds rise from the field in a cloud around them, the calves skip and frolic. A row of white-capped peaks in the distance look down with their slower form of delight.

Finally, we get back into the car and continue north. Our second delay is caused by the word "bakery" on the Polebridge Mercantile sign. We each get a fresh-baked huckleberry "bear paw" pastry. These are the sorts of delays I don't mind. We have a few other shorter delays for irresistible photos, and despite a relatively early start we don't arrive at Bowman Lake until almost 11:00am. We park next to a sign warning of cougars in the area, then head toward the trailhead.

As I know from my earlier trip, the view across Bowman Lake is too beautiful to pass up. We stop at the beach for yet another delay. As Deborah sits on the bench, one of many deer in the area steps into the bushes behind her for a perfectly timed photobomb. I continue to take pictures as it walks up behind her, perhaps checking out the edibility of her hat. I think the deer aren't so much tame as they are smart; they know that predators are not as likely to come after them in the midst of a crowd of humans. The cougar, however, must sense the increased density of deer in the campground, and so it's come closer for the sake of a meal. Yet another way our presence has impacted this seemingly wild area.

Our round trip to Lower Quartz Lake makes for a long day. Our hiking guidebook tells us it is a three-mile hike. We hike across the bridge over Bowman Creek where I spent an earlier day writing and fishing. A half mile past the trailhead, a sign says it is 3.1 miles to Lower Quartz. This sort of arithmetic is not in our favor. Still, we keep on. Soon we are ascending a ridge. One guide book lists this as a 1000-foot climb followed by a 1200-foot descent to Lower Quartz. It isn't especially demanding, but the weather is warm and by halfway up we could use a short rest. For only the second time of my Glacier National Park stay, however, the mosquitoes are dense and combative. We keep moving. Near the top, flashes of yellow and bright orange flitting through the trees catch my eye. I spot a western tanager. It lands on a branch about twenty feet away. I see another one a hundred yards beyond it. I slowly lift my camera. It flies off before I can even point the camera. At least I have seen it, unlike the invisible thrushes whose songs fill these woods.

We crest the ridge and the trail provides just enough gap in the trees for a view south. We find more bear grass, but it is a week or more behind the flowers below. A breeze blows in and the density of mosquitoes drops. We pause for a trail bar and water, and then begin a steep descent through a section of forest that looks like it burned four or five decades ago. We have to watch our footing, and Deborah makes good use of her new hiking poles. Not far down I spot another pair of western tanagers. This time the near one doesn't fly away, but flits from branch to branch. I get a much closer look. Nearly its whole body is yellow, but both the wings and tail are black. It has yellow bars near the front of its wings. What I particularly note, though, is its beautiful face, bright orange-red around the beak, and up the forehead along both sides past its eyes where the soft color fades slowly to yellow, almost like it was airbrushed. I bring my camera slowly to my face and the bird stays where it is for several seconds, which turns out to be about one half second less than I need. The auto-focus of my DSLR won't work through the trees so I manually focus. Just as I get almost focused, the bird jumps to a new branch a few feet away. This repeats several times. Eventually I manage three shots before it flies off into the deeper woods.

The hike up the ridge was not along a stream. Wendell Berry's statement about paths and streams isn't always true, even in a national park. Partway down the south side, however, we come upon a small spring bubbling up near a patch of soft and inviting moss. I am thirsty and wish I could trust it enough to drink. As a child I would have filled my water bottle at such a place. Forty years ago, it might have been safe. Now I am not willing to risk it. I am reminded that my older brother got giardia just a few weeks before his wedding while backpacking with me in the Colorado Rockies, drinking from a clear stream far above the timberline where we couldn't imagine beavers spreading giardia.

The spring becomes a little stream and we follow it for a while. It is different than the hike up Avalanche Lake, or even my walks around Johns Lake. The trees here are close and thick, and I can't see far. Only the steepness of the path at my feet gives a sense of terrain. It will bring to mind a different passage from "A Native Hill"—one that seems to perfectly describe the difference between this morning's hike and yesterday evening's.

> There is no longer the possibility of seeing very far. The distances are closed off by the trees and the steepening walls of the hollow. One cannot grow familiar here by sitting and looking as one can up in the open on the ridge. Here the eyes become dependent on the feet. To see the woods from the inside one must look and move and look again. It is inexhaustible in its standpoints. A lifetime will not be enough to experience it all.[17]

17 Berry, p.16.

I want to become more familiar with this park where I have been given the gracious gift of residence. I realize this will almost certainly be my only visit to Lower Quartz Lake. I will have to settle for experience rather than familiarity, and know even then that a lifetime will not be enough. I look and move and look again. I look often at my feet, which keep finding stumps and rocks.

We arrive at the outlet of Lower Quartz. The mosquitoes have gone from bad to ferocious. It is brutal even stopping to remove our packs and dig out our lunches. The foot bridge is more primitive than the one at Bowman. It crosses from stone pylon to stone pylon. I walk out on the bridge. A refreshing breeze sweeps across the water—not so stiff as to be uncomfortable or even to upset somebody fly casting, but enough to keep off the mosquitoes. With our feet on the boulder pilings, the bridge makes a comfortable bench, and we eat lunch in the mosquito-free zone. We admire the lake as we eat. It is quiet, nestled in a valley surrounded by low wooded hills. Unlike Avalanche Lake, it boasts no spectacular mountain views. Still, it's a near-perfect spot.

When I see a few fish rise, I rig up my fly rod, change from hiking boots to sandals, zip my pant legs off, and head fifty feet up the shoreline to the head of the creek. The fish continue to rise. Looking more closely, I see dark gray mayflies coming off the surface. I tie on a gray Wulff and wade out into the cold water. The drop off is quick and the shore is tangled with fallen trees. I can only get about five feet from shore. With trees leaning over behind me, I have to roll cast. I shoot my line out fifteen feet past the edge of a log. A large trout emerges from under the log, slams my fly hard, and breaks my line. I tie on a new leader and a new fly. Over the next forty minutes I land six cutthroat on the same fly. The first three are thirteen to fourteen inches long, which is larger than I'd expected. While I'm fishing, Deborah sits on the bridge and reads. She points out a loon cruising the lake behind me, probably also looking for trout. I work further up the shore, and then out deeper above the creek mouth. My fourth trout is smaller—maybe nine inches. The last two are just seven-inch fish. Some are still rising, but the noses I see breaking the surface also look small. I decide it's time to depart. We leave the bridge, brave the mosquitoes long enough to pack up our gear, and start back up the trail. As we hike up the ridge, Deborah hears the echo as the loon sings its beautiful and mournful song.

SCARS AND DIVIDES:
"THE DIFFERENCE BETWEEN A PATH AND A ROAD"

JUNE 17.

My alarm sounds at 5:30am. I resist the temptation to hit "snooze". We want to make the most of our time spent driving over the continental divide. It would have been easy to spend the entire month on the west side of the park, even staying in the Lake McDonald valley and sticking to trailheads off the Going-to-the-Sun Road. I would not have run out of places to visit or revisit. Yet my trip would be incomplete if I didn't get over to the east side at least once. My wife's visit is a good excuse to do so.

At the recommendation of one of the Lake McDonald Lodge staff, we have a list of places to see. We finish breakfast, and head out toward the west entrance before 6:00am. US-2 takes us along the Middle Fork of the Flathead upriver toward its source, following the boundary between Glacier National Park and the Flathead National Forest. Except for one short stretch where the road crosses into the park, we drive on the south side of the river—the national forest side—along a busy railroad track. For the first several miles the road cuts along a gorge a hundred feet above the water. I glance down from time to time when it is safe. The river still rages whitish green from snowmelt and the past twenty-four hours of rain. It looks like a kale smoothie still being mixed in a blender. Thankfully, though, the rain has stopped and the morning is beautiful. The peaks to our left are draped in clouds. Ephemeral mist clings to the lower slopes like flimsy lingerie.

Though we are on a route labeled East US-2, much of our journey takes us more southward. We pass through the settlement of Nyack and a few private homes and lodges grandfathered into private land in the midst of the national forest. Though I know the Middle Fork must be getting smaller as we follow it upriver, past tributary after tributary, for many miles it is difficult to see any difference in size. In Nimrod—a village that shares its name with a great-grandson of Noah, a great hunter of biblical times—we come to the confluence of the Middle Fork with Bear Creek. Here US-2 turns back east along Bear Creek toward the Continental Divide. The Middle Fork flows down from the south and the Great Bear Wilderness. I look up the Middle Fork with some longing. I would love to get backcountry into this wilderness if it were a little later in the year when the higher elevations were no longer snowbound.

Now we follow Bear Creek for several miles. This is not a big valley river like the lower Middle Fork, but a tumbling cascading mountain creek narrow enough that the riparian canopy from opposite banks nearly touches overhead. We cross the Continental Divide, passing from the Pacific Ocean watershed into the watershed of the Mississippi River and Gulf of Mexico. Soon we come across another small creek and for the first time today we are driving in the same direction as the flow of water. The landscape opens up. Ridges no longer tightly enclose the road. The slopes have shed their lingerie. Snow and not clouds now whiten the higher elevations.

✦   ✦   ✦   ✦   ✦   ✦

I have not spent any time on the eastern side of Glacier National Park during my residency. It is not merely that any trip to the east side and back requires several hours in a car—hours not spent writing. It's also the fish. Cutthroat making their way up the Columbia River colonized many waters on the western side thousands of years ago by. That strain of westslope cutthroat has been lost through much of its native range, even in parts of Glacier National Park, such as in the Flathead River system where cross-breeding with non-native rainbow trout has diluted the westslope cutthroat genes. What has come to light only recently through the work of scientists like USGS biologist Clint Muhlfeld is that genes of the Yellowstone cutthroat sub-species—a strain not native to Glacier National Park, but introduced decades ago to a couple lakes—have also spread far into the native westslope population. Some isolated westslope populations still persist, but they are rarer than thought. Learning about them, and about their place in and dependency upon the greater Glacier ecosystem, is part of what brought me to the park, and why I have focused my time on the west. The future of westslope cutthroat may rest in those remaining westslope waters that still protect that wild and native strain.

Yet as I have heard, and as I now begin to discover, the east slope is just as magnificent as the west with some subtle and not-so-subtle differences in character, based in part on higher elevations and a dryer climate. In the town of East Glacier, we turn north and follow Highway 49 around a steep winding mountain slope, enjoying stunning views past fields of wildflowers and over Lower Two Medicine Lake back toward the park. We stop briefly to take in the view. Once driving, however, I am more aware of numerous windings of this road. As we go up, over, around, and down Two Medicine Ridge, we seem to be following the path of a spaghetti noodle through a plate of pasta. We turn onto US-89. It is a wider and straighter road, but even this route takes a big bend to circumnavigate a ridge. This surprises me, since the ridge doesn't appear especially steep. I wonder that parts of the road were not carved in a more direct route. That flash of impatience, however, is only momentary. I am not in any hurry, and the drive is beautiful. All of Highway 49 is itself a seasonal shortcut, saving us from heading all the way east to US-89 in Browning.

Not for the last time, my thoughts turn back to Berry's essay, and one of my favorite passages from it.

> The difference between a path and a road is not only the obvious one. A path is little more than a habit that comes with knowledge of a place. It is a sort of ritual familiarity. As a form, it is a form of contact with a known landscape. It is not destructive. It is the perfect adaptation, through experience and familiarity, of movement to place; it obeys the natural contours; such obstacles as it meets it goes around. A road, on the other hand, even the most primitive road, embodies a resistance against the landscape. Its reason is not simply the necessity for movement, but haste. Its wish is to *avoid* contact with the landscape; it seeks so far as possible to go over the country, rather than through it; its aspiration, as we see clearly in the example of our modern freeways, is to be a bridge; its tendency is to translate place into space in order to traverse it with the least effort. It is destructive, seeking to remove or destroy all obstacles in its way.[18]

I know this road is in some ways a scar on the hillside. I am glad, at least, that it winds more like a path, more in obedience to the hill's contours. We wonder aloud whether the road was an old wagon path. I'm glad no highway designer blasted a straight route through the center of the hill. We will remain patient and delight in it.

---

18 Berry, p.12.

At the bottom of a long slope, a view opens up of a windy Saint Mary Lake. This last ridge we wound over had another significance. Though less than an hour earlier we crossed out of the Pacific Watershed, we cross another divide here, passing from the Gulf of Mexico into the Hudson Bay watershed that reaches to the very edge of the Arctic. In just an hour or so of mid-morning, we will have driven beside waters from all three divides on this Crown of the Continent.

Though we now look at some of the same peaks from the opposite side—and are just three dozen miles away from my cabin if we had come over the Going-to-the-Sun road, and less if we were crows—I'm still aware of the difference in landscape. We now see forests dominated by deciduous aspens rather than cedar and hemlock. When the road winds around the east side of the hill we catch glimpses of endless high prairie, and I appreciate Montana's claim to a Big Sky.

We stop at the St. Mary's entrance and visitor center, and spend time reading the words and thoughts of leaders of three different native peoples who used to roam freely on what is now Glacier National Park, hunting, fishing, and worshiping. These are peoples who are no longer free to use that land in the same way. Some of their words and thoughts will haunt me through the day. I am thankful to the park for its honesty in sharing the words. To say that I am glad for the existence of Glacier National Park would be a dramatic understatement. I have no doubt that I will be marked and shaped by this time I get to spend here, and will be forever grateful for it. Even apart from my own visit, I am glad for the work of conservation and preservation that goes on because of the park. I am also deeply saddened that the joy and delight of so many who visit here has come out of the pain and loss of peoples who once experienced that same delight and are now largely excluded from it. I wonder if and how it would be possible for the park still to be a "national" park without excluding those whose ancestors once dwelt here.

Wendell Berry wrote of the same haunting. "I am forever being crept up on and newly startled by the realization that my people established themselves here by killing or driving out the original possessors... by the sense of the violence they have done to their own kind and to each other and to the earth."[19]

✦　　✦　　✦　　✦　　✦　　✦

We leave the St. Mary Visitor Center and drive first to the pull-off for the Jackson Glacier View. This is as far as the road is open today. Logan Pass is still buried. Some of the peaks are now dusted with yet more new snow that fell during the night. Though I'd hoped to see them dusted instead with morning sunlight, this different dusting is also beautiful. Yet our eyes search not for new snow from last night, but for snowfall that is centuries old and packed by the weight of time. We are looking for Jackson Glacier. In a dozen or so years, visitors to Glacier National Park won't see glaciers. They will have melted in the air of a warming planet. Maybe this will be my own last chance to see the glaciers of this park. I don't want to miss it.

We look at a deep pack of white snow in the direction where the signs point to the Jackson Glacier. We think it is the glacier, but covered by the same dusting of new snow that covers the mountain peaks it's hard to tell where the glacier ends and the winter snowpack begins. I think now, not of Wendell Berry's words about road-building, but of the words of one of the leaders of the Kootenai posted at the St. Mary Visitor Center. "The Kootenai recognize the irony of the Going-to-the-Sun Road. It is a huge scar on the landscape that cuts right through the heart of Glacier. But without it there would be fewer visitors and less support for keeping Glacier National Park pristine." This is one of the ironies I have wrestled with increasingly over my time. It lay

---

19 Berry, p.8.

behind my conversation with Jessica on my third day in the park. The irony could be broadened from the road to the entire park.

Elsewhere on that wall I read more words of Kootenai elders addressing similar issues:

> In Glacier National Park, our elders are appreciative of a national desire to preserve the area in its pristine condition.
>
> We are thankful for the preservation of an area that has 500-year-old cedar trees who listened to our ancestors sing and dance long before the Kootenai were aware of Europeans. Yet, we are also aware that this place has not been preserved because of its significance to us. It is preserved because of the many visitors that come to the area.

Deeply thankful for the preservation of this area, I have both delighted, and been awed, to walk in the midst of those 500-year old cedars. Reading these words, however, I hold this thankfulness with mixed feelings—feelings that apply not only to the scar of the Going-to-the-Sun Road, but the park in general. I realize again that "pristine" is a relative word. I hope that in years to come the benefit of the amazing work of preservation will benefit the Kootenai people. And the Blackfeet also, as well as the Pend d'Oreille. The words of Pend d'Oreille elder Snacé Earring nearly a century ago as he stood atop Logan Pass—which his people call the "Pass of the Mountain Goat"—must ring even more true today: "To the Salish and Pend d'Oreille elders, the park now feels like another place dominated by non-Indians. But the elders still like to come here when they can, and they still feel the power of the place." I think he must have felt the strength of the hills far more keenly than I ever will. Maybe his sense of that strength was more akin to that ancient Hebrew poet who first sang that hymn we now refer to as Psalm 95.

After staring at what we think is a shrinking glacier, and pondering the significance of it, we drive back down the road and hike to St. Mary Falls. As we walk, we look across the lake at Virginia Falls thundering down the other side of the valley. We have a clear view because we are walking through another forest burned by fire. The south-facing slope is blanketed with an array of wildflowers of many varieties and colors including lupines and some variety of paintbrush. Once again, I thought as Wendell Berry did when he came on the wildflowers in Kentucky, "I was also exultant that I saw them now—that they were here."[20]

Like so many other walks over the past week and a half, our soundtrack is mix of songbirds and the low thrum of a thundering river and a pair of waterfalls. At the falls, a water ouzel flies past and lands on a piece of moss almost behind the falls. It then flies out through the spray, down the river below our footbridge and out of sight. I wait for it to return, but it doesn't.

Our drive from St. Mary's back around to Many Glacier at the foot of Swift Current Lake takes us back outside the park again. It is windy at Swift Current Lake. We decide to sit inside and enjoy the view from behind glass rather than go for a walk. We stay for only an hour. On the drive out we come to a wildlife traffic jam. A dozen cars are pulled off on both sides. Visitors stand roadside holding cameras and binoculars. We join the crowds and spend twenty minutes watching a large black bear munching his way across a meadow with a lake behind him and a row of jagged peaks behind that. This is an iconic Glacier National Park scene. It helps give the impression of pristine. Except I know this bear has been influenced by human presence. He is unperturbed by his human audience. His meandering brings him steadily closer to the line of cars.

---

20 Berry, p.24.

A pair of rangers stands by keeping close watch. I suspect they are here primarily to keep the humans from doing stupid things. When the bear gets within fifty yards of the road, a ranger—holding a can of bear spray as a precaution—runs into the field waving his arms and shouting at the bear. The bear gets the point. He turns and runs off a hundred yards. He soon realizes, however, that the human is no longer chasing him. He stops running and resumes munching on whatever he is munching on. Flowers? Clover? Insects in the grass? As we drive away, he is already beginning to meander back toward the road. He has clearly learned that humans are not a threat, and probably also that where there are humans there is food.

The Peace of Woods and the Names of Streams: "Things Fall Into Place"

June 24.

My wife's too-short visit is over. I am alone. As our last backcountry outing together, we took a horseback ride up to Snyder Lake. Snyder Lake, and Upper Snyder Lake above it, are important parts of a few stories. They are among the remaining waters where native westslope cutthroat still reside above the reach of invasive rainbow and brook trout. They are also important to the story of Snyder Creek. They are its source.

Today I awake again to a 4:30am alarm. I will begin my morning where Snyder Creek gives up its name—where it flows into, and becomes one with, Lake McDonald. Before the day is over, however, I hope also to visit the creek farther upstream, closer to its source. If Snyder Creek were a story told only in the direction of its flow, I would be reading that story out of order, skipping ahead to the ending before reading the middle. But its story is told in myriad different ways, and my life moves too fast to read more than a few words. Someday maybe I will return and bushwhack to Upper Snyder Lake, and then follow the whole course of Snyder Creek down to Lake McDonald. This summer I must be content visiting just a few spots, remembering that the creek's story is told over time more than space.

I skip breakfast, and take only enough time to brew coffee while I tug on my waders. Then I am out the door walking down the road toward the Lake McDonald Lodge where Snyder Creek empties into Lake McDonald. I've already rigged my fly rod with a dry fly imitating a small hatching midge, and added a little imitation midge nymph a foot and a half below that. At 4:55am I stand knee deep in the lake, casting where the waters of creek and lake mingle. This is my second morning in a row here. For an hour at sunrise yesterday, trout taunted me by sipping natural flies off the surface of the lake while ignoring every artificial fly I threw at them. Last night I went to bed thinking about the noses of those insect-sucking fish ignoring my attempts to deceive them. Unlike yesterday morning, the sky is cloudless today. A rich golden glow halos the peaks at the northeastern end of the lake. I even get a hint of pink on the lower hills on the southwestern end, away from the mountains. Though it's barely light enough to see my flies inches from my face, and certainly too dark to tie another one on, swallows are already busy over the water swooping and rising and darting this way and that.

Trout are rising also, just like yesterday. They hit the surface hard all around the alluvial fan of this little tributary. A few chase the natural insects so aggressively they come partway out of the water, letting me see not only their lips, but their heads as well. This behavior suggests trout feeding on *emergers*: aquatic insects in the process of hatching from their underwater nymph stage to their winged adult stage. Emergers are vulnerable to fish as they swim toward the sky, or as they sit briefly on the surface drying their wings before flying away. Then they become vulnerable to the swallows. The trout must come fast, and get them before they become swallow food. This is what I expected, and why I am fishing a midge nymph as a *dropper* below my other fly. The dry fly is there primarily as a float for the little nymph, and to act as an indicator letting me know if a fish takes my nymph below the surface. At the end of each cast as my line grows taut, that submerged fly should swing upward toward the surface like an emerging midge.

It was a promising plan, or so I thought. I fish for half an hour without a single strike. Though whatever insect is hatching is too small for me to see, the fish continue to rise and the swallows continue to feed. When it is light enough to tie a knot, I go through some of my other small flies hoping to find something close to what is hatching. They all prove equally unsuccessful. By 5:45am the sky is light and the fish have stopped rising. I give up and head home for oatmeal, defeated by the trout.

Tired from my early morning start, I consider napping. Then I reflect that seven days from now I will drive out of the park, board an airplane, and fly home to Vermont. This may be the most beautiful day of my trip. I make lunch and walk out the door with a fly rod, iPad, camping chair, water, and an extra layer of insect-repellent clothing tucked into my pack. It is a relatively easy round-trip hike of seven miles. Despite its name, I don't plan to fish in Fish Lake, but the hike will bring me across three small mountain streams. One book mentions that Snyder Creek, the first of the three I will cross, holds invasive brook trout in the lower stretches. I'm curious to find some of these exotic eastern implants and see what kind of water they have colonized, and where they have competed with and possibly displaced the native cutthroat trout.

Fisheries biologist Kurt Fausch, in his early research on the impact of invasive trout, helped lead an extensive study of Rocky Mountain streams in Colorado and Idaho. His research compared waters holding only native cutthroat trout with comparable waters that had been invaded by brook trout. The research found that "the density of insects emerging from brook trout streams was only about two-thirds of the amount from the paired streams with native cutthroat trout." To verify this, they ran additional studies in lab-controlled streams, and the results were even more pronounced. "Brook trout... could reduce the density of emerging insects by more than half compared with native cutthroat trout, when the two species were at the same density and other factors were controlled."[21] This, of course, would directly impact any other animals that fed on emerging aquatic insects such as riparian-dwelling birds and rodents. Indirectly it would impact everything further up and down the food chain, which is to say, the entire ecosystem. Based on their studies, for example, a brook trout invasion (as a result of human stocking) of an alpine cutthroat trout stream would result in a 20% reduction in spiders. If I find and catch any brook trout in Snyder Creek, I will happily remove it from the water. Although that action alone won't save the stream and its spiders, I won't feel guilty eating a fresh brook trout for supper.

The hike to Fish Lake begins up the Sperry Trail along the same route I took on horseback a few days earlier. Most of the thousand-foot gain in elevation comes in the first two miles as the trail follows the edge of the steep ravine carved by Snyder Creek. Several openings in the trees provide scenic overlooks across Lake McDonald toward Howe Ridge. Despite the gorgeous panorama, my eyes are continually drawn downward toward the creek. A hundred and fifty feet below me I catch glimpses of tumbling cascades of white water. In one spot, where direct morning sunlight reaches the creek, a thick insect hatch comes off the water. A column of fluttering white wings climbs dozens of feet into the air, above the tree tops. I'm too far away for a clear identification. They could be caddis or mayflies.

As I expected, plenty of other hikers travel the trail. One threesome runs past me in serious training mode. Others meander along at slower paces. A few parents have young kids on their

---

21   Kurt D. Fausch, *For the Love of Rivers: A Scientist's Journey*, (Corvallis: Oregon State University Press, 2015), p.179.

packs or beside them holding hands, but they still move quickly enough to overtake me when I stop to gaze down at Snyder Creek looking for more insects and scoping prospects for trout habitat. Folks are friendly with greetings. When I lose my views down into the gorge, I begin to move more quickly. I reach the trailhead to Snyder Lake on my left, and continue past it. The Sperry Trail makes a short descent toward the creek, which has been climbing up a steep gradient to meet me.

I like that, in the opening paragraph of "A Native Hill", Wendell Berry names not only the Kentucky River at the bottom of the hill, but also Gullion's Branch and Cane Run, two creeks whose valleys lead down to the larger river valley. For several days, I've pondered a small mystery. I've always loved maps, and it's their blue lines that draw my attention most. I love looking at the names of streams and rivers (even small ones), and studying the paths they follow. I've done so since I was young. I'm curious about the boundaries of watersheds. Maybe this also explains why "A Native Hill" speaks to me so much. I can relate to his reflections on the confluences of waters and the sounds of streams.

It's been thirty years since I last called "home" the rural New England town where I went to elementary and high school. I've forgotten the names of most of the streets, and even of my teachers and classmates. I might struggle to navigate the back roads if I were to visit there again. Yet given a town map, I could draw in the waterways and ponds. I can picture where three year-round streams eventually come together to flow out through the woods on the eastern edge of town, and where another passes through marshes and comes out the southern boundary. It helps that I spent countless hours traipsing along them as a teenager, usually with a fishing rod in my hand. If walked along them today, I'd be saddened that many once-favorite stretches now flow through housing developments, but I could still map them.

Part of what I love about Glacier National Park is being only a few miles from the divide of three watersheds. I've spent a lot of time sitting at the table studying maps, paying most of my attention to streams, rivers, and lakes, and connecting what I observe as I hike and drive to their cartographic representations. I remember arriving on my first day and driving northeast along the south shore of Lake McDonald. Approaching the lodge, I crossed three little creeks in the final mile. The first and westernmost flows into the lake at Sprague Creek Campground. The smallest of the three, it is easy to drive across without noticing. The campground name was my primary clue to the creek's existence, but the topology also hints at it. Most of the drive runs along the base of a steep ridge with no space to put a campground along the lake shore. Sprague Creek Campground sits on a rare flat jut of land, maybe three hundred feet wide and a thousand feet long, sticking out into the lake. When I first saw it, I wondered if it was an alluvial fan, built up over thousands of years by a creek carrying loads of gravel as the snow melts the mountains. I assumed also that the creek whose alluvial deposit made Sprague Creek Campground would be called Sprague Creek.

A few hundred yards further along, however, I came to the second of the three creeks. A sign labeled it as Sprague Creek. I made a mental note of this. I soon learned that this middle creek flows into the Lake McDonald only a few dozen yards from my cabin, and I thought about it often, wondering where it comes from, and whether fish swim in it. For my first two and a half weeks in the park, it flowed high and wild with melting snow, spilling over its banks and threatening to spill over the road.

Lastly, I crossed Snyder Creek, the third and easternmost of the trio, which flows into Lake McDonald just behind the lodge where I have now spent two mornings in unsuccessful pursuit of trout. Synder Creek is also marked by a roadside sign. After observing this all on my first drive in, and on several subsequent trips, I checked it out carefully on two different maps. Here was the curious thing: the maps and roadside signage were at odds. According to the maps, the creek flowing into Sprague Creek

Campground is, indeed, Sprague Creek. The middle creek has no name. Yet all three creeks follow a parallel path down the mountain and pour into the lake near one another. Is it possible I was misreading the map? I double-, triple-, and quadruple-checked. I kept finding the same thing. The creek with the Sprague Creek sign on the roadside has no name on the map. The creek labeled Sprague on the map has no name on the roadside. Creeks are not highways. They can't cross over or under one another.

I kept meaning to ask somebody about this. Just a couple days before my Fish Lake hike, however, the sign for Sprague Creek disappeared altogether. I looked for it. I asked several park employees about it. Nobody knew what I was talking about. A few folks looked at me like I was deluded with tales of disappearing signs—or possibly disappearing creeks. But though I often confuse the names of my own children, these are the sorts of things that stick in my brain. So I take this hike today with the mystery still hanging over me. Now is my chance to get closer to the origins of these streams.

The trail crosses over Snyder Creek at a place labeled on some maps as Crystal Ford. I stand at the bridge and look into the water, hoping for a glimpse of a trout. I see nothing. Above the bridge the creek looks like it could be small-trout water. Downstream the gradient steepens quickly as it drops into the ravine. I leave my fly-rod in my pack and continue on. Immediately across the bridge, the trail to Fish Lake turns right off the Sperry Trail. I climb a short distance over the last lip of a ridge, and find myself standing in a thick stand of fir and larch. Though the sun has been staring hard at me all morning, unblinking, I now move through cool refreshing shadows. I hear the gentle murmur of a creek somewhere nearby, but I don't immediately see it. The top of the ridge is almost level and nothing in the contour suggests an obvious stream. Everything feels muffled and mysterious, but strangely alive. It's like a scene of out of the *Chronicles of Narnia*, maybe from *Prince Caspian* when Lucy senses the woods just on the verge of waking up. This would be a good place for a dryad, or possibly an ent.

I think again of Wohlleben's *The Hidden Life of Trees* and wonder what these trees are communicating to one another. I think about a tree's consciousness—whatever that might be—and of its different time scale, how it takes several hours for a nerve impulse to travel the height of a tree from root to branch, or for a tree to speak with a neighboring tree. In the 1999 film *The Matrix*, Neo Anderson learns to move at "bullet time", like his nemesis Agent Smith. It is portrayed as a power in the film, but it could also be a horrible limitation. Other humans become mere statues. If Neo's own consciousness remained in bullet time, he would be unable to communicate with other humans. He could deliver a long oratory, and it would be just a blip in the ears of another human, while their uttering of even a single syllable would seem to Neo to take hours. If he always lived in bullet time, he might not even recognize humans as conscious. He must slow himself back down again, or else he will miss out on life.

Maybe we need to do the same thing, if we want to hear the voices of trees, or read the story of Snyder Creek. What richness a tree has, when its life spans centuries! In "A Native Hill", Berry writes that when we are aware not only of the physical extent of the forest, but of its temporal extent, then we "come into the presence of mystery. After all the trouble one has taken to be a modern man, one has come back under the spell of primitive awe, wordless and humble."[22]

✦   ✦   ✦   ✦   ✦   ✦

As I walk, attentive to the hint of running water and scanning for a nearby stream, I become aware of intense bird activity. Flapping wings and darting shadows fill the trees ahead of me. I continue forward several steps. Soon everywhere I look—left and

---

22 Berry, p.26.

right, low and high—I see dozens of little brown birds fluttering from branch to branch. It's busier than the swarm of swallows on the lake in the morning. Some land on trunks at eye level only ten yards from the trail, but I become aware of many more high in the canopy where the treetops are full of bright red cones. I take out my camera and try for a photo, but it's nearly impossible. The birds are constantly moving, appearing and disappearing, darting in and out of shadows, landing on a cone only to take one little peck and then fly off. I try focusing on a cone, but there are so many cones that the birds never land on the one I am aimed at.

After several minutes, I give up with the camera. My attention drifts back to the other part of the soundtrack: the nearby stream. Following the gentle sounds, and hints from the contour, I wander southward away from the trail and deeper into the quiet of the woods. I almost trip into the water before I see it. It is the most gentle and unique—and in its quiet way, beautiful—creek I have seen in Glacier National Park. I sense that I am near the source. To my left I see a slight depression in the hill. It isn't quite a meadow. Trees grow there. Yet the trees are less dense. The stream emerges from there. It seems to pour out of the ground, from springs and wetlands in this secret wood. Though the creek flows past only thirty yards from the trail, I'd never have spotted it from more than a few feet away. The surface is almost level with the ground, but branches and grasses lean over and blanket the water.

If I lived nearby, I would return often. Berry speaks of the importance of places like this, and of the wisdom we gain from striving less to live in bullet time, and more in forest time.

> Sometimes I can no longer think in the house or in the garden or in the cleared fields... And so I go to the woods. As I enter in under the trees, dependably, almost at once, and by nothing I do, things fall into place. I enter an order that does not exist outside, in the human spaces. I feel my life take its place among the lives—the trees, the annual

plants, the animals and birds, the living of all these and the dead—that go and have gone to make the life of the earth. I am less important than I thought, the human race is less important than I thought. I rejoice in that. My mind loses its urgings, senses its nature, and is free. The forest grew here in its own time, and so I will live, suffer and rejoice, and die in my own time.[23]

I take a few minutes breathing the moist woodsy air. Then I return to the trail and continue to walk slowly through the woods, listening to birds, listening to the stream, trying to listen to the trees. The trail bends back to the right and down a gentle slope. The creek, which had followed a parallel but invisible path to my left, takes the same turn. The course of the stream now emerges clearly, free from its low blanket of branches. The stream and trail converge at a bridge a few dozen yards ahead. I am just below a transition point: a threshold or liminal space. The stream escapes from its secret wooded glade and prepares to tumble down the hillside through cascades and plunge pools like a traditional mountain creek. Eventually it will pop out of the woods near my artist cabin. I wonder how many people have walked alongside this stream or followed its course down the entire hillside. Very few, I guess. I would like to do so one day, perhaps after I have followed Snyder Creek.

I continue over the bridge. A short distance later I come to a much smaller creek that—despite the road signs at the bottom—is Sprague Creek. I know from the map that it flows down from the small lakes above Sperry Chalet, and on down the mountain toward its namesake campground. Only a few dozen yards past this creek I emerge at Fish Pond.

✦   ✦   ✦   ✦   ✦   ✦

---

23 Berry, pp.24-25.

Unlike Avalanche Lake, Fish Pond is quiet and out of the way. I saw no other hikers on my way in. Though I'm told trout live in the lake, it does not look like trout water. The nearby edge is covered with lily pads. It looks shallow and warm. I take out my camera, but not my fly rod. As I drop down a little slope from the trail to the shoreline, I discover I'm not alone. A photographer sits by the shore, his camera on a tripod with his big lens aimed down toward lily pads. We talk for a while. He points out two frogs on pads just a few feet away. They are the first frogs I've seen in the park. Suddenly he starts snapping photos. One of the frogs has just caught a dragonfly. It hangs out of the frog's mouth. I want to get photos too, but I'd feel guilty; he had been working so hard, and waiting so patiently, for that shot.

After a while, I turn and move along the shoreline. Several male and female yellow-rumped warblers hop and flutter from lily pad to lily pad. The colors of the males are striking. Along with a rich assortment of shades of blue, slate, and gray on their backs and wings, and some brown on their tails, they have bright yellow throats, yellow caps, soft yellowish underbellies, and yellow wing bars. And, of course, they have yellow rumps: little patches of yellow on the top of their tails. The females are more muted in their bodies, but still sport soft yellow throats and shoulder bars, and yellow on their undersides. When one of them manages to snag a dragonfly, it pauses on a lily pad to enjoy the snack, or flies off with it into the woods, perhaps to a nest and waiting young. Otherwise they are constantly moving, pin-balling between pads, never staying on a pad more than a few seconds. They are mesmerizing to watch.

A chipping sparrow also makes an appearance. In the sunlight, its crest appears slightly raised and takes on a deep chocolate hue. While the birds flutter and chirp and dine around me, I sit and eat my own lunch and enjoy the peace. Nobody else shows up at the pond during the hour and a half I am here. With the exception of my occasional pre-dawn outings, this is as much solitude as I have experienced in the park. After lunch, I watch a pair of ducks in the distance. Then I pack up my chair and head out.

I cross back over Sprague Creek—it looks too small to hold fish—and continue on. A few minutes later I arrive once more at the middle creek. I stand on the footbridge and look down into the water. This stretch of creek looks beautiful. An oxygen-enhancing and insect-friendly riffle gives way to a soft pool, then a log jam, a bend, and another pool. It looks like a perfect stretch of water for some small cutthroat trout. A thick canopy shades the stream, offering numerous places for a fish to hide from a bird or mink. Beyond the bend and second pool, the stream plunges over a rock and around some boulders before it takes another sharp bend. After that it descends more quickly and disappears from view. Upstream of the bridge it looks shallower, but still promising.

I get off the bridge and find a spot to lean my pack against a tree. In a few moments, I have all nine pieces of my old L.L. Bean pack rod put together. I haven't yet seen any fish or even any rising insects, but I have no doubt that the stream has plenty of food for a trout. Remembering the thick cloud of insects coming off Snyder Creek in the late morning, I tie on an elk hair caddis with tan wings and an olive body. Within three minutes I catch two cutthroat trout right below the bridge. One is six inches long. The other is seven. I put my hand into the clear water to release them gently. The creek is refreshingly cool, and given the canopy I imagine it will stay that way all summer even through July and August. What lovely habitat for a small wild cutthroat trout!

That is my thought today. Several weeks from now, however, I will read that this ridgeline is burning. A brutally hot and dry July will be followed by an even hotter August. Much of northern Montana will be on fire, along with Idaho, Washington, and

Oregon. Smoke will fill the skies of the Pacific Northwest. It will make for beautiful sunsets, but it's hard to think of much else that is positive. The fire will burn the famous Sperry Chalet—a tragic loss—and I will see photos of fire trucks in front of Lake McDonald Lodge. I will think of various hikes I took up this ridge. I will weep at the loss of these old trees that filled me with peace and mystery and awe. My thoughts will turn also to this little stream that flows off the ridge, and to the small, wild, fragile cutthroat trout in it. Their canopy is gone. I will wonder what the heat of the fire has done to them.

But none of that future knowledge is present to me as I stand on the bridge. I spend a few more minutes exploring downstream and up, but I get only thirty yards in each direction before the brush dissuades me from pushing further in my hiking shoes. I hook and lose one more fish in a pool below a boulder. Then I set off down the trail again. Moving in human time, I arrive back at Snyder Creek. I wonder if I can have success at two creeks today? If I catch anything in Snyder, will it be a native cutthroat trout or invasive brook trout? Keeping the same elk hair caddis imitation on, I fish first below the bridge. The creek still runs high from melting snow. The main current looks too swift for a trout, but I drop my fly into some likely looking seams near the edges. Nothing moves for the fly. I follow the trail thirty yards up to the next corner and fish a couple spots. I meet no success. I climb along the bank on the downstream side until the thick brush blocks my path. There I manage to drop a fly in a pool behind a boulder and a small fish grabs the fly the instant it touches the water. I find a cutthroat, only about five inches long. I release it carefully. I'm happy to have found a native fish, and only slightly disappointed I won't be able to remove an invasive fish for supper.

I set my rod down by my pack and return to the bridge. There I stand, enjoying the stream as hikers pass by every few minutes. Looking down with polarized lenses into the stretch of current I hadn't bothered to fish because it had looked unpromising, I'm surprised to spot movement in current near the tail of a small pool. I watch more closely, and the hint of movement becomes a fish, appearing and disappearing as it wanders back and forth between current too swift for me to see into and the softer water on the side. After watching for a couple minutes, I grab my GoPro and bungie it to a long stick I find lying on the ground. I start a video running and—lying on my belly—slip the camera down into the swift current behind the fish. As I watch more closely, I see not just one, but two, and then three little trout. I spend several minutes taking underwater videos and photos. Then I return with my fly rod. I dangle a caddis fly over the eddy from the bridge, straight below my fly rod. Before the fly even touches the water, the two trout simultaneously leap out of the water like synchronized swimmers in cutthroat competition for my fly. I catch the one with the better aim, lead it to the near shore and observe it for a moment, then release it gently back to its home.

+   +   +   +   +   +

I hike back down the mountain glad to have found native cutthroat rather than invasive brook trout in both streams I fished. I'm also delighted to have gotten close to the source of one of them, and to have turned lines on a map into a real thread of water beneath trees full of singing birds. As for the mystery of the stream names, it takes me three more days to solve it. After an evening paddling a canoe on Bowman Lake with Ranger John, I share my riddle with him. Though I feel foolish telling him so, I claim certainty both in having seen a roadside sign labeling the middle creek as Sprague, and later having that sign disappear. The next day, John gets back to me. At the start of the year, the Glacier National Park sign people had put the Sprague Creek sign up in the wrong place. They didn't discover the error until after I arrived. Then, of course, they took it down. That middle brook—the creek flowing out of a spring in a small bird-filled wooded bowl between Sprague and Snyder Creeks that had briefly been mislabeled, where I caught two small cutthroat trout just below a footbridge—was Jackson Creek.

I will continue to refer to these three streams by their names, now. If I speak of them to others who have visited this place, they may know the streams I speak of. Perhaps the names will elicit some memory of their own visits. In the end, though, despite my illusions, I realize that knowing the current English name of this stream does not mean I know the stream or its story. Wendell Berry was right in "A Native Hill": "In order to know the hill it is necessary to slow the mind down, imaginatively at least, to the hill's pace."[24] I wonder if I have even begun to slow my mind down enough, or if I'm still striving in the other direction of moving in bullet time.

INVASION OF THE BULL-TROUT SNATCHERS: "HUMILITY AND REVERENCE BEFORE THE WORLD"

COFFEE WITH CHRISTOPHER DOWNS, JUNE 28.

My morning begins with a drive to Montana Coffee Traders in Columbia Falls to meet with Christopher Downs, a National Park Service Supervisory Fisheries Biologist and Program Manager. Downs is a coauthor on several research papers I've used as sources, and has also worked on numerous projects related to the protection of native fish in Glacier National Park. These include studies of the genetic status of westslope cutthroat, projects related to the prevention and suppression of invasive lake trout, and a conservation translocation project moving remnant bull trout to waters not infested with lake trout. I am interested

---

24 Berry, "A Native Hill", *The Hudson Review*, (**21**:4)1968-1969, p.630. (Note: this sentence appears in *The Hudson Review* edition of this essay, but not in the version appearing in *The Art of the Commonplace* cited elsewhere.)

in all of these, and in hearing the general thoughts about the past, present, and future of this beautiful place of one who knows the park waters intimately.

I also learn quickly that Christopher enjoys casting flies for trout. For that reason, our ninety-minute "interview" proves almost too enjoyable. I make an effort not to get sidetracked talking about fishing. I begin with a question many have raised with me: What is the difference between one species of trout and another? They all live in cold rivers. They are all beautiful. Why does it matter whether cutthroat, rainbow, or brook trout live in some small mountain stream? Why make the effort to prevent non-native fish from colonizing park waters, or to suppress them once they are there?

Christopher's answers are knowledgeable and articulate. He is also passionate in explaining why protecting native bull trout and cutthroat trout is so important. He enumerates a number of ecological, economic, and also cultural reasons. As a biologist, he can speak at length about ecological interdependencies. Not only are aquatic ecosystems finally tuned over millennia, but what happens in rivers has a profound impact on what happens in the adjacent forests and vice versa. "Cutthroat trout are a link even to a terrestrial food chain," he says, mentioning several fish-dependent animals such as otters, loons, and osprey. "Cutthroat are a very easy prey to secure [as food for other animals]. They are up on top of the water. They're visible from the air. Along with whitefish they make up a big portion of the diet" of several birds and terrestrial mammals. Even bald eagles, he points out—though they vary their diet more than osprey—depend on cutthroat.

Downs then goes deeper into ecological issues. Tremendous diversity exists among the native cutthroat that have evolved in these waters over thousands of years. Some are adapted to an *adfluvial* life history: hatching from eggs in streams and rivers, returning to lakes in adulthood to take advantage of a more abundant food supply and deeper colder water in the summer, and then returning to the rivers to spawn. Even among the adfluvial strains of cutthroat, some spawn in the outlets of lakes, while some spawn in tributaries; some are well adapted to mountain tarns, and others to big lower elevation lakes. Other strains of the same species are adapted to a fluvial environment, spending their entire life in moving water. Even among the westslope cutthroat with fluvial life histories, some are adapted to bigger rivers such as the South Fork of the Flathead, and others to small headwater streams like the hand-sized fish I caught in Snyder and Jackson Creeks. Some will live their entire lives within a few yards of where they hatched from eggs, while others may swim dozens of miles making use of a variety of habitats over their lifespan. A similar comment can be made about the native bull trout. When those native genes are replaced in the ecosystem with genes of hatchery rainbow trout, that diversity and the corresponding fitness, resilience, and adaptability get lost. This is a point that USGS fisheries biologist Clint Muhlfeld will also make to me repeatedly later in the day.

As important as the issues are, Downs is aware that ecological concepts don't motivate everybody. After all, somebody who doesn't care about the presence of native cutthroat might not care about the collapse of osprey or otter populations. Thus he turns next to the economic importance of the native fish. "You go to the airport here and you see more rod cases than suitcases sometimes," he points out. "People aren't coming here to catch rainbow trout and brown trout. There are far better places to catch those. They don't grow well here to begin with. They have different habitats that you're not going to get in these mountain streams… What you get [in Glacier National Park] is the optimal growth of westslope cutthroat trout. It's the best westslope cutthroat fishing there is. We have big rivers that support them, and smaller streams. It's an economic driver." Downs goes on to put cutthroat trout into the perspective of a larger picture. "People come here for the native natural resources. [In some places] that's a primary objective of our management and it's a wonderful mandate to have: to preserve the natural environment for the benefit of the public." A moment later he adds an important point. "And it's supposed to be in perpetuity."

Down also mentions the cultural and social significance of native species. Cutthroat trout are an important part of the heritage of native peoples as well as of early settlers to the area. In order to protect that cultural heritage, we need to protect important aspects of that landscape that are central to that heritage, include flora and fauna. Speaking of the importance to those cultures of harvesting food from the land, he adds, "Cutthroat trout reach abundances in some places such that folks can keep some without having a major [detrimental] impact on the cutthroat population." Ensuring healthy populations of cutthroat for generations to come is part of preserving the culture.

Our conversation turns to the threats these native trout populations face. The biggest concern, Chris says repeatedly over the course of our conversation, is non-native fish. No matter how good the environment is for native cutthroat and bull trout—and the habitat in the greater Glacier National Park ecosystem is fantastic—once invasive fish get into the system it is almost always impossible to selectively remove them. Unfortunately, non-native lake, rainbow, and brook trout have all invaded various waters in the greater Glacier ecosystem, as have non-native Yellowstone cutthroat trout. At least the first three of these invaders have proven devastating to native fish populations. Lake trout have arguably caused the most harm. While in the famous waters of Yellowstone Lake, the cutthroat population has suffered the most from lake trout, in Glacier National Park the bull trout are most negatively impacted. Bull trout are close cousins of lake trout. Both are members of the char genus *Salvelinus*. A paper on which Downs and Muhlfeld collaborated explains, "Lake trout and bull trout share similar feeding strategies, morphology, growth rates and diets, indicating similar trophic positions as top-level piscivores and creating a strong potential for competitive interactions."[25] Downs later points out that the problems extend beyond competitive interactions; lake trout prey directly on juvenile bull trout. However, the life histories of bull trout and lake trout have two important differences. Bull trout are adfluvial; though they spend much of their adult lives in the lake, they spawn in cold running water, often migrating long distances up to small headwaters. Lake trout, by contrast, are a lacustrine species; they spawn in the lakes and not in running water. (That they spawn in deep lake water is one reason lake trout are not an available source of protein to terrestrial or aerial predators.) A second difference is that lake trout can live thirty to forty years, while the bull trout lifespan is only a dozen to fifteen years. This provides a significant advantage to lake trout in terms of population sizes.

Lake trout were introduced to Flathead Lake, downriver of Glacier National Park, in 1905. For a few decades after their introduction, lake trout seemed benign; there was no evidence that they moved up the Flathead River to colonize connected waters, cutthroat remained the most caught fish in Flathead Lake, and bull trout continued to thrive as the apex predator. Lake trout were not the only 20th century introduction to the lake, however. The stocking history in Flathead is one that has been repeated in waters all over the Rocky Mountains west, with environmental impacts felt keenly a century later. Kokanee salmon—a landlocked strain of Pacific sockeye—were introduced fifteen years after the lake trout. By 1940 the kokanee had displaced cutthroat as the most caught fish in the lake. The runs of kokanee up the Flathead River into Glacier National Park were famous. The human-introduced fishery was an abundant one, and though it certainly had numerous ecological ramifications, at the time many considered it both commercially and recreationally successful.

---

25 Fredenberg, et al, 2017.

But the story of human tinkering didn't end with kokanee. In order to provide an additional food source for the salmon, Mysis shrimp (also called "opossum shrimp") were introduced into the drainage in the 1960s. The introduction proved disastrous at many levels. By 1981 the shrimp had appeared in Flathead Lake.[26] Though they thrived there, they did not provide food for the salmon as hoped. Kokanee fed in the daytime near the surface. The shrimp are vertical nocturnal feeders, coming to the surface at night to feed, then returning to deep water during the day. Even worse, the shrimp competed with the salmon for zooplankton causing the kokanee population to collapse. The effect on lake trout, however, was the opposite. Monsters of the deep, the lake trout greedily gobbled up the shrimp during the day, and with the abundant new food supply their population exploded. Soon overpopulating Flathead Lake, lake trout for the first time began to move up the Flathead River to colonize new waters. The west slope of Glacier National Park had twelve lakes with an historic native bull trout population. Lake trout found their way into nine of those, and in eight of the nine extirpated the bull trout within a few years. The introduction of lake trout in Flathead Lake, and later shrimp, led to the tragic loss of bull trout in eight park lakes several decades later and dozens of miles upriver.

I reflect on yet another passage from Berry's essay.

We must learn to acknowledge that the creation is full of mystery; we will never entirely understand it. We must abandon arrogance and stand in awe. We must recover the sense of the majesty of creation, and the ability to be worshipful in its presence. For I do not doubt that it is only on the condition of humility and reverence before the world that our species will be able to remain in it.[27]

---

26 Fredenberg, et al, 2017. Also *High Country News*, Feb.3 2014, referenced on 4/4/2017 at http://www.hcn.org/issues/46.2/the-great-flathead-fish-fiasco.
27 Berry, p.20.

I think of the history of indiscriminate human stocking of species from fish to birds to mammals. I consider the notion of being worshipful in the presence of nature—an easier task when standing in the "majesty of creation" so evident in Glacier National Park. Speaking with Christopher Downs, I think more of the survival of species—not so much our own species, though that too is at risk, but the ability of other species to remain on earth with us. I think of how much more my own race needs to practice humility and reverence. How might the history of Flathead Lake looked had those of European descent come to the area with less arrogance and more awe?

This history led to our conversation about Quartz Lake, one of the most interesting and important projects Downs has worked on. In 2003, lake trout were discovered in Lower Quartz Lake. Lower Quartz is the furthest downriver of four important native bull trout lakes connected to the North Fork of the Flathead. I had a mental map of this lake from my hike with my wife a week and a half earlier. A lake trout (or any other fish) coming from the North Fork to Lower Quartz must swim about seven miles up Quartz Creek, gaining over 700 feet in elevation. Then it gets tougher. Continuing past Lower Quartz, that migrating trout must gain over 200 feet in elevation in only a mile of river—roughly twice the average gradient of the lower portion—to reach Middle Quartz Lake.

Quartz Lake is only a few hundred yards above Middle Quartz. At roughly four miles in length, it is the largest lake of the group. A mile and a half up upper Quartz Creek and then Rainbow Creek from Quartz Lake, Cerulean Lake sits in a bowl surrounded by Cerulean Ridge, Rainbow Peak and Vulture Peak. One 2008 study listed Quartz and Cerulean lakes as among the more productive bull trout lakes in Glacier National Park.[28] They are important waters for conservation of the species. Thus in 2004, the year after the discovery of lake trout in Lower Quartz, the USGS immediately began to build an artificial fish barrier just below Middle Quartz to protect the three upper lakes from the impending invasion. It was tough backcountry labor, Downs opines. No roads wind into Quartz Lake. Cement trucks were not an option. They worked with logs and lots of rocks trying to create a barrier impassable to migrating lake trout. In 2005, however, before the barrier was even complete, they discovered lake trout already in Quartz Lake. Given the elevation gain in the creek between Lower and Middle Quartz, this came as a surprise to Downs. "Quartz Creek is a high gradient stream. We didn't know lake trout would be able to get there."

The only good news was that the invasive lake trout were still in low abundance, suggesting that the invasion was recent. "We still have a chance to do something," Downs thought. The first step was to prevent further invasion. "The horse is out of the barn. We've already got reproducing lake trout there. We just don't want more to come in." He worked with the USGS to finish the barrier. It wasn't perfect, he admitted, but for a backcountry barrier made by hand it was pretty good. "It may not keep every fish out, but most of the time, most years, we're going to keep most fish out."

The question then was what to do about the lake trout already in Quartz Lake before they devastated the bull trout population as they had done in eight other lakes. Suppression efforts of invasive species are difficult and costly. Even invasive weeds in lakes have proved impossible to completely eradicate, and fish

28 Meeuwig MH, Guy CS, Fredenberg WA, "Influence of landscape characteristics on fish species richness among lakes of glacier national park, Montana. Intermt J Sci (2008) 14:1-16 *Cited in.* Lora B. Tennant, Robert E. Gresswell, Christopher S. Guy, and Michael H. Meeuwig, "Spawning and rearing behavior of buill trout in a headwater lake ecosystem," *Environ Biol Fish* (2016) 99:117-131.

are more difficult than weeds; fish can swim away from you. The other challenge to suppressing invasive fish is doing so without damage to the native populations. Unfortunately, traditional techniques for removing invasive fish have a by-catch. "If you want to get rid of lake trout, but you pull up a net and it's mostly whitefish, then it's failure," Downs said. "If we're having an adverse affect on the native fish, then what's the point? It's just adding to their problems."

Downs was part of a careful study to see if suppression efforts—which would involve considerable labor as well as factors like having a motorized boat in a water managed as wilderness— were justifiable. According to his paper with Muhlfeld and others, four factors suggested the possibility of successful suppression at Quartz Lake:

1. At 1.36 square miles (870 acres), it is relatively small compared to other invaded lakes like Lake McDonald;
2. Thanks to the new constructed barrier, it could be isolated from further invasions;
3. The lake trout were recent invaders and their population was still low; and
4. The lake has a low biological productivity (including no Mysis shrimp), which provides a sort of built-in assistance to human efforts.

After careful study, Glacier National Park and the USGS began an extensive experimental lake trout suppression effort in Quartz Lake—one that could potentially lead the way to suppression in other waters through the Rocky Mountain west. They made use of a variety of techniques. At the core was the old technique of gill-netting, but it was greatly enhanced using modern telemetry. During spring, when lake trout are nearer to the surface, they captured thirty of them via traditional angling and surgically implanted them with acoustic transmitters before releasing them again. They then tracked the fish daily from late September through early November to find spawning concentrations. Quartz Lake is glacially formed and like nearly all of the park's lakes it sits at the bottom of a steep valley. Cerulean Ridge rises nearly 3000 feet above the lake on the north side, and Vulture Peak to the south towers more than 5000 feet above the lake. They discovered that the lake trout preferred to spawn at the bottom of steep avalanche chutes on the deposits of cobble and boulder. They leave the deep water and come into shallows at night to spawn. The team thus focused the gill-netting efforts at the locations and depths suggested by the telemetry data. They recaptured a remarkable 93% of the tagged lake trout. They were also able to target juvenile lake trout in the spring when they are in deep water where few other fish dwell. Over the course of five years, the suppression efforts removed a total of 352 mature lake trout in the late fall, while spring gill-netting removed 1457 juvenile lake trout. Only 33 juvenile bull trout were incidentally killed as by-catch.[29] "Management ideas are the same all over," Downs said. "We're all trying to remove invasives. We're all trying to build barriers. We're all using gill-netting." Their 2017 research paper describing the work and data at Quartz Lake from 2009 through 2013 can provide a future model for more effective efforts on lakes all over the west where invasive lake trout are a problem.

Downs and his team have already applied some lessons from Quartz Creek to protect another lake in Glacier National Park so that suppression efforts might never be necessary. Akokala Lake sits about five miles to the north of the three Quartz lakes, over two ridges. "Akokala is a small lake that doesn't have lake trout yet," he explained. It is smaller than any of the Quartz lakes. "It's got bull trout and cutthroat trout—only native fish. We are trying to be proactive at Akakola. Keep the lake trout out. And rainbow

29 Fredenberg, et al, 2017.

trout also. It's a multispecies project. We went in there learning what we did on the Quartz system. We built a really big barrier there out of logs.... It looks like two log cabins on the side of the creek." Like at Quartz, the whole thing was built by hand in the backcountry. It will have to be maintained and constantly checked. Downs said he now is past the age of hauling big rocks himself, but he spoke with pride about his team out using snorkels and diving in freezing water stuffing rocks into holes.

As with the suppression efforts, the creation of artificial barriers has a potential downside of fragmenting the ecosystem. Connected river systems are important for a number of reasons. They are important for continued genetic diversity as different subpopulations of native fish interact. And some native fish— including populations of bull trout—have life-cycle histories in which they may travel hundreds of miles to different habitats. In the case of protecting native bull and cutthroat trout from invasive lake and rainbow trout, however, the advantages of the barriers far outweigh the costs. Indeed, the barriers are probably the *only* hope. Downs acknowledges the negatives of river fragmentation caused by artificial barriers, but then he points to Hungry Horse Dam built on the South Fork just a few miles outside of Glacier National Park in the 1950s before the invasion of lake trout up the Flathead River. "That [dam] is why we have a native cutthroat population and a strong bull trout population there [in and above the reservoir]."

In addition to the efforts to suppress lake trout in Quartz Lake, Downs has hope for restoration of bull trout in at least one more lake, though it will be a more roundabout and long-term process. Logging Lake is one of the more famous lakes in Glacier National Park. It is also remote, accessible only via a hike of several miles. At one time, Logging Lake was a great bull trout fishery. As with eight other lakes in the system, however, invading lake trout found their way in. Now nearly all the bull trout are gone. This has led to an effort that for some is controversial, but to Downs is both reasonable and practical: the translocation of bull trout to a lake where they were previously not present.

Translocation is "the human-mediated movement of organisms from one area with release in another." They are "increasingly becoming an important management tool for the conservation of native fishes that are threatened by accelerating human stressors, including invasive species, habitat loss, and climate change." Translocation of fish has been used for reintroducing a species to a water where it once was native, reinforcing an existing population of the same species, and introducing a species to a water where it was not historically present to establish a conservation population. This last type of translocation, known as *conservation translocation*, is the most controversial because it introduces a non-native species to an ecosystem.

"Conservation introduction is the deliberate, human-mediated movement of organisms to establish new populations in habitats (1) that are not known to have been previously occupied and (2) where conditions are predicted to be more suitable for persistence. This approach differs from reintroduction (re-establishment of a species within previously occupied habitats) and reinforcement (restocking of a species to supplement previous translocations)."

As the proponents of the effort in Glacier National Park admit, like all forms of stocking or introduction of non-native species, "translocations have resulted in severe biological, social, and economic impacts."[30] Indeed, the very problem Downs and

30 Benjamin T. Galloway, Clint C. Muhlfeld, Christopher S. Guy, Christopher C.Downs & Wade A. Fredenberg (2016) "A Framework for Assessing the Feasibility of Native Fish Conservation Translocations: Applications to Threatened Bull Trout", *North American Journal of Fisheries Management*, 36:4, 754-768, DOI: 10.1080/02755947.2016.1146177

others are trying to solve was caused by the introduction of a non-native species.

Ecological risks suggest some important guidelines for conservation translocation. The paper describing the study at Logging Lake cites five from the IUCN.

1. "suitable habitat and donor populations exist,
2. other endemic or threatened species will not be extirpated,
3. hybridization is unlikely to occur,
4. the dispersal potential of the species has been identified and deemed acceptable, and
5. all possible threats to the long-term persistence of the population have been identified and are considered acceptable."[31]

The team conducted a careful study at Logging Lake and found that it met all these conditions. The translocation project moved forward. During spawning season, they captured 110 young bull trout in Logging Lake, transported the juveniles upriver above a natural impassable barrier to Grace Lake, and released them to form a new population in a water previously uninhabited by bull trout. The exact impact of introducing a new species of fish to Grace Lake can never be known. Several factors led to the decision, however. One was the dire situation of bull trout. They had already been extirpated from many lakes, and the remaining population in Logging Lake was so small they had no real future there. Genetic studies of the few remaining bull trout showed that they all came from the same adult breeding stock. This was a case of helping to save a population by providing a new home. There is also hope that the new population in Grace Lake can one day be used to repopulate Logging Lake if efforts at suppressing the introduced lake trout prove successful.

---

31 Galloway, et al, 2016.

Of equal importance is that Grace Lake already had an introduced species. Although most of the Pacific watershed of what is now Glacier National Park had native westslope cutthroat, more than ninety years ago non-native Yellowstone cutthroat were introduced into Grace Lake. Thus, the additional introduction of bull trout wasn't putting an exotic fish into a previously all-native body of water. In fact, the healthy well-established population of Yellowstone cutthroat in Grace Lake would provide a food supply for bull trout. Bull trout are piscivores. They feed on cutthroat trout as well as whitefish. They have co-existed with various strains of cutthroat trout for millennia. A final important factor is that Grace Lake is in the same drainage as Logging Lake, and is only a short distance away. The Logging Lake population of bull trout is more likely to be adapted for the particular environment at Grace Lake than they would for a lake in a different drainage, or than fish from another drainage would be for Grace Lake. Hearing all this, I thought of the words of Berry. It seemed to me like a project done with great "humility and reverence", not so that our own species could remain in the world, but so that another species could.

Downs ultimately had a succinct summary. Bull trout face many threats including climate change and habitat loss as well as invasive species. Protecting threatened populations of bull trout—indeed, protecting the species itself—in many places involves ongoing expensive efforts. It may be, for example, that suppression of invasive lake trout will never fully extirpate them in Quartz Lake and the efforts will have to continue for as long as we want to protect bull trout. By contrast, the translocation of bull trout from Logging Lake to Grace Lake is a "one and done" effort. The trout were captured, hauled up to Grace Lake, and released. Though scientific studies of the effectiveness of the effort will continue as a way to gain knowledge, no additional work has to be done. It's up to the bull trout now to survive and colonize this water.

Stoneflies, Melting Glaciers, and Other Shocking Stories:
"the wilderness of a place"

Lessons from Joseph Giersch, Clint Muhlfeld, and Wendell Berry, June 28.

Departing from my coffee with Christopher Downs, I arrive mid-morning at the U.S. Geological Survey field office for the Northern Rocky Mountain Science Center. It is situated in a small two-story building within the Glacier National Park headquarters in West Glacier. I'm here to spend a day with biologist Clint Muhlfeld as he makes a guest appearance teaching a summer university field biology class. First, however, I get to meet Joseph Giersch, another USGS biologist who works with Muhlfeld studying two imperiled stoneflies: the small black meltwater stonefly and the glacier stonefly.

Giersch and I talk about stoneflies. Though grizzly bears, wolves, elk, and even game fish like cutthroat trout have been more romanticized in our imagination, and thus their plights receive more attention in the press, stoneflies and other insect species are ecologically at least as important as these big mammals. How important? And why should we care about them? Giersch answers by sharing data from his study. Within 100 meters of a melting glacier or snowpack—such as on Lunch Creek near the top of Logan Pass off the Going-to-the-Sun Road—meltwater stoneflies can reach an astounding density of nearly 1500 individuals per square meter. As you continue downstream, however, the density declines rapidly. At a mere 427 meters from its source, Lunch Creek hosts only 360 stoneflies per square meter. The density continues to drop farther from the source. The species thrives in abundance a short distance below a melting glacier or snowpack, but *only* in that environment.

That abundance is vital to the ecosystem. Joe said the high population densities near a glacier made the meltwater stonefly similar to a keystone species in its impact. They are an important food source for many creatures ranging from other aquatic insects like caddis flies to terrestrial spiders, voles, and birds. They are therefore also important to anything farther up the food chain that feed on those spiders, rodents, and caddis flies. The alpine ecosystem has evolved to be dependent on these almost microscopic little stoneflies. They provide an important link in the food chain between algae that gets its energy directly from the sunlight and the animal world.

Yet despite their importance, these rare insects have only recently been studied, and much is unknown. Joe said he still wasn't sure exactly *how* the stoneflies fed. What is certain is that they are imperiled. Unfortunately, 80% of the parks eponymous glaciers have disappeared in the last century and a half. Climate change has had its most dramatic impact on alpine and arctic environments where warming happens at two to three times the global rate. It is predicted that the last glaciers will be gone from the park by 2030. This bodes badly for the stoneflies. "Climate warming is causing rapid loss of glaciers and snowpack in mountainous regions worldwide," Giersch wrote in a research paper he published with Muhlfeld and others. "These changes are predicted to negatively impact the habitats of many range-restricted species, particularly endemic, mountaintop species dependent on the unique thermal and hydrologic conditions found only in glacier-fed and snowmelt-driven alpine streams."[32]

32 Giersch, J.Joseph, Scott Hotaling, Ryan P. Kovach, Leslie A. Johnes and Clint Muhlfeld. "Climate-induced glacier and snow loss imperils alpine stream insects", *Global Change Biology* (2016), doi: 10.1111/gcb.13565.

Both stonefly species he studies are under consideration for listing in the endangered species act—along with the polar bear—as creatures endangered because of climate-change-induced loss of ice. They face at least regional extinction. Though some creatures further up the chain *may* be able to find another replacement food source, the stoneflies are still an important part of the ecosystem's biodiversity. The system will be less resilient if they disappear.

Late morning I say goodbye to Giersch, feeling both excited about a cool pair of insect species living in such a fragile environment, and sobered at their plight and its consequences. When Wendell Berry wrote about the net of the sea that slowly but constantly pulls the mountains down, I doubt he was thinking about insects in the waters at the farthest reaches of that net. From now on, when I think of the melting glaciers that melt mountains, I will think of the meltwater stonefly.

I think also of something else Berry wrote in the same essay about the importance of understanding, and the oft-repeated human failure to live with indigenous knowledge of the land where we dwell. Referring to human practices, he writes, "surely there could be a more indigenous life than we have. There could be a consciousness that would establish itself on a place by understanding the place's nature and learning what is potential in it. A man ought to study the wilderness of a place before applying to it the ways he learned in another place."[33] I am glad for the work of Giersch and others who live and study this place of wilderness—or the wilderness of this place. I am glad to learn of the potential in a tiny stonefly. I hope that learning has not come too late.

✦   ✦   ✦   ✦   ✦   ✦

Clint Muhlfeld stands by the front door of the USGS building waiting for me. Ten university students enrolled in a summer class,

---

33 Berry, p.26.

along with their professor, wait outside. I'm excited to sit in on the class, to learn more about the native trout in and around Glacier National Park—to gain a deeper understanding of the nature of *this* place. I'm also looking forward to the conversation with Clint as we drive from location to location. Muhlfield was a central figure in the work I've been hearing about all morning from both Christopher Downs and Joseph Giersch. His name appears as a lead investigator on many of the studies I've read. His research on cutthroat trout is groundbreaking.

We drive a short distance to Apgar where we find a quiet spot on Lake McDonald. There, as a mother loon swims quietly past with two chicks on her back, and the jagged peaks still holding remnants of winter snow glare down from the background —and two young female visitors lay on a dock sunbathing in bikinis with their backs to the mountains oblivious of passing loons—I listen to a fascinating introduction to the history, biology, and lifecycles of the park's most famous native fish. The students interact, alternately asking and answering questions. Muhlfeld is engaging in his presentation. I'm sucked into the discussion. Some of what I hear about trout I've already learned in the past, but some is new and will inform my writing.

After an hour, we leave and drive north up the Outer North Fork Road into the adjoining national forest. As we drive, Clint tells me more about his work, some of which involves the fitness of native cutthroat. When the genes of invasive rainbow trout dilute the genes of the native westslope cutthroat, adapted for millennia to these waters, it causes a clear decline in all measures of biological fitness. In particular, hybridized cutthroat trout—the "cut-bows" as they are often called—are less successful at reproducing.

We stop at a small camping area in the national forest and eat lunch. I get a chance to talk with some of the students. I'm intrigued by the story of one young man who identifies as an indigenous person. He has ancestors from a native Alaskan people, as well as from a tribe that used to live in the area near what is now Glacier National Park. Taking this class, he tells me, is a way for him to get closer to the land where his ancestors once dwelt—and from which their people have now been excluded. A large tattoo covers his neck. I want to study it, but I'm afraid to ask. It is, like all tattoos, a self-inflicted scar. It is also a work of art. He tells me it is a symbol of his ancestors. I think of the Going-to-the-Sun road as a tattoo: a scar on the land, and also a story, and something that reveals beauty.

After lunch Muhlfeld describes to the class in more depth the project his team has been working on in a tiny tributary creek to the nearby river, which in turn flows into the North Fork. For several years they have been periodically shocking the little creek to catch juvenile fish, and then implanting Radio Frequency Identification (RFID) tags, also known as Passive Integrated Transponders, or PIT tags. On return trips, they attempt to recapture those fish and see how they're doing and how much they have grown. They also taken scale samples for genetic testing, trying to understand just how far the rainbow trout genes have traveled into the cutthroat population.

After the introduction, we pile back into cars once more and drive up a dirt forest service road into the hills. We park, and the students haul the electro-shocking equipment down a steep bank and push through grass and brush toward the creek. I follow with my video camera. The creek we will be working on is small. It wanders knee deep through brush and tall grasses, with undercut banks and plenty of fallen trees. I could easily leap it in many places. After Muhlfeld provides an important safety demonstration, the students break into two groups and get down into the water ready to do their part in the study. One group moves upstream quickly with sensing equipment looking for tags on existing fish. The other group moves more slowly with the electro-shocker, periodically sending a current into the river, which temporarily stuns nearby fish. A team trailing behind the designated shocker is ready with nets to scoop up stunned fish. I stay with the second group. Over the next hour or so, they manage to net, measure, weigh, and release live back into the stream thirty small cutthroat fry plus three juvenile bull trout. Four cutthroat have PIT tags from an earlier survey. They weigh and measure the previously tagged cutthroat and all three bull trout.

I don't get involved in the weighing or measuring. I'm interested in what they discover, but at present I'm more invested in watching the students and letting them do the work. They are learning science not in a classroom or indoor lab, or from a textbook, but in the field. Their enthusiasm, smiles, and readiness to help reveals their growing engagement. This is the best way to learn, I think. I think also of the importance of this work for the fish they are studying—how the research may impact management policy that may ultimately help these native fish survive.

I think also of an earlier conversation I had with one of the park rangers. He told me the entire annual budget for the park was only $12 million. He shared how a student in a local school grumbled about how much money was spent on the national park, until the ranger expressed that amount in terms of the salaries of professional athletes. A single above-average major league pitcher, or a really good NFL cornerback or wide receiver, makes in a year the entire park budget needed to manage a million acres including all the road and building maintenance as well as the salaries of the seasonal and year-round employees. The ace on an MLB staff or a star quarterback will make double the budget of the entire park. Muhlfeld works with the USGS and thus is not dependent on those funds, but Christopher Downs is, and so are the many projects and studies he supervises. I understand now why many who work in the park speak of it being underfunded. Thinking of the importance of their conservation efforts, I agree. I realize why Muhlfeld has to spend so much time writing grant proposals in addition to his actual research work project leadership on lake trout suppression, translocation of bull trout, genetic studies of cutthroat trout, and work with stoneflies.

I ponder again the importance of understanding the wilderness of a place and learning its potential. Close to the end of "A Native Hill", Berry laments,

> "We haven't yet, in any meaningful sense, arrived in these places that we declare we own. We undertook the privilege of the virgin abundance of this land without any awareness at all that we undertook a responsibility toward it. That responsibility has never yet impressed itself upon our character; its absence in us is signified on the land by scars."[34]

Will the absence of stoneflies and glaciers be felt as a scar? Will the loss of bull trout? The presence of invasive lake trout? Or will we find a way to avoid those scars? Maybe it will require the development not only of more *individual* character and responsibility, but also of a different *national* sense of character and responsibility. What is our responsibility? What are our scars? How will those shape us?

· · · · · ·

I end my month-long stay at Glacier National Park with an early morning drive up the scar of the Going-to-the-Sun Road, just the third day it is open in 2017. I am the first to arrive at Logan Pass to an empty parking lot. I watch the sun rise while listening to the songs of mountain chickadees and watching voles rush out from holes near the edge of a patch of snow. Across the road, slightly down the valley, meltwater stoneflies munch on algae

34 Berry, p.26-27.

in Lunch Creek, converting the photosynthesized energy of algae into a form that will benefit creatures farther up the food chain.

When the parking lot starts to fill, I take a three-mile hike through snow back over the Continental Divide to Hidden Lake, passing goats and marmots. The lake is still mostly covered with ice, and my plan of wading in sandals quickly proves painful. So after a short but intense chill, I move to the shore and back into my wool socks and hiking books. Despite the tree canopy now immediately at my back, making it a challenge to wield a fly rod trailing forty feet of fly line, I cast flies for non-native Yellowstone Cutthroat trout. I yield my spot when a grizzly bear walks up the stream. Neither the bear nor I am successful in getting close to the easily-spooked trout cruising around the outlet. When I lose my reading glasses and can no longer see to tie on new flies, I give up.

I watch a family fly a drone. I tell them drones are illegal in the park. They move away out of my sight, but later they are flying it again. No rangers are around to stop them. I wonder at this notion of their coming here and hiking three miles into the wilderness because it is *wilderness*, but with so little thought to what makes it so. I take a nap in the sunshine. I talk with a young man and woman sitting near me. The woman, Meredith, is from Idaho. I note the tattoos on her feet, forearm, and wrist. She is beautiful, confident, joyful. I ask her to tell me about her tattoos and their significance. She tells me their story, which is really her story. The tattoos on her feet are of birds in flight. They came from a hard time in her life, and helped remind her that she was meant to fly—a word of encouragement from a friend. The tattoos on her left wrist and right forearm are from a happier time, symbols of her love of the outdoors. A few days later Meredith will find me on Facebook. She and Chris, the guy who'd been sitting next to her, had just gotten engaged. They have redeemed for me the last hour that the drone family had briefly diminished.

I didn't bring quite enough drinking water for the day, and I stay longer than I should, but tomorrow I will catch a flight home. I ignore the voice of wisdom telling me to leave. My foolishness pays off in a way. After watching for several hours how they are feeding on tiny nymphs on the silty lake bottom, I change my tactics and eventually catch and release three fat and brightly colored trout.

I was the first to arrive at the lake in the morning. I am almost the last to depart at the end of the day. I drink my last drop of water before I'm even a quarter of the way out. I consider drinking from a stream of melting snow. I decide to leave it for the stoneflies.

POSTCARDS FROM ALASKA

"Alaska, where there's nothing to fear
but fear itself.
And the bears."
—Seen on a t-shirt

INTRODUCTION: A LOVE AFFAIR WITH DOLLY VARDEN

I have a love affair with Dolly Varden trout. For a time, I tried to keep the affair secret from the love of my youth, my long-time partner, the one I come home to: the wild native brook trout of New England and Appalachia. But brook trout and Dolly Varden are cousins in the char genus. Secrets turn into rumors, and rumors make their way up the river like a hatch of *Ephemeroptera*. I hesitate to call this a confession. The term implies some assumption of guilt. This is more of a defense, an *apologia*, or even an accusation. I could begin blaming my father, and a fishing guide named Brad Roche who hosted my father and me for a 2003 visit to his lodge on Iliamna Lake and some headwaters of Bristol Bay. After a multi-day float down a tundra river flowing east from Wood-Tikchik State Park into the Nushagak River (where I spent most of those long Alaskan July days sight-fishing for, occasionally hooking, and sometimes even landing, thirty-pound king salmon) we took a short day-trip up the Iliamna River. There I set aside my big salmon rod, pulled out my 5-weight, and spent a day casting for resident Dolly Varden—a species I had never before caught and knew little about. Although Brad had proven an excellent guide in helping me catch several large salmon on a fly rod, and had good tips for rainbow trout fishing as well, he acknowledged that he'd not spent much time fishing for char.

Not long after Brad pulled the jetboat onto a gravel bar, I spotted some Dollies finning in knee-deep water on the inside of a sweeping gravel bend, with a school of sockeyes claiming the deeper part of the current near the farther bank. Brad identified the trout as Arctic char—a common confusion even today—and I would only later learn from an Alaskan fisheries biologist who studied my photos and heard where I had caught them that they were certainly Dolly Varden (*S. malma*) and not Arctic char (*S. alpina*). It didn't matter to me. Both were foreign to my home waters, and different from the salmon I'd been catching. Unfortunately, Brad's rainbow trout techniques proved unsuccessful. So I changed my approach. I began to fish as though for brook trout in one of my favorite mid-sized Maine rivers. I got rid of my egg-sucking leech patterns and tied on a little weighted nymph. I didn't have a strike indicator, but the fish were visible in the clear water and I was able to mend my line and get a natural drift. The approach worked, and I had a great and delightful day catching these Alaska "trout" under the shadows of Mount Iliamna. Fifteen years later I still have clear memories of the stream and the fish, which I thought were the most beautiful I caught over my ten-day visit.

I had saved for a couple years to take that trip with my father, eager to do it while he was still fit enough for the challenges—such as the eleven miles of hiking needed to make several trips back and forth across the tundra from the pond where the float plane dropped us to the river, hauling our steel bear box, heavy-duty raft, food, tents, and gear. I thought that trip would be my once-in-a-lifetime Alaskan wilderness trip. And, indeed, the experience with my father was a once-in-a-lifetime memory. Half a decade later, however, my brother, Ted, his wife Susie, and his sons Brad and Michael moved to Anchorage. Once Ted settled in, I found a way to visit him, and then to keep visiting him or his sons, over and over, almost every year for close to a decade.

We enjoyed a variety of outdoor activities ranging from hiking to sea-kayaking to biking and berry-picking, but fishing was unquestionably a central part of all the visits. From time to time, Ted and I fished in famous salmon and trophy-trout waters on the Kenai Peninsula, enduring combat fishing for the sake of big fish. We caught silver salmon, steelhead trout, rainbow trout, and a fair number of fat Dollies on the Kenai River, Anchor River, and Quartz Creek. I thought the Dollies were the most beautiful of them all, though chrome steelhead were close. We mostly sought out the quiet and solitude of backcountry fishing. That usually meant smaller fish, most of which were Dollies, and in addition to their own beauty I associated them with the stunning splendor of the places we caught them. So I also hold my brother and his family to blame for taking me to so many beautiful remote lakes and rivers around the Kenai Peninsula and Chugach State Park.

Over three visits in 2015 and 2017, the extraordinary pilot and guide Glen Alsworth, Jr. from the Farm Lodge in Port Alsworth also helped stir up my steamy love affair with Miss Dolly. My memory is still haunted by the memories and mysteries of three not-to-be-named rivers in the Bristol Bay watershed where Glen has taken me to chase two-foot long Dollies who were themselves chasing spawning sockeye salmon. Flights over herds of caribou, brown bears splashing in the river, and the tang of blueberries picked by the riverbank and plopped fresh into my mouth does not hurt the memory. Neither do the glaciers, towering waterfalls, or majestic volcanic peaks seen from the air.

Ultimately, however, it is Alaska and her Dolly Varden who themselves shoulder the full weight of blame. They have seduced me with beauty and lavish colors and sweet whispers in my ear. I think no person with any aesthetic sense could have resisted.

So, because a true lover delights to speak and boast of his or her beloved, I must share a few things about Alaska and its Dolly Varden. Though Dollies are often called "trout", they—like the native brook "trout" of the east—have been classified in a different genus than both the European brown trout or the numerous North American rainbow and cutthroat trout. The European brown trout belongs to the genus *Salmo*, along with the Atlantic salmon. Both the rainbow and cutthroat trout are in the genus *Oncorhynchus* along with all five species of Alaskan salmon. Dolly Varden belong to the genus *Salvelinus*, commonly referred to as *char* (or *charr*). Alaska has three native species of char, Dolly Varden, Arctic char, and lake trout, as well as a few non-native brook trout. Of these, Dolly Varden are the most widespread, varied, and adaptable. As I read in Kurt Fausch's fascinating book *For the Love of Rivers: A Scientist's Journey* and a few other sources, they have an evolutionary history almost as interesting as their name, which comes from a character in the Charles Dickens novel *Barnaby Rudge* who in the fashion of the 1870s wore a bright colored petticoat. Originating in Japan (where they can still be found) or eastern Russia[1], they likely first found their way to North America along the Bering land bridge formed during the last ice age some 40,000 years ago. Upon reaching what is now Alaska, some turned north and made their way along the coast of the Chukchi Sea. Others turned south and found their way down as far as British Columbia. When sea-levels rose with the melting of glaciers, and these northern and southern populations became isolated, they adapted into distinct strains or subspecies. Like brook trout, Dolly Varden can now be found in large fresh water lakes as well as small beaver ponds, in little alpine streams far from the ocean, and in large coastal rivers where some move back and forth between salt and fresh water.

I was particularly interested in Dolly Varden—more even than lake trout or Arctic char—because of how many different

---

1 Fausch, p.37

places they have managed to thrive, and because they get so little attention (at least compared with salmon), and in no small part because of their beauty. For many years after the salmon industry really took off, the state of Alaska put a bounty on Dolly Varden in an effort to decrease their numbers because it was believed that they preyed upon juvenile salmon and salmon eggs in such significant numbers as to hurt the salmon populations.

There, then, is my defense. But here is the wonderful thing about this type of passion: my care for the Dolly Varden and the rivers where they swim and make their lives has not lessened my love of brook trout, or of any other river. Learning to care for the particulars of one fish and one place may be necessary for learning the love of all fish, all rivers, and all places. I love my brook trout and the rivers and streams of Vermont and Maine not less, but more. And maybe, because of my experience with Dolly, I am better equipped to care for the rivers of my home.

RETURN TO THE SOUTH FORK OF THE EAGLE RIVER[2]

CHUGACH STATE PARK (2009, 2015, 2017)

Wild blueberries are strewn across the alpine meadows stretching for thousands of yards in every direction. The ubiquitous fireweed paints brushstrokes of magenta on the rise in front of me. Further up the slope, blueberries give way to the black spheres of milder crowberries. To my New England born eyes the needled crowberry shrubs look nothing like a plant that should bear edible fruit, but the flavor of their berries blends nicely with the tang of bright red low-bush cranberries that also dot this breathtaking landscape.

I am sitting at the edge of a small footbridge over the South Fork of the Eagle River in Alaska's Chugach State Park. With me is my good friend and fellow teacher David O'Hara along

---

2 This essay has been slightly edited from a version that first appeared in *The Written River* 10 (2016).

with nine Middlebury College students taking our summer nature-writing class. It is the most diverse groups of students I have taught in my twenty-six year career. They come from seven different countries and represent a variety of majors including history, architecture, film and media studies, computer science, geology, and environmental studies. A fun and curious group, they are all in Alaska for the first time. Fresh from our three-mile hike, they have scattered along the riverbank in both directions, each choosing a different place to sit and observe, or to meander and soak in the scene. For a short while, I remain on the bridge breathing in the air of this place and watching them. My eyes are drawn alternately between the water flowing beneath me, the jagged ridges rising to the skyline on three sides, and the students whose safety has been entrusted to me.

Tumbling down from the glaciers further up the valley, the river is full of gray-green glacial flour. I can see no more than a few inches through the milky current as it passes on down the valley. As poor as the visibility is below the surface, however, when I lift my eyes from the water, my view stretches for miles. At two thousand feet of elevation, we are just above the tree line. Only a few scrubby evergreens and poplars dot the landscape. I can see all the way up to the five-thousand foot ridgelines where the alpine flowers, grasses, and berries give way to lichen favored by the Dall's sheep, and eventually to bare rock.

Back closer to my feet, my eyes rest on smaller dots from a variety of yellow and white flowers. The yarrow and monkshood are almost as ubiquitous as the fireweed. As for the variety of other flowers, however, I would not know their names except that Julia, a history major with a special interest in environmental history, has become enamored with identifying them. Since that task requires close observation, I happily encourage her newfound passion. "*Achillea millefolium*," she concludes with pride. Then she moves from a lacy white flower to a yellow one. Here Julia falters briefly. The plant bears something in common with single delight, alpine buttercup, and alpine avens, but it is not any of these. My own heart is full without knowing the name of this particular flower. I look at the other students. Michael, an environmental studies major focusing on religion and philosophy, sits on a rock in the middle of the current. His barefoot venture across invisible rocks through icy water must have left those feet numb, but he looks content. A few students sit writing or sketching in their notebooks. Some gaze intently at the river. Others study the vegetation. Some sit. Some stand or walk slowly around. Obeying their professor's instruction, they don't stray too far.

Brenden, a geology major, has picked up his fly rod. He is trying to catch one of the Dolly Varden char that live in the river. These salmonids are one of the narrative lenses through which we are studying this environment. What do they eat, and how do they find their food in this opaque water? How are their lives intertwined with the lives of other creatures around them, both above and below the surface? What threats do they face in our quickly changing world? Dollies further down the valley feast through the summer months on salmon eggs and in the winter months on rotting salmon flesh—much like bears and gulls and eagles and nearly everything else in the Pacific Northwest within striking distance of a salmon stream. Even the trees eat salmon, though it comes to them more indirectly. But here in this alpine meadow we are above the reach of even the strongest and most acrobatic salmon. These char depend on aquatic macro-invertebrates, or the occasional terrestrial insect blown into the water by the constant breezes in this nearly treeless place. I will later turn over some rocks in the river and find nymphs of small golden stoneflies and mayflies clinging to the stream bottom. They are beautiful little creatures. They are also potential food for a Dolly Varden.

I know some Dollies live in this stream. I have been to this spot once before, nearly six years ago, with my brother Ted, who lives nearby in Anchorage. I have wanted to return ever since, and it is a delight now to finally do so, and to share it with others. I have been to many beautiful scenic and wild places in my life, but two others in particular evoked a particularly powerful response of awe, delight, and humility—moving me so profoundly that simply being there left me in tears of joy unable to speak for many minutes. One was standing amidst giant redwoods on the northern coast of California—trees as tall as a football field is long, so big that my wife and I could not come close to touching each other's fingertips if we reached around the trunk, and old enough that they were alive for the first Christmas. Yet mere size and age did not capture the sense of holiness and silence of that place. The other location was Painter's Point overlooking the Grand Canyon of the Yellowstone on the first day of our family visit to Yellowstone National Park after ten days of driving. Tears streamed down my face at the beauty and wonder that can still be found in the world. When I looked at my wife, I saw her crying also.

There is a Welsh word, *hiraeth*. It is said that the word has no direct translation to English. It describes a powerful sense of longing for something good and beautiful. It conveys also a sense of grief or sadness over something lost, or perhaps something that hasn't yet even existed. *Desire* may be the closest English word, but for many people desire has other connotations—such as mere lust—that do not capture the notion of *hiraeth*. The German word *sehnsucht* might be closer in meaning.

Sitting on the bridge, surrounded by such beauty, I am left with that overpowering and indescribable sense of wonder and longing. But it is tinged with sadness. I am also aware of what has been lost, or what is yet to be fulfilled. I see signs of human-made trails on both sides of the stream where my kind has trampled the delicate alpine flora with heavy hiking boots. I know that my mere presence here, along with the ten fellow travelers I have brought with me who now explore this stream, adds to that damage.

My previous trip is also why I know Dollies live in the water. My students have been learning about this fish. They have learned from Kurt Fausch's wonderful book, *For the Love of Rivers: A Scientist's Journey*, that this freshwater species so common throughout Alaska probably traces its evolutionary history back to Japan or far eastern Russia. I have also learned from another Alaskan fisheries biologist, Brenden Scanlon, of an anadromous strain of northern Dolly Varden that move back and forth between Russia and Alaska without thought of passports. Some overwinter in Alaska and spawn in Russia. Others overwinter in Russia and spawn in Alaska. All of them get fat in the rich Arctic waters. They can grow to twenty pounds before moving back into freshwater.

The Dollies in this stream will rarely grow longer than seven inches, but they are as beautiful as their bigger cousins. The only way to see one in this nearly opaque water is to entice it with a fly. Some of the students have no desire to angle for a fish, but a few will attempt this enticement—and succeed. They will carefully hold a fish in wet hands at the surface of the stream, and admire the beauty of this silvery char with its bright red fins. The students will look at Dolly's petticoat, and at the magenta pearls along Dolly's sides. Then they will gently unhook and release the fish, which will disappear back into the milky current.

My thoughts again jump back six years ago when I hiked and camped with my brother three miles further up this verdant valley on the ridge separating Eagle Lake on the left and Symphony Lake on the right—when the beauty of the place overwhelmed me in the same deep way that the giant redwoods and the thundering falls at Painter's Point once moved me. I sat at the edge of my tent on that day and in a single square-foot cluster of ground picked a handful of blueberries, crowberries, and cranberries and let their mix of flavors burst in my mouth. It was a perfect harmony, giving meaning to the name of the lake on the right. I looked out over its green water at the glacier whose melting waters fed the stream, and the jagged ridges behind. I also knew the meaning of *hiraeth* or *sehnsucht*.

On that day, my brother Ted stood down by the lakeshore casting flies for grayling. After a couple minutes fishing, he realized that a willow ptarmigan sat beneath the bushes only a dozen feet behind him. It had made no effort to flee when he approached. Hiking in the past, we'd seen numerous ptarmigan showing no apparent fear of humans even in relatively wild places. Given the species' reputation for tameness, after admiring it for a moment, my brother returned to fishing. After several minutes, however, the bird still sat there. For even a ptarmigan to stay put for so long and not meander off into the brush seemed unusual. It was not sitting on a nest, or guarding young. It didn't appear to be eating. Eventually my brother took a closer look. Then he understood. The bird was not able to flee; its legs were tangled in a mess of fishing line. Some careless angler had dumped his unwanted snarl of monofilament on the shore, and this ptarmigan had been ensnared by that carelessness. We don't know how long it had been there. Other than its understandable distress at the large two-legged mammal scrutinizing it, the bird appeared uninjured.

Ted approached slowly, keeping quiet, trying to appear non-threatening. I'm sure the bird was terrified. It had no knowledge of his kind intentions. Ted bent down and took a gentle hold of it. As it tried to peck him, he reached in with his fishing knife and cut away the line about its feet. As soon as the bird was free of its snare, it ran off into the brush and disappeared.

In the introduction to his book, Kurt Fausch quotes Aldo Leopold, who noted that to study ecology is to "live alone in a world of wounds." The words are true. It is also to live in a world of unspeakable beauty and awe and interconnectedness. When my class packed up to leave, David had all our students spend five minutes picking up some of the trash left around the bridge by previous hikers so that we could pack it out with us. As we filed back down the trail I couldn't resist frequent glances over my shoulder, wondering if I would ever be back there. And what it would be like if and when I did.

Afterword

I did return to this spot, just over two years later. Dave came with me again, along with his son, Michael, the student who'd sat barefoot on a rock in the river. Michael had since graduated from college and this time he came as a photographer and not as a student.

We'd traveled far that day to get to the South Fork. We began the morning down on the Kenai Peninsula in the town of Soldotna. Coming up the Sterling Highway and then the Seward Highway, we detoured to the village of Hope for a quick visit and a late-morning snack of homemade pies at Tito's. Realizing we were nearly out of gas and might not make it to the station in Girdwood, I inquired for local options and was sent to a sketchy-looking "gas station": a rusty old Tesoro pump at the end of a road in a front yard decorated by junked tractors and the rotten shell of an old wooden boat. A note was posted on the door: *if you want to buy gas, call this number.* We called and spoke with somebody who said he'd come up and sell us some. Twenty minutes later, a man appeared and sold us $20 of gas. He was friendly, humorous, and something of a "character" in the best sense of that word. After buying gas, we spent nearly an hour listening to his fascinating stories about how his brother had moved to Hope in 1963 only a year before the earthquake, about all they had done to get by during lean times, about his teaching welding in the local high school, and how the town of Hope (and the state of Alaska) had—and had not—changed in the past half a century.

The stop did mean, however, that we didn't arrive at the trailhead until 4:30pm, and we didn't start our six-mile hike up the trail along the South Fork of the Eagle River until closer to 5:00pm. We hiked in a steady rain the entire way. After we crossed the familiar bridge where our class had met two years earlier, the trail grew muddier. My newly re-waterproofed hiking boots turned out not to be very waterproof. Neither were my hiking pants. We all got soaked. Trudging through mud and cold rain, carrying a pack with too much gear, it was hard to enjoy the landscape that had delighted me so much in the past—in part because the clouds and rain occluded much of that landscape. At the outlet of Eagle Lake, we finally got above the lower cloud layer. Views opened up of the dead-end valleys on both sides. The ridges grew higher and more sheer with jagged stone. Yet though the view had improved, the hiking and camping conditions hadn't.

We arrived at our destination between the lakes after 7pm. Three tents already stood along the ridge, spread out in the prime locations. Our heavy wet legs had to carry us some distance further along the lake to find an unoccupied flat area. We set up our tents in rain. I switched to a dry shirt, we cooked dinner, and then I crawled into my sleeping bag. We woke to more rain, which lasted all morning. We got a two-hour break at midday, and did some fishing, but I caught only a few small grayling. Then the rain settled back in. That night it turned cold, and we woke to find the peaks around us covered with fresh snow.

Yet somehow, despite the bleakness of the weather, the raw chill in the August air that had caught me by surprise, and the soreness of my legs and back, the beauty still overwhelmed me at times. It seemed even bigger than I remembered it. Maybe this bigness was felt because we set off to walk along the near shore of Eagle

Lake and barely made it a third of the way. Or maybe the falling of fresh snow on the ridges made the mountains appear higher and sharper. Maybe the very bleakness of the weather exaggerated what a big and desperately beautiful landscape we had entered. As beautiful as it was, however, it did not feel hospitable on this long August weekend. We could appreciate that beauty, but the place itself was indifferent to us.

Except for the blueberries. They were still hospitable. And they were everywhere, just as I'd remembered. Crowberries too. I picked a cup of them and pulled from my pack a pint of half-and-half—one of the unnecessary items I'd brought that had made my pack too heavy and my legs too tired. I discovered to my delight that all the shaking from the miles of hiking had partially whipped the cream. I sprinkled a little sugar in with it, shook it some more, and poured it over my freshly picked blueberries.

Sehnsucht.

The Mining of Zinc,
the Changing of the Climate, and the Arctic

Sea-Run Dollies of the Wulik River, August 2015

I'd been in leaky waders all day and didn't want to put them on again. So I stood barefoot, knee-deep in the icy waters of the Wulik, an arctic river flowing westward across windy tundra into the Chukchi Sea. My shins and ankles ached. My feet were numb. At the moment, however, I was barely aware of the pain. My heart pumped with adrenaline because I'd just seen that the big leaping dancing fish at the end of my fly line was not another chum salmon, but the first sea-run Dolly Varden I'd ever hooked.

I hoped it would become the first I landed, but I'd been battling the fish for several minutes without progress. My usual big-fish fears splashed around my head as wildly as the fish yanked and tugged in the current. Would it break my line if I put too much pressure on it? Or perhaps spit the hook if I didn't?

My first full day north of the Arctic Circle was coming to an end. The August sun, following a path slanting more sideways than downward, glowed through the cloud layer low on the horizon. The afternoon before, my friend David O'Hara, my nephew Michael, and I had taken a commercial flight from Anchorage to the small city of Kotzebue. There, while Michael hauled our camping gear to Arctic Backcountry Flying Service, Dave and I intended to connect to a Ravn Alaska commuter flight hopping up the coast to the native subsistence fishing village of Kivalina on the mouth of the Wulik to spend a day observing the rhythms of life, interviewing people, and photographing an historic, challenging, and potentially vanishing way of life. At the end of the afternoon, Michael and our bush pilot Eric Sieh would pick us up in Kivalina and continue up the Wulik to a camping location suggested by a North Slope fisheries biologists with the Alaska Department of Fish and Game—the same biologist who'd recommended Eric as a safe and knowledgeable pilot.

Unfortunately, we landed in Kotzebue to discover that our flight to Kivalina was canceled. Fog had socked in the coast to the north. The only later Ravn flight was already booked full; the governor of Alaska had chosen that same day to visit Kivalina, and between the official state retinue and all the press, every seat was taken. So we hauled our gear bags to the Arctic Backcountry office to find Eric and maybe get out to the Wulik a little early. Again, we were stymied. The fog that kept us out of Kivalina stretched inland. The bush planes weren't flying either. We weren't the only ones stuck. Another small party sat in the Arctic Backcountry lounge waiting for a flight to the Brooks Range for a camping trip they'd been planning for at least a year. To our dismay—and to theirs—they'd been waiting since the morning of the *previous* day. They still hoped to make adjustments and salvage their trip, but their plans were slipping away with each passing minute. We wondered if the fog would do the same to us.

Eric wasn't happy, either. The long days of Alaskan summer are bread and butter for bush pilots. Every hour his planes sat on the ground meant money fluttering away in the wind. To make matters worse, an FAA inspector had picked that day for an apparently-unannounced inspection—and I've never met anybody who moves to rural Alaska because they like regulation and bureaucracy. The inspector was auditing Eric's books to make sure he was keeping up with the mandatory aircraft maintenance. Instead of flying over beautiful country earning money, Eric was flipping pages in his record book and answering questions. We would later learn, overhearing bits of the conversation, that Eric had been servicing his aircraft *more* frequently than necessary. Maybe that conscientious safety was why the biologist had recommended him. While this news reassured us, however, our soon-to-be-pilot looked grumpy and frazzled.

Anxious to escape the tension of the waiting area, we decided to clear out for a while and wander the small city. We had a few errands to run—errands Michael would have run alone if our Kivalina flight had not been canceled. Mostly we just wanted to see this remote fishing city surrounded by the Chukchi Sea, and try to make up for our missed visit to Kivalina. Leaving our gear in the hangar, we started down the mostly-empty orthogonally-arranged streets. We walked past husks of old pickups, barbed wire fences, and more than one building with a collapsed roof. We also saw homes recently painted and well-maintained, and a couple newly renovated playgrounds with colorful modern slides and swing sets. It was a dry town so there were no bars. We passed a small Episcopal church and a Church of God advertising Sunday morning services and Tuesday evening prayer. We also saw ATVs and snowmobiles as numerous as the working cars, and several boats parked in driveways and side lots. Satellite dishes decorated the rooftops and yards. This was not a land reached by cable television. Yards and driveways held large shipping containers instead of sheds, plus quite a bit of trash, attesting to the challenges of getting stuff on or off the remote city.

Our first stop was at the National Park Service office for the Western Arctic Parklands, where we borrowed a couple bear barrels to protect our food. To protect ourselves, we had brought a shotgun. However, our shotgun shells had been confiscated at the Anchorage airport because they were not in original packaging. We next found a hardware store and bought new shells for three times what we would have paid in Anchorage. We had a delicious but equally expensive pizza at a little restaurant called Little Louie's. When we passed a grocery store, Michael and Dave decided we didn't have enough granola bars, and they bought more. We wandered a few more side streets, and got a look at the waterfront. Then we headed back to the lounge to wait and hope for word that the fog had cleared.

When word came a couple hours later, Eric leapt up like a man grabbing at that $100 bill fluttering past in the wind. "Get your shit," he announced. That was all. Without further explanation, he was out the back door heading toward his planes on the tarmac. Dave, Michael and I glanced at one another, not sure what had just happened. The other party also gave curious glances.

"Time to go," somebody else in the office explained. "Bring your gear out to the planes." That was all we needed to know. Grateful that our wait had been a few hours and not a day and a half, we hustled out into the hangar after our pilot. Eric was clearly in as much of a hurry as we were, and as quickly as we hauled stuff to the tarmac, he loaded it into his plane: four days' and three nights' worth of food, camping gear, fishing gear, cameras, and video equipment. As it turned out, he loaded *almost* everything we had flown to Kotzebue with—everything *except* for Michael's waders, which still lay in the hangar hidden beneath a tarp the other departing party had tossed atop them in their own hurry to be on their way.

The flight took us across the mouth of Hotham Inlet off Kotzebue Sound and up the winding Noatak River, between the Cape Krusenstern National Monument to our west and the Noatak National Preserve to our east. For the first part of the flight, up past the town of Noatak, the landscape below held nearly as much water as land: tidal flats, rivers and streams, marshes, wetlands, and countless nameless ponds. Many waters were dotted with white shapes of swans, whose broad wings and large graceful bodies were visible even from the plane. We also saw the shells of abandoned boats and old hunting or fishing cabins that may or may not have been abandoned. I kept an eye open for bears or moose, but didn't see any.

At first, a few forested areas spread out across the river valley, but the further north we went the fewer trees we saw. When we angled north-northwest off the Noatak River, the trees disappeared altogether. The ground below became a wide expanse of gray-green tundra with splotches of rust red brush and yellow blossoms. Farther to the right and in the distance ahead, rolling hills gave way to higher peaks, but the ground below was flat. As we crossed the Red Dog Mine access road—a big dirt scar visible from miles away—I saw a massive mining truck with ten rows of heavy duty wheels lumbering toward us from the distance hauling a load of ore.

Finally, we came over a low bluff and caught our first glimpse of the Wulik. Eric took one pass along the river, trying to spot a school of Dolly Varden for us, but we saw only mottled chum salmon. On the second pass he dropped the fat-tired bush plane down on a riverside gravel bar. We were barely out of the plane stretching our legs before he started tossing our gear out to us. Unpacking the plane was even quicker than packing. We soon had a big pile of belongings near the brush on the edge of the gravel. Eric was ready to depart. "I'll be back in three days *if* I can get here," he said. Then, as an afterthought, he asked, "Do you have a satellite phone?"

We shook our heads. "Do we *need* one?"

He shrugged. "It would have been nice if I could have called you to get a report on the weather here before trying to come," he commented. But he knew as well as we did that it was too late for that now. "Have your stuff ready by 10:00am. I can arrive any time after that, depending on the conditions."

"And if you *can't* get here?" one of us asked, a little nervously. It was not the first time I had pondered that possibility.

"I'll come when I can," Eric replied. "Sometimes it can take a few days, though."

Then he was up in the plane with the engine starting, taxiing back down the riverside gravel. He turned eastward. The engines roared and the small plane accelerated quickly. In not much more distance than I can cast a fly with an 8-wt rod, the plane was off the ground and arcing off over the bluff across the river.

"Hey," Michael said, as the plane disappeared. "Where are my waders?"

When the plane was out of sight and the last sounds of the engine faded, we turned our attention to setting up camp. We found a flat stretch of well-drained gravel above any reasonable risk of flooding and set up our tents. We then established a cooking area near the shoreline a reasonable distance from where we would sleep, and also moved the bear-resistant food barrels away from the sleeping area.

Then I stopped and let the reality of our setting settle in. We stood by a river inside the Arctic circle. I didn't think another human stood within a dozen miles. Across the river to our south, directly out the front flap of our tents, a flat bluff rose steeply twenty or so feet above the river's edge with a rocky outcropping overlooking a deep eddy. I remembered the biologist telling me to stand on that bluff and look down into the river. In the right conditions, he'd told me, a spotter could pick out fish in the current and direct an angler where to cast. A thick stand of thin willows and brush stood in a sheltered hollow at the base of the bluff on the downstream side. They were the only trees we could see in any direction. It looked like a place *not* to walk, if we wanted to avoid bumping unexpectedly into large mammals.

Behind the tent to the north, across a wide expanse, a few rounded foothills rose out of the tundra. Far beyond them to the northeast, at the edge of our sight, stood the blue-gray outlines of higher ridges. This was a glimpse of the DeLong Mountains on the western end of the Brooks Range. We thought about the adventures the other party would be having somewhere up there. I looked upstream, to the east. A dozen or so miles away stood a closer line of foothills. Nestled back in there stood the Red Dog Mine, the largest mine in Alaska, one of the largest zinc mines in the world, and part of the reason we had chosen this particular river for our three-night excursion. The strain of northern sea-run Dolly Varden in the Wulik River was the other reason. Asking questions about these fish was a means of asking broader questions about the rivers in which they lived, and everything impacting and impacted by those rivers.

This arctic excursion was the sixth and final week—the last big adventure—of the summer trip to Alaska. Most of the places I had visited over the previous five weeks were in public lands: national parks, national forests, national preserves, and also state and city parks. Though the system of public lands is not perfect, all of these important types of lands offer vital protections against exploitation, especially of fragile areas, ecologically important areas, or areas of unique wilderness value. This visit was an exception. Though the Noatak National Preserve, and beyond that the Gates of the Arctic National Park and Preserve, lay somewhere further to the east, our camp was outside the boundaries of both of these protected lands. So were the Wulik River and its tributaries. Ikalukrok Creek in particular, one of the major tributaries of the Wulik. was fed by two branches of Red Dog Creek, which drained the area of Red Dog Mine.

Not long after Red Dog was opened in 1989, and the top-load of earth was removed exposing more of the big zinc deposit, a significantly increased load of toxic heavy metals was discovered in the creeks downstream of the mine. Discolored heavy-metal-laden water flowed down Red Dog Creek into Ikalukrok Creek and from there into the Wulik. A fish kill was reported in the Wulik twenty-five miles downriver.

Though I could not see the mine from where I stood, I knew that if I followed the correct branch of this river upstream far enough, I would come to it. In one sense, though, it wasn't the upstream direction that mattered, but downstream. We all live downstream. This river flowed down from the hills to where I now stood, carrying the stuff of those hills, including any stuff spilling, leaking, or leaching from the mines, its tailings ponds, and the rain-washed grounds exposed by the mining. And then the river flowed on past me, carrying with it whatever it had picked up in those headwater hills, whatever had not settled out with the silt and gravel, all the way down to the mouth of the Chukchi Sea. Westward, downstream of our little gravel bar, the river curved to the right away from the bluff, split around a brushy island, then took a big broad sweeping bend back to the left where it piled up once more against the bluff a mile or so beyond us, before it disappeared from sight. A single low hill stood against the sky to the west, but the terrain was mostly flat that way.

Roughly the same distance downstream from us as we were from the hills, the Wulik poured out into the Chukchi Sea near Kivalina. The river is the lifeblood of that village; the existence of Kivalina depends on the Wulik. The fish that made their annual upriver migrations provide the basis for a subsistence lifestyle—not only the livelihoods of the villagers, but their culture and way of life.

And that migrating fish was the Dolly Varden that we had come to look for. The Wulik River is a seasonal host to a northern strain of sea-run Dollies that claim dual citizenship. Some spawn in Russia, swim out to Arctic seawater to get fat on the same sort of rich diet as their salmon cousins, and then move into fresh water of northern Alaska to overwinter and to feast on salmon eggs, before returning to Russia to spawn the next generation. Others reverse that transnational pattern, spawning in Alaska while overwintering in Russia. And while a Dolly Varden in a mountain stream in Chugach State Park might not exceed eight inches, many of these ocean-going Dollies reach eight pounds. Some exceed fifteen or even twenty pounds. If the Wulik is healthy and conditions are right, the sea-run Dollies enter in such sizes and numbers that their presence sustains the community of Kivalina in the same way that salmon are the staple of other fishing communities across Alaska.

So, not too long after setting up the camp, I rigged my 8-wt L.L. Bean travel rod, tied on a fly, pulled on my waders, and walked down to the river. Dave and Michael got their rods rigged also. Soon the three of us stood in the Wulik casting flies in the pools and calmer water above and below a swift chute. Dave and I waded thigh-deep out into the current. Michael, devoid of his waders, fished from the shoreline or near to it, limited to the depth of his rubber boots.

Over the first few hours we caught several grayling, ranging from twelve to eighteen inches. They hit hard on any pattern imitating a salmon egg, but also took flies imitating leeches, especially egg-sucking leeches. Grayling are a beautiful fish with large prehistoric-looking dorsal fins. They fight well and are fun to catch. In the sunlight, their silver scales shimmer with red or purple. Unlike the Dollies, they remain resident in the river year-round. Observing them, seeing what sorts of locations they occupied in the river, and what they ate or did not eat, was interesting and helpful as well as delightful. At times, though, it was hard to keep them off my hook. Eventually I tried to avoid them.

I also hooked some big chum salmon, weighing at least ten pounds. The second largest of Alaska's five species of salmon, chum take a fly aggressively and are hard fighters. In southern Alaska, where most folk consider their meat inferior to that of red salmon (sockeyes), king salmon (chinooks), and silvers (coho), they are not much prized despite their size and fighting spirit. However, northern Alaskans value them and call them *silverbrites* and *keta*. There is a good market for keta in Japan, and their eggs (and flesh) are a food source for the Dolly Varden as well as the grayling, bears, and birds. They are arguably as important to the ecology of the Wulik as the Dollies, and directly or indirectly as important to Kivalina.

The presence of the chum was a promising sign that we might find the Dollies we sought. Although, as our pilot Eric would later acknowledge, large numbers of chum also made it challenging to get a fly to a Dolly. The first chum I hooked broke my line before I could bring it close. It didn't take long to hook a second. Even without the current, the big fish was capable of putting a hard bend into my heavy-weight salmon rod. In the swift current, I had my hands full. I fought it a little longer, and managed to lead it to shore, but it broke me off right at my feet. My supply of egg-sucking leeches was quickly disappearing. I tied on another and kept fishing. After a long battle, I finally landed the third chum, which ran close to three feet long. I revived it and released it. Over the next two days I would land several more until I grew tired of them interfering with my fishing for Dollies and began to avoid them also.

We crawled into our tents that first evening, however, without seeing a single Dolly. After watching through the back of the tent as a late and colorful sunset spread across a vast horizon, I crawled deeper into my sleeping bag and went to sleep. When I next opened my eyes, I opened them very wide. Somewhere close by, I could hear the heavy footsteps and snuffling of a large animal. Michael picked up the shotgun and held it. The steps got steadily louder, as did the beating of my heart. We expected at any moment to hear a ruckus as a bear ransacked our gear. After the eternity of a few minutes, however, the steps moved away. The regular night sounds of river and breeze returned. I lay awake several more minutes imagining bear sounds, but whatever had come did not return.

When we stepped outside the next morning, the first thing I did was check our food. The barrels sat where we had left them, with no prints in the area to suggest the bear had even looked at them. We weren't wrong about the middle-of-the-night visit, however. A fresh set of bear tracks went right through the soft sand thirty yards from the tent. I wondered where that bear was now. I expected to see one looking down at me from the bluff, or from the willows across the river.

After breakfast, we set off downstream to explore the river. Since Michael had no waders, we kept along the bank with our fly rods and shotgun. The going was slow. On several occasions, we had to drop through a thick brushy gully of a dry stream-bed. It might have been a more pleasant hike if it were not for the mosquitoes, and the concern for bears in the gullies. Anytime we were not in the water or on gravel where the breeze was constant, the mosquitoes were ferocious. The ground was covered with blueberries, but stopping to pick them was deadly. We did drop down to the water at several places to cast, and we found plenty more grayling, but no sign of Dollies. Eventually we trudged back up to our campsite.

Twenty-four hours had passed since the plane dropped us off with no sign of a trout. The water level had come down noticeably, however. On the first day, it was too swift for me to wade across the river at the camp. By late in the second day, it looked crossable either near the island or upstream of the bluff. Remembering how the fisheries biologist had suggested scouting, I carefully made my way across a stretch of slower water and climbed the higher bluff on the opposite shore. The extra feet of elevation have a significant impact on the wind as well as my visibility into the water. Blueberries were still plentiful but both brush and mosquitoes were absent. I had a great view of our campsite, and the river in both directions. Looking down into the water I spotted chum salmon by the hundreds, and a few grayling in among or behind them, but still no Dolly Varden.

Which brings me back to the start of my story. By dinner time my feet were cold and turning to prunes. Though having waders was a good bit better than not having them, after twelve hours tromping around in them I was ready to have them off. When I hung them up on a bush to dry and we cooked our dinner, I assumed I was done fishing for the day. Sitting by the river as evening fell, however, I saw a fish leap out in the current. Though it was too far away to identify clearly, I'd seen none of the tell-tale purple mottling of a chum salmon. The fish I'd seen leap looked more silver and torpedo-like. I stood up and watched more closely. Another fish leapt—or the same one leapt again. I felt a rush of adrenaline much as I had the previous night at the sound of heavy footsteps. A third fish leapt, and then a fourth. I picked up my rod, waded barefoot out into the numbing water, and began to cast my big heavy egg-sucking leech.

Somehow, I managed to make the right cast with the right drift, and the fish hit hard. I eventually landed my first sea-run Dolly Varden, a twenty-eight-inch chrome-bright fish with bright red fins and magenta spots. I would land one more slightly smaller Dolly that evening before my feet got too cold. Michael also landed one casting from the shallow water near the shoreline. I went to bed that night nervous about the prospects of another nighttime visit, but excited in anticipation of a morning of continued fast action landing one big Dolly after another, now that they had moved into the river.

Both expectations proved false. Some sound woke me in the middle of the night, and I stuck my head out the tent flap. The arctic night never really grows completely dark in the summer; evening fades through a long sunset into a short period of twilight, and then back to the slow sunrise. In the twilight, I could make out the glow of wet gravel on the bar where we did much of our fishing, and the soft gray twinkling of light on the ripples in the current. To my relief, no big brown shadows lumbered past. Instead I caught a glimpse of the mysterious white shape of a large snowy owl standing at the water's edge. Enchanted, I watched it for several minutes. When I reached for my camera, however, the owl took flight. I captured only a single blurry photo of the bird with its flecked brown and white wings outstretched and a spray of water coming off its tail. Then it was gone.

The Dollies were gone too. Next morning, before I even ate breakfast, I waded out into the river to cast. I saw no sign of them. Though we couldn't have guessed it the previous evening given how fast that one flurry of action was, the three Dollies we had landed were all we would see on the trip. It may be that the fish had been further upriver where chum were more actively spawning, and were simply passing by on their way back down to the sea, perhaps headed toward Russia. Or maybe some other factor had brought them upriver for only a quick visit, and they had turned and departed as quickly as they came. Or maybe they were in the river all along, staying out of sight and not feeding. We would catch as many more chum and grayling as we wanted, but no more Dolly Varden.

✦ ✦ ✦ ✦ ✦ ✦

"It's all fucked up," Eric said. "Everything's fucked up."

Two mornings after my encounter with the pair of sea-run Dollies, Eric dropped his little bush plane expertly down on the little strip of gravel that had been our home for three days, almost exactly when he said he'd be there. As we loaded the plane, he asked us about the trip, and whether we'd gotten into any big trout. At first, he acted surprised that we had caught only three, but then he went into a strongly worded lament about how messed up everything was. The lack of Dollies was disappointing, but not really surprising—just one more bit of evidence for him. It was the last week of August. Usually the Dollies didn't move upriver in large numbers until September, he told us, echoing what the state fisheries biologist had said a few weeks earlier. But this year, Eric explained, they'd come into the river in *early* August and were already disappearing.

He went on to complain that the caribou seasons were also messed up. Having lived in the area for more than a quarter of a century, Eric had gotten used to seasonal patterns and migrations, and had never seen anything like the changes and unpredictability of the last couple years. Chum salmon were multiplying like crazy, but the dolly populations were down and their seasons were haywire. It would be hard on the people who lived here and depended on the caribou and trout.

◆　　◆　　◆　　◆　　◆　　◆

We had paid Eric extra to fly us over Red Dog Mine on our way out. We headed there now, following the Wulik upriver, east into the hills. For a few minutes, the landscape below us was much like what we'd flown over on our way in: a wide expanse of gray-green tundra, with hints of red I now associated with changing leaves of blueberry bushes. Near the river bottom, the green was darker and richer, with patches of yellow. There was less water here, though. Only a few small ponds dotted the landscape, along with little streams draining the tundra and flowing into the Wulik.

The hills loomed ahead, however, and soon we were flying through them. From a distance, they had looked worn and rounded, but the slopes proved steeper and the valleys between the hills deeper than I'd guessed. Brush gave way to thin grasses and lichen, with wide bare patches of gray ground where nothing grew. The landscape held a stark beauty, despite how barren it appeared. As we got higher into the hills, the soil and rock took on a hint of red. Mist and low clouds swirled through the deeper valleys, occasionally revealing more patches of yellow grasses or flower.

My first glimpse of Red Dog Mine was of the massive tailings pond—an earthen-works reservoir more than a mile long and half a mile wide. "Pond" was too small a word; it was a lake. We came in from the south, and could see the large cluster of red buildings across the water. Beyond those, the mountain was carved up by more quarries, roads, and ponds. Since the deposit of zinc lay close to the surface, it was extracted via open-pit mining. I'd used the term "scar" to describe the haul road we flew over three days earlier, but the scar of the road was nothing compared to this.

My real concern, though, was not the impact of the mine on this one part of the landscape, which in the vast scale of even this one Alaska borough was relatively small. I thought more about the potential for a spill from the tailings pond, as well as leakage into the watershed of the heavy metals exposed on the surface of the earth. I thought of the impact of that on everything downstream, all the way down the Wulik to the sea.

I'd read a lot about the mine before the trip, and continued to read more after. We also talked to several people impacted by it. Though I didn't encounter much discrepancy in *facts* about Red Dog Mine, the narratives and opinions varied. The NANA Regional Corporation, one of thirteen Alaska Native organizations, owns the mine, which in addition to zinc also extracts a smaller amount of lead and silver. Teck Cominco Alaska, a subsidiary of a Canadian company, operates the mine under contract. NANA receives 25% of the mine royalties, and the mine employs almost five hundred workers, most of whom come from local mostly-native communities. With the entire population of Northwest Arctic Borough only a little over 7,000, that makes Red Dog a major employer. A lot of money flows into local hands. In the city of Kotzebue, where much of that money flows, folks are hesitant to say anything bad about Red Dog Mine.

Indeed, the record of Red Dog is arguably quite good compared with other mines. Defenders point out that Cominco responded quickly to the contamination that occurred during the first year of operation resulting in the fish kill in the Wulik. The mining company engineered solutions by which underground springs and sources of Red Dog Creek bypassed the zinc, and also added protection to keep ore stockpiles and other exposed mining systems from contaminating groundwater. The Alaska Department of Fish and Game and the EPA have closely monitored the downstream waters since then, with both chemical and biological sampling, and there have been no indications of further spills or significant impacts to aquatic life. In particular, flesh samples of Dolly Varden and chum salmon in the Wulik and other nearby waters found no detectable difference in levels of heavy metals between fish downstream of the mine and those in other nearby rivers.[3] There is even evidence that Red Dog Creek is cleaner than it was before the mine, at least in terms of heavy metals and related acidity. Prior to the mine construction, high concentrations of heavy metals naturally leached into the water; discoloration of that creek, and barrenness of the land because of high soil acidity, is what led to the discovery of the zinc in the first

---

3 Alvin G. Ott, Phyllis K. Weber-Scannell, and Matthew H. Robus, "Fish Monitoring Study, Red Dog Mine in the Wulik River Drainage, Emphasis on Dolly Varden (*Salvelinus MalmaI*)" Technical Report 91-4, Alaska Department of Fish and Game, Division of Habitat.

place. Grayling now live in the creek where there was no historical record of them.

The narrative told from Kivalina—which, unlike Kotzebue and other communities is directly downriver—is a little different, however. Kivalina not only depends on the annual migrations of Dolly Varden up the Wulik, but they also get their drinking water from the river. When the seepage of heavy metals into the river was first discovered in late 1989, the mine operators denied any culpability or connection with mining operations. People of Kivalina as well as the Department of Fish and Game had to pressure Cominco to take action. Fortunately, the whole community of Northwest Arctic Borough, which has an ownership stake in the mine, depends on a subsistence lifestyle, which in turn depends on the region's ecological health: on the runs of Dolly Varden and chum as well as the annual migrations of caribou. Local involvement in ownership of the mine, and in labor at the mine—even if mine management is leased out—may be the most important hope for continued operation without major disasters.

Even so, there are still concerns. Part of the mine's water treatment involves the addition of lime and sodium sulfide to precipitate zinc, lead, iron, and cadmium. Though this removes the heavy metals and lowers acidity, it increases concentrations of dissolved solids in the river. There have also been air quality and soil quality violations around the mine and the haul road. Dust of zinc carried along the roughly fifty-mile-long road has contaminated plants and soil along the road, and that will also inevitably find its way into local waters. In a 2004 study, the EPA reported 487 million pounds of toxic compounds released from Red Dog Mine, which is more than any other mine in the nation. Not surprisingly, Kivalina residents continued to pressure for additional testing and safeguards and continued vigilance is the key.

I flew away from Red Dog Mine with mixed feelings. The gaping wound on the earth stuck with me, along with the sight of the tailings pond and the recognition of how catastrophic a spill could be. The list of historic mine spills is long. Yet I also thought about the importance of those jobs to area, the importance of zinc to the world, and my impression that this collaboration between NANA and Cominco has resulted in an operation committed to safeguarding all that is downstream.

But then I thought of the proposed Pebble Mine in the headwaters of Bristol Bay and my heart sank. Pebble Mine, if it is approved, would be over 50 times larger than Red Dog: an astounding 28 square miles of mine area compared to 0.5 square miles of pits I had flown over which seemed massive even from an airplane. In addition to having 56 times more area, Pebble Mine would also be roughly twice as deep. This puts the volume of Pebble Mine roughly 100 times greater than Red Dog. This level of devastation to a landscape is hard to fathom. And the potential impact of Pebble Mine is far greater even than those 28 square miles. Indeed, in every way, both the impact and the risk of Pebble Mine would dwarf Red Dog. Pebble Mine would use 35 billion gallons of water per year, which is 28 times as much water as Red Dog. And while Red Dog currently is the largest waste-producing mine in the country, Pebble Mine would produce well over 50 times as much waste.

Geologic and hydrologic studies have also shown that the potential environmental damage caused by contaminated water in Red Dog Mine is mitigated because of 100 to 600 feet of permafrost below the mine, resulting in minimal shallow groundwater to link the mine waste. The area of the proposed Pebble Mine has no such protection. The receding and melting glaciers left porous glacial till and little to no permafrost. The risk of ground water contamination is thus much higher at the proposed Pebble Mine even without the tremendous difference in scale.

And lastly, we come to the tailings ponds for Pebble Mine—not one, but at least two. Like everything else, they would dwarf Red Dog's 585-acre impoundment. Pebble Mine proposes building the largest dam in North America, 4.5 miles long and over 700 feet high, constructed of earth. This would all sit near the headwaters and ground waters of three different river systems all of which flow into Bristol Bay, the most important salmon fishery in the world. The leakage of heavy metals from Red Dog Mine into a small creek that had already been naturally contaminated would be nothing compared to a spill or even the seepage of multiple massive impoundments of Pebble Mine. And the vast destruction of landscape of the Pebble Mine would be on a whole different scale. The international ownership of the Pebble Mine also has no real stake in the land and waters on which that mine would be built.

✦　✦　✦　✦　✦　✦

All that brought me back to the story I had come to the Wulik to write, which turned out *not* to be the story I needed to write. The Wulik River is indeed threatened, as are the livelihoods of the people of Kivalina and all western Alaska. Red Dog Mine is not the greatest threat, though. It is climate change. The thing I didn't know when I planned the trip was that, as concerned as the people of Kivalina are about the impact of the zinc mine on the health of their river, many have become even more concerned with global climate change. This was emphasized in the dramatic changes in caribou migrations, the changes and declines in the runs of Dolly Varden, in the thawing of permafrost, and especially in the rising sea levels that threatened to drown the coastal village. In the words of our pilot, everything was "fucked up."

Out of the Frying Pan and Into the Fire

Farm Lodge and the Bristol Bay Watershed, August 2015 and August 2017

Early on an August afternoon Dave O'Hara and I took a one-hour Lake Clark Air flight from Merrill Field in Anchorage along the northern and western edges of the Cook Inlet and inland through Lake Clark Pass to Port Alsworth, a community of private land amid the vast landscape of Lake Clark National Park and Preserve. Remote rugged mountain peaks and the thick masses of hanging glaciers loomed over us on the flight, so close it seemed we could reach out and touch them. Below us, the landscape was carved by silty glacier-fed rivers swollen by one waterfall after another pouring down ridges on both sides. Then the turquoise waters of Lake Clark opened up beneath us, and soon we touched down on the gravel airstrip.

In the language of the Dena'ina people who have dwelt for centuries around its shores and in the surrounding areas, Lake Clark is known as *Qizhjeh Vena*, which means a "place where people gather" or the "Place People Gather Lake."[4] When we stepped off the plane and became one of the gathering persons, the Farm Lodge porters already stood waiting with carts to haul our gear to our cabin. "Would you like to do a little fishing before dinner?" one of them asked, as they unloaded the plane. I needed no convincing. We followed them to our cabin and dug through our duffel bags for waders, fly rods, and tackle. Barely quarter of an hour after I first set foot on the ground in Port Alsworth, the porters hauled me on an ATV to the far end of the runway. From there, only five more minutes of lakeshore walking took

---

4 *Dena'ina Elnena: A Celebration: Voices of the Dena'ina* edited by Karen E. Evanoff, Published by the United States Department of the Interior, National Park Service, Lake Clark National Park and Preserve, August 2010. Except where otherwise noted, further Dena'ina place names and their meanings from this source.

us to the mouth of the Tanalian River, or *Tanilen Vetnu* in the Dena'ina language: "flows into water stream". It is a fitting name. Lake Clark filled the expanse ahead of us, stretching beyond sight to the right and left, disappearing into the blue-gray of distant cloud-wrapped hills. We spent two delightful hours landing one fat grayling after another in the cold, green-tinted water of the Tanalian, where its swift current clashed with the winds blowing in across the lake. Though the gravel river-bottom provided good footing, I waded cautiously, knowing that with a single misstep I could easily be swept off into the darker blue-green depths of the lake. The ridgeline of Tanalian Mountain and wilderness hills of Lake Clark National Park, with low-lying mist swirling around their feet, looked down on us from behind, indifferent to our presence or fate.

After a shower, a feast awaited us up in the main Farm Lodge building where we gathered with other lodge guests. We dined luxuriously, filled out menus for the next day's breakfast and lunch, and were then given the simple schedule for the morning: come to breakfast at 7:30am ready to depart at 9:00am for our long-anticipated fly-out fishing day. I went to bed full of eager, nervous anticipation. When we arrived at breakfast—a feast almost as grand as the previous evening's dinner—we were told our departure time had been moved up to 8:30am. Though I wasn't quite as ready-to-go as I should have been, the earlier departure time still excited me. I wanted to get the most I could out of this potentially once-in-a-lifetime experience: the first time in my life, and possibly the last, when I would have a one-day fly-in Alaskan fishing trip. I needed no urging to get ready sooner. We finished the meal and rushed back to our cabin to gather our waders, wading shoes, spare clothing, rods and gear. We were still getting ready at 8:20am when one of the workers knocked at our door and said the plane was ready to go as soon as we could get there. We handed him our duffel with waders and boots and he disappeared.

I stepped out the cabin door and looked out at Hardenberg Bay, whose waters lapped a beach just a few steps in front of our porch. I tried to spot our transportation. A raft of blue and white Cessna float planes lined the cove, but no activity buzzed around them. I looked further down the boardwalk onto the gravel airstrip and noticed a small black plane with big fat tires sitting at the near end. A few folks stood around it. That, apparently, was our ride.

We walked the short distance to the airstrip. There, we met Glen Alsworth Jr., the grandson of the Alsworth who homesteaded this place some seventy years ago, and after whom the town got its name. Though we had interacted with Glen Jr. via e-mail, I hadn't realized he personally would be taking us fishing. I was delighted. It took only a couple minutes to load our gear into the back of the plane. "Do you have any bear spray?" Glen asked. We responded in the negative. Though we had some back in the cabin for our camping trip the next day, we hadn't brought it with us, assuming our guide would be in charge of our protection. I grew worried. Were we supposed to bring some? Apparently not, because Glen replied, "Good. This is the only plane in our fleet without wing storage, so you aren't allowed to bring any." I would only later make the connection. A canister of bear spray going off inside the cabin of an airplane would incapacitate a pilot immediately. Spray was only allowed in wing compartments. As with all issues of safety, the Lake Clark Air pilots carefully enforced this. At the time, though, bears still concerned me. I nervously inquired as to whether Glen had some sort of deterrent. "Yeah," he said with a smile. "I've got bear spray: the kind that sprays lead."

We seat-belted ourselves in the plane. Dave gave me the front, next to the pilot. Glen went over the safety features and emergency protocol. No flight attendants or additional crew would be there to direct us should some unfortunate or unforeseen event arise. It would be up to us. Though I had no expectation that any of this information would prove necessary, I paid careful attention to the details of where to find the fire extinguisher and survival kit. I thought about my wife Deborah, who is fearful of small planes. I was glad she was not there listening or she might have begun imagining all the scenarios in which those protocols would be required.

Glen went through his final safety checks and started the engine. As it idled, I pulled out my DSLR and made sure I had my telephoto lens handy. Glen saw the camera. The Farm House Lodge specializes in wilderness and wildlife photography. Glen explained that if it wasn't raining, I could open the door during flight and avoid the distortion caused by the glass windows. I was both eager and afraid to try. "We won't be going over Frying Pan Lake on the way over," he explained. "It's too foggy. Hopefully these clouds will lift and we can do a fly-over on the return."

I understood Glen's comment. Dave and I were interested in the ecology of the area that would be impacted if Pebble Mine were ever approved. Frying Pan Lake was at the center of that area: the equivalent of ground zero. Under the proposed mine plan, the lake would cease to exist; it would be replaced by a massive tailings impoundment behind one of the world's largest dams. The lake, and everything downstream of it in all directions, was imminently threatened. Dave and I wanted to see that area: to get a clearer and more concrete experience of space and place: to replace the abstraction of maps and reports with the sight of real trees and lichen, bears and caribou, rivers and lakes and beaver ponds, hillsides and valleys, blueberry bushes, and especially salmon and Dolly Varden. So Glen had suggested we spend a day on a river whose headwaters came out of the area, with a fly-over of Frying Pan Lake if weather permitted.

The present weather did not permit, and Glen's announcement turned out to be the last bit of conversation we would have for over an hour. Once the engine revved up, it was much too loud to talk. We all donned headsets to protect our ears. Glen had told us about past photography and filming flights when his passengers had created a system of elaborate hand signals to indicate what sorts of animals they were seeing. "I thought I was going to get to see my first Alaskan elephant," he'd joked, putting his hands in the shape of what might be the neck and head of a trumpeter swan— or in a different context the trunk of an elephant.

Soon our little black Stinson raced down the airstrip, and within just a few beats of my own racing heart we rose into the air, lifted above the level of the trees, passed over the Tanalian River, and climbed out over the green vastness of Lake Clark, the place where people gather. The flight brought us southward along the lake, past Sixmile Lake, and down the Newhalen River toward Lake Iliamna. Soon we were flying over a largely treeless tundra. We were so much closer to the ground than in a commercial jet— even closer than on our flight the previous day—that it seemed we could almost drag our hands along the soft spongy surface. We could spot not only beaver ponds by the dozens, but were so low I expected to see the eyes of beavers looking up at us. Back in Vermont, over the course of several months leading to this trip, I had studied maps. I knew the river we were headed toward: a headwater of the Nushagak on its eastern side. I had a mental picture of the landscape and the river in relation to Lake Clark and Lake Iliamna. Or I thought I did. We flew much further south than I had imagined we would, and soon we were traveling along Iliamna. The second largest lake entirely in the United State, Iliamna is impossible to miss. We flew along it for many minutes. Several times we appeared to turn north away from the lake, but then we ended up back in sight of it.

And then Glen got really close to the ground. The wheels touched down and we coasted to a stop. That was when I learned the reason for our flight path. The clouds hung too low that morning for Glen to cross the pass up into the valley we were trying to reach. Rather than continue burning through his supply of gas while waiting for the clouds to lift, he dropped down on a ridge overlooking Iliamna. We got out, stretched our legs, uncovered our ears, took a few photos, and found some wild blueberries, crowberries and cranberries to munch on while we waited. Silently, I hoped and prayed the trip would not be canceled altogether—that the clouds would lift and we would make it to our destination. But it was out of my hands.

✦   ✦   ✦   ✦   ✦   ✦

In his book *A 20th-Century Portrait of Lake Clark, Alaska*, National Park Service historian John Branson describes some of the inhabitants of the area around Lake Clark National Park and Preserve who preceded Glen's grandfather, "Babe Alsworth". The earliest record of human habitation on the shores of Lake Clark dates to roughly 4,000 years ago, but there is evidence in the broader area of human habitation going back at least 10,000 years.[5] I think of how challenging it would have been to settle here just a hundred years ago. Even in the summer, I am dressed from toe to head in modern high-tech fabrics to keep me warm and dry and comfortable. The lack of plants taller than a few inches bears witness to the harshness of the climate: wind, cold, and even extreme dryness during winter months when all is frozen.

Thanks to the salmon that carry millions of tons of nutrients from the ocean up into this watershed every year, food is plentiful—salmon, caribou, and the myriad berries blanketing the landscape—but only during the summer. There must be a frenzy of activity to gather it all in to prepare for the long, cold winters of short days and long nights. I am amazed that various peoples succeeded and prospered here. In her ethnohistory of Lake Clark National Park and Preserve, Karen Gaul summarizes a few conclusions from current archaeological evidence. Prior to a

---

5 John B. Branson, *A 20th-Century Portrait of Lake Clark, Alaska: 1900-2000* (Anchorage: U.S. Department of the Interior, 2007), 5.

thousand years ago, the chief source of food was caribou, and so the people who dwelt in the land lived a more nomadic hunting lifestyle keeping with the rhythms of migrating herds. Then the runs of salmon increased dramatically, perhaps due to a warming trend. Though hunting of moose, sheep, and caribou as well as gathering berries and other plants remained significant, this brought about a shift toward fish as the predominant food source. The development of weirs and fish traps led to more permanent settlements around lakes and places of annual salmon spawning runs.[6]

This did not suddenly make life easy, however. Even in the early twentieth-century, when commercial fisheries had come to the area and modern firearms could make the harvest of meat simpler, subsistence lifestyle was full of challenge and hard work for the full-time inhabitants of Tanalian Point, nestled just a few hundred yards down the lake from my Farm Lodge cabin on Hardenberg Bay. Branson describes the community as diverse, with Dena'ina and Euro-born Americans living in community together.

> Life revolved around the seasonal round of subsistence activity to put food on the table.... Residents had to have put enough potatoes and rutabagas away in root cellars, salted enough water fowl and moose meat in wooden barrels, and smoked enough fish in caches to survive the long Alaska winter. Subsistence activities continued year around: [spring] vegetable gardening... followed by Bristol Bay commercial salmon fishing (for an infusion of cash), subsistence salmon fishing, berry picking, sheep and moose hunting, fire-wood cutting, trapping and wood-hauling with dog teams.[7]

---

6 Karen K. Gaul, *NANUTSET ch'u Q'udi Gu: Before Our Time and Now: An Ethnohistory of Lake Clark National Park and Preserve*, (Anchorage: U.S. Department of the Interior, 2007).

7 Branson, p.8.

I know that many now dwell in various communities nearby, and some—including Dena'ina people—still practice a traditional subsistence lifestyle, salting and smoking meats to preserve for the winters, and preserving berries from the brief but abundant harvest. I'm thankful that Lake Clark National Park has as one of its central management purposes supporting that continued tradition. But as much as I enjoy the stunning beauty of this place, I'm glad I don't have to do that sort of hard work. I don't think fly-fishing all day to catch (and release) three or four Dolly Varden trout would fit in very well. Even the modern technology of an airplane does not free one from the whims of weather, as I experienced at the moment.

We continued to stand on the tundra, looking back and forth between Lake Iliamna to the south and the clouds on the low valley passes to the north. Under most circumstances I would have been impatient to get out fishing, but the flight had been so enjoyable and such a unique experience that my patience was only mildly tested. We even had a chance to create a few hand gestures. Dave had spotted a family of three brown bears running along the river. The sow was sprinting at a full gallop, and the cubs were far behind struggling to keep up. He also saw two caribou and another family of three bears. Sitting on the wrong side of the plane, I had missed them. But at least we now had a complex hand signal for "sow bear running in the river followed by two cubs."

Eventually, the cloud layer lifted. We got back into the plane, took off, and made it through the pass. When we flew over the river, I spotted a brown bear splashing around below us, presumably chasing salmon. This one was on my side, but since it had no cubs I wasn't able to use the new hand signal. I also took several photos of another big brown bear rushing across a shallow stream. My attention was so focused on the bear in the river, it wasn't until later—looking at the photos on my larger computer screen—that I noticed three smaller black bears on dry land a hundred yards ahead fleeing from the big brown. Finally, I spotted a pair of swans and was able to give the elephant signal.

Twenty minutes after taking off, Glen once more dropped his fat-tired Stinson on a level patch of gravel on a bluff overlooking the river we had come to visit and to fish. Now my impatience kicked in. I'd been anticipating this moment for months. In less time than it might take for a Dolly Varden to snap up a mouthful of drifting salmon eggs, I leapt out the plane and began pulling on my waders. Soon I had my rod together and a big purple egg-sucking leech tied to my 3x tippet. Glen tied on a similar fly. Dave decided to go with a bead-head prince nymph. When we finished rigging, Glen led us a short distance along a bluff overlooking the river. There we paused again to study the water. It didn't take Glen long to spot fish. He pointed out several grayling and thought he saw one large Dolly Varden in the pool where two braids flowed together below an island. I saw the grayling, but I didn't see a trout.

Glen led Dave to the head of the pool, and sent me down the bank to the middle, so we could cast to different sections without interfering with each other. Finally, all the anticipation bore fruit. With the bluff behind me, I had no room to back-cast, but by lifting my rod up high I managed to propel my heavy fly out to roughly the spot where Glen had seen—and I had failed to see—the big Dolly Varden holding in the current.

My pilot and guide had not been wrong. I hooked into the big fish immediately. Almost as quickly, the fish tore off down river and broke my line. I stood staring at the river for several seconds, like one whose lover has just slammed the front door with a parting shot that can't be mistaken for anything other than a final goodbye. After a long moment of heartbreak and pondering what might have been, I tied on another fly, determined to get into a rebound relationship as quickly as possible. I managed to elicit a strike from another big Dolly, but I never got the hook set on the second one. After two misses, I worried Glen would judge me unworthy of the spot to which he brought us. I also worried that I'd lost my only chance at romance. The second worry proved well-founded. There is a cliché, usually spoken to jilted lovers: "There are plenty of fish in the sea." The saying simply isn't true. Or, rather, it may have been true of the sea at one time, but it isn't always true of trout in rivers. We fished another forty-five minutes in that first hole. Dave landed several large grayling and I landed a couple, but we saw no more Dollies.

Following a bear track along the shore, avoiding the litter of half-eaten salmon carcasses and fresh dung, we moved upstream to a stretch of thigh-deep current between two undercut banks. Glen told me to cast against the near bank. I did, and finally hooked and landed a Dolly Varden over twenty inches. It was my first Dolly of the day, and one of the biggest of my life. I could see it was the same species of fish I had caught in mountain streams and lakes in Chugach State Park and on the Kenai Peninsula; it wore the same magenta pearls, and sported tell-tale red fins. Yet it was much more stunning in its display of colors than most of its cousins I had seen in the past. It had a much darker green back, and the red on its fins and bellies was more of a deep cranberry than the burnt orange of the mountain dollies. Only on the Anchor River in October had I seen a Dolly Varden this colorful, and perhaps only on the Kenai River had I seen one close to this big.

Now that his guest had finally succeeded, Glen began to cast his own rod in earnest. It did not take him long to land a Dolly enough longer and fatter than the one I landed that I conceded the contest with no measurement needed. But I measured anyway, using the sections of his rod as he held the fish in the water. It was a full two feet long.

We continued upriver toward the next corner, mostly fishing undercut banks. We all landed grayling after grayling—strong and fat from an abundant diet of salmon eggs and aquatic insects— but I hooked no more Dollies in that stretch. Dave, still casting his bead-head nymph, landed the most grayling; he couldn't keep them off his hook. Eventually, he switched to a streamer with a bead in front of it. Right away he hooked and landed a bright and plump Dolly. He stuck with the fly for the rest of the day.

Around midday, we hiked back to the plane and ate our lunches atop the bank looking down at the river. I noticed again the stark contrast between the tundra where we sat and the narrow stretch of land along the river just a dozen feet below us. The tundra, though mostly covered by spongy moss and lichen, with a few scattered delicate lavender wildflowers and an occasional patch of blueberries, was nearly barren of trees, bushes, and even grass. Almost nothing grew more than a few inches off the ground. Yet where the river made its narrow cut below the level of the tundra, tall grass and flowers, thick brush, and even some willow trees grew thickly in the swath of land along the shoreline. A steady supply of water, rich nutrients in the soil from an abundance of rotting salmon—some preprocessed by bears and other creatures—and just enough shelter from the wind, was the difference for this band of abundant life in the midst of a harsh landscape.

Eating lunch, we were thankful for the wind as it kept off the mosquitoes that were thick in the streamside brush. Despite the mosquitoes, however, I was eager to be fishing again. I inhaled my sandwich, guzzled a bottle of apple juice, and was soon ready to fish more. After lunch, we turned our attention downstream where the river wandered away from the edge of the bluff into a wider meandering cut with several braids. Thinking of all the fresh bear sign, we skirted the edge of a patch of willows and thick underbrush, and made our way to another pool Glen liked, where two braids flowed back together at the base of an island. We spent the rest of the afternoon in the fifty yards above and two hundred yards below that pool. I landed and released three more trout, all over 16", and hooked and lost three others. Dave also landed three.

Though a good bit of my attention focused on the Dollies and the places I (or Glen) thought they might be, I continued to observe other life in and around the stream. Fortunately, we did not observe any bear, despite the numerous bear signs. The mosquitoes were a different sort of threat, but as long as I stayed in the water they weren't bad. From time to time we came up on a king salmon sitting like a half-submarged submarine in the current over a run of gravel, or trying to hide against an undercut bank. It is hard to hide in knee-deep water when you are three feet long, weigh forty pounds, and are bright red. However, the tracks, scat, and salmon remains on the bank suggested why the fish might want to hide. Some of the kings were solitary, but several were paired up. The patches of white rotting flesh mottling their red-scaled sides signaled that these fish were in the final stages of life, destined to become nutrients in the ecosystem soon, even if a bear didn't catch them.

I also saw a few sockeye, working upriver on their long spawning journey. Their bodies had a similar rose-hip coloring to the kings, but the sockeye heads were dark green. The male sockeye also sported noticeable humps on their backs and a more pronounced kype than the kings. Had I come upon a salmon of either species that had still looked fresh, I might have been tempted to cast for it, though with my lighter trout rod I wouldn't have had much chance to land a big salmon.

When the sun had sunk half way down toward the horizon in the downriver direction, Glen gave us a "last cast" warning. Since it often takes me a least a dozen casts to make the cast that actually counts as last, I was ready to go about ten minutes later. We climbed up the bank onto the flat expanse of tundra to the plane that had sat waiting patiently all day. With a sigh, half of contentment and half of longing, I took off my slightly-leaky waders and packed my rod. The clouds lifted, and as we got into the plane Glen announced that we should be able to fly back over Frying Pan Lake. We put on our headsets, he revved up the engines, and after a short taxi our fat tires bumped down the flat of the tundra then lifted in the air.

✦   ✦   ✦   ✦   ✦   ✦

One geological report of the area surrounding the proposed Pebble Mine offers a description of the landscape.

> The surficial geology of the map area is dominated by arcuate end moraines, meltwater deposits with abundant kettle depressions, broad outwash aprons and elongate valley trains, and striking meltwater channels. Former glacier-dammed lakes are marked by broad expanses of unusually smooth, poorly drained, and gently sloping terrain that terminate abruptly upslope at consistent altitudes and are commonly bordered by beach and deltaic deposits.[8]

I appreciate the poetry in these words: the mix of scientific terminology with descriptive adjectives getting at the broad, striking expansiveness, gentle and smooth in ways and yet abrupt in others. I would not be able to identify an "arcuate end moraine" if it bit me. However, as we flew along various dividing river valleys making our way east, and scouted for bears and caribou while admiring the work of beavers, I admired the kettle depressions. Most were full of water, making them kettle ponds. Some looked like mixing pots for paints, each with its own unique color based on local chemistry and minerals.

I had a clear hint that we were approaching the proposed mine area when I began to see ATV tracks marring the landscape below me and churning up the fragile tundra. I thought of the contrast between these and the meandering caribou tracks we had flown over earlier. Despite the fragility of the tundra soil, I thought

---

8 Thomas D. Hamilton, "Surface Geologic Map of the Pebble Limited Partnership's Pebble Project", Anchorage Alaska, 2007, p.1.

these tracks would heal eventually. I tried not to imagine what the landscape would look like if the ATVs were replaced with all the equipment needed for one of the world's largest open pit mines. That scar that would not heal in a thousand lifetimes.

We flew on. I recognized Frying Pan Lake from satellite photos even before Glen pointed it out to us. The Pebble Mine base camp sat in an expanse of tundra not far from the lake. A handful of hard-sided dwellings as well as a few canvas or soft-sided structures stood near numerous rows of red, gray, and yellow shipping containers lined up side-by-side, and what looked like stacks of pipes and pallets and other building supplies. Some sort of network of pipes connected buildings to one another and to what looked like covered pits in the ground.

I know that Pebble Mine—like many other environmental concerns today—is highly politicized. When I later mentioned the mine to the staff at Lake Clark National Park and Preserve, they were careful not to offer personal opinions or even to articulate the official park position in their own words. Instead they directed me to a publication that park officials had worked collaboratively to draft. The publication does not even mention "Pebble Mine"; it is titled "Concerns Regarding Large-scale Mining on the Western Boundary of the Park." Though the brochure does not explicitly oppose the mine, it outlines several serious concerns:

1. The health of the watershed to support returning red salmon;
2. Ecological systems that depend on the return of sockeye salmon for food and nutrients;
3. Wildlife migrations that depend on wilderness land in and around the Park such as caribou and other species;
4. The cultural and food security integrity of communities dependent on the subsistence resources of the Park.

I shared those same concerns. Bristol Bay is the most important and prolific salmon water in the world, providing roughly half of the world's sockeye harvest. And, as I have repeatedly seen, those salmon provide the nutrients to support the terrestrial ecosystems of Alaska, even as the terrestrial ecosystems are a necessary component of the marine ones. Even apart from a spill or "disaster", just the upsetting of the area's entire hydrology from an open pit mine of that scale and depth could be devastating. The potential for contamination of the water is considerable also, even without the inevitable spill at the tailings compound. "Copper is the most toxic element to aquatic life and even at very low concentrations may affect a salmon's ability to return to its spawning ground," the park brochures states, in elaboration of its first concern.

I asked Glen Jr. about Pebble Mine. He also understands how politically charged the topic is, and he hesitated to answer too quickly. One doesn't need to be around him long to realize how deeply and profoundly he loves this land and the people who live on it. There is no place he would rather be. I'm sure he took as much or more delight flying over that landscape and seeing the caribou and brown bear for the ten thousandth time as I did doing it for the first time. Though he is quiet and reserved, his joy and delight is contagious. He also knows the land about as well as a person can know such a vast place. His deep love both comes from, and feeds back into, deep knowledge. He is the third generation of his family to live in Port Alsworth, but his roots are even deeper than those three generations. Glen's great-grandmother Agrifina—the mother of his paternal grandmother Mary—was a Yup'ik Eskimo from the Nushagak Bay area where the river we had just spent the day on eventually drained. And he looks into the future not only of his five children, but also of any grandchildren who may one day arrive. The river where we spent the day, he said, "is part of my back yard and a place that I hope my grandchildren will be able to enjoy as much as I have."

In some ways, then, I think the proposed Pebble Mine would be an anathema to somebody with Glen's passions and concerns. "The Farm Lodge offers access to some of Alaska's most wild places," he told me. "Our primary purpose as a business is to help people safely experience the most wild and untamed parts of our state. Because we are stewards of land, we offer low impact activities designed to let people enjoy the resource without depleting it. On a more personal level, we exist to minister to and serve others. The Farm Lodge is a wonderful tool that we can use to help people get closer to creation." With regard to the importance of salmon and the rivers where they spawn, he went on to add, "Much of our tourism focuses around fishing, bear viewing, and photography. These are all activities that are directly affected by the water and salmon runs. The salmon are the cornerstone for much of the plant and animal life as well as an attraction themselves."

That last sentence resonated with everything I had learned. Yet still Glen hesitated to jump into a debate that is so polarized. As a business person in a hospitality industry, he probably needs to avoid alienating any potential clientele on any pole. But his hesitancy to give a defining answer seemed even more deeply rooted in both his personal humility and also in a resistance to polarization in and of itself. "It is probably a question better put before a group of hydrologists, fish biologists, engineers, etc.," he said. "Unfortunately, the debate has been monopolized by those who believe that large scale development is either inherently evil or those who believe it is the end-all to be pursued at any cost (or perhaps any profit)." I continued to push questions, and eventually he elaborated:

> Unfortunately many people on both sides of the issue have convinced themselves and others that a very specific future is inevitable based not on science, logic, observations, or research; but on preconceptions and speculation. Why

not ask, *Can this be done in a sound way? If so, what can we do to ensure that it is done in that way?* The answers to these questions are probably more critical to an informed and responsible decision than the speculations so eagerly offered by individuals who refuse to vacate their soap boxes.

Honestly, I don't know the answers myself. And I fear that it will be increasingly hard to wade through the political mire surrounding this subject in order to draw close enough to the real issues that should be the basis for finding those answers.

✦   ✦   ✦   ✦   ✦   ✦

When I flew away from Port Alsworth a few days later, after a two-night camping trip with Dave on Lake Kontrashibuna in the wilderness area of Lake Clark National Park, I was sad at the thought that my first trip to the Farm Lodge and Lake Clark National Park might also be my last—that it really was likely just a once-in-a-lifetime trip, like my float trip down to the Nushagak River with my father had been more than a decade earlier. But I also left Alaska that summer with news that the Pebble Mine project was officially dead; it had been dealt two fatal wounds: the EPA had denied the permitting for the mine, and the voters of Alaska had also rejected it at least symbolically. The death certificate was so clearly written that the head of one of the conservation groups that was among the strongest opponents of the mine had already moved on to a new project.

It turns out that both conjectures were wrong. Two years later I would return to the Farm Lodge in Port Alsworth for an eight-day trip that would include two days flying down to Katmai National Park (also in the salmon-rich headwaters of Bristol Bay) as well as a return trip to the same river I had visited with Glen and a return camping trip to Kontrashibuna. The hospitality of the Farm Lodge was every bit as lavish as I remembered. The landscape of Lake Clark National Park and Preserve, including the flight into the Port Alsworth, was every bit as spectacular. And the fishing around both national parks was even better.

With respect to the future of Bristol Bay and its ecological health, however, prospects had changed for the worse. To say that November of 2016 brought big changes in Washington would be an understatement. The EPA that had been protecting the important salmon waters of Bristol Bay was being gutted, and the extraction-based economy of Alaska was in shambles because of a collapse in oil prices; many industries (and people) were desperate for anything that might bring new income (and the potential for jobs) including a large-scale pit mine owned and operated by a foreign company.

On three occasions on this return trip, Glen was my pilot for outings to headwaters of Bristol Bay, and on two of those he was also my fishing guide for the day. We discussed a lot of different topics including the spiritual value of nature and what it means to see the world around us, and especially the beauty of Alaska that surrounded us, as "creation"—as the result of a meaningful purposeful act of a loving creator instead of the result of some grand cosmic accident of meaningless random forces. We didn't talk much about Pebble Mine. Maybe I was afraid to bring it up, since I have found myself moving closer and closer to one of those poles.

Eating Salmon Eggs in Katmai

Katmai National Park and Preserve, August, 2017

We step out of the float plane and onto the shore of a small lake. A chill wind blows across the water behind us, across our cheeks and necks, across our bare fingers. I look over the alpine tundra painted green with dapples of pale yellow, toward a steep barren hill of rock and sand. I am surprised to see patches of snow in a gully all the way down at the base of the hill. It is mid-August. Though I expect snow year-round on the higher mountain peaks of southcentral Alaska, I'm surprised to see so much remaining down low near the rivers and lakes. I ask our pilot what our elevation is. His answer surprises me. We are a thousand feet higher than I thought. That explains the snow.

I look out again over the tundra, taking more careful note. Not a tree can be seen in any direction. Other than along the lake shore, I don't even see a bush. I look down at my feet. Tiny green leaves mixed with occasional bits of lichen cover the terrain, giving the tundra its patchy colors. A dense bunch of blueberries lies scattered on the ground. More scatterings lie to my left and right. At first, I don't see any blueberry bushes. It looks as though some unlucky berry picker tripped and spilled her can on the ground. I reach down to pick up a berry or two and find they are still attached to a plant. The bushes are there, but they are barely "bushes" at all—just thin vines a few inches long, creeping along the ground, clinging low and out of the constant wind that blows across these high places. Our elevation becomes even more of a reality to me.

We take a short walk toward the end of the lake. The tundra is soft and spongy. We try to stay on lakeshore gravel as we make our way around, both for the better footing and to minimize our impact on the fragile terrain. Soon we stand next to a shallow river at the lake's outlet. The brisk wind makes its presence felt on this overcast Alaskan day. We are bundled in hoods or hats, jackets and fleece. It is August, but I feel summer only in the long hours of daylight. Though we only finished breakfast an hour and a half ago, the sun has been up for several hours and will remain in the sky for many more.

My attention, however, is no longer on the snow, berries, wind or cloudy sky. It is on the river. Dozens of fat red sockeye salmon—the males sporting humps and pronounced kypes—are visible in the short stretch of water in front of me. It is so shallow in places that their fins stick up like those of a shark in a horror film. The undulations of their powerful aquatic bodies are barely perceptible as they hold their places along the gravel bottom. They are in the last stages of their long spawning journey. From time to time, a female does a vigorous shaking dance either to help form her redd, or to shake eggs loose from her body. Those eggs are the final thread holding her to life. When she has released them, she will die. Males stand ready nearby, jockeying for position and the privilege of fertilizing those eggs.

Just downstream of those sockeye, fat Dolly Varden char and rainbow trout hold in the current waiting to suck up any eggs that drift loose. At least I hope they do. In their dark green camouflaged skins, they are much more difficult to see than the bright red salmon that stick out of the water. Moving close enough to spot them is often also close enough to spook them away.

The presence of salmon in the river is what makes me surprised at our high elevation. I think of how long of a journey these fish have taken—not just the number of miles from the ocean, but the elevation they have gained up high-gradient rivers in swift-moving water, leaping cataracts and waterfalls—to get to this very spot where they are now trying to start a new generation with their offspring. In a few years, those offspring will repeat the same journey to the same spot. Some small percentage will, that is. These salmon lay eggs by the tens of thousands. On average, only a couple eggs per female will survive to adulthood. It is a potent lesson in biology. It is also an insight into the ecology of Alaska. The dozens of salmon I see in front of me are only a fraction of the number in this river. Over a mile or so, as we fish our way downstream through the morning, we will see not just dozens but several hundred—perhaps even a few thousand. And even those hundreds to thousands pale in comparison to the number of fish that have entered this river from Bristol Bay and the Pacific

Ocean, which in turn is only a small portion of the multitides that have swum up dozens of other tributaries of the richest salmon water in the world.

Once again, Glen Alsworth Jr. is leading this adventure. I am in the midst of a week staying at the Farm Lodge in Port Alsworth with my friend and frequent co-author David O'Hara and Dave's son Michael. We've been exploring both Lake Clark National Park and Preserve and also Katmai National Park and Preserve. Today Glen has flown us to Katmai to spend a day trying to hook up with one or two of the trout that have followed the salmon upriver to feast on an egg-buffet. The flight from Lake Clark was stunning, and as much a part of the allure of the trip as the trout we are casting flies toward. As our plane made its approach up the river, I looked down and saw big red smudges in the clear water below us. The smudges—massive schools of sockeye salmon— filled whole stretches of river, fifty, seventy, a hundred yards long. We saw several big brown bears splashing through shallower portions of the river, chasing after the salmon like first graders chasing a soccer ball in gym class. We also got a close look at a dozen big caribou bulls carrying massive racks on their heads. These, also, we had come to see.

So this day has already been a wonderful success before we even step out of the float plane. The fishing proves challenging, however. As we saw on the flight in, the sockeye—and the trout following them—have not had an easy journey. In addition to their long-distance swim, they have run a dangerous gauntlet of predatory bears. The fish that have made it this far have probably had to scoot past more than one furry ursine. After a series of narrow escapes from the proverbial jaws of death, they are easily spooked by shadows or movements. The shallow sparkling clear water makes them even more wary. We have to guess where the trout and char are without getting too close to either them or the salmon. Since the trout have come to feed on eggs, we look for actively spawning salmon. We need to cast heavily-weighted flies into the midst of those salmon and let them sink to the bottom and drift downstream to (we hope) a waiting trout. Several times through the day I hear—or I emit—a groan of despair as a fly inadvertently snags one of the big sockeye. The line goes taut. The salmon feels the tug and takes off upriver or down. The rod bends hard. And then…

Well, one of three things happens. We are fishing with trout rods. They are 5-weight rods meant for a two-foot long fish weighing perhaps three to six pounds, not the 8-weight rods we might use for three-foot long salmon weighing ten or more pounds with the strength to swim hundreds of miles upriver. Most of the time, therefore, an inadvertently hooked sockeye breaks our line. The salmon then goes back to its spot in the river as though nothing happened, perhaps sporting a new decorative body ornament for the final day of its life before it spawns and dies. We anglers must then go up on the shore with the blueberries and spend precious minutes tying on a whole new set of terminal tackle. Sometimes we are lucky and the hook comes loose before the line breaks. Or the third option: we let the salmon pull us downstream until we can lead it to shore and remove the hook—a processing typically requiring more time than tying on all new gear.

We all begin fishing large flies imitating leeches or egg-sucking leeches. I focus on deeper pockets, pools, and undercut banks. After fishing several stretches of water with no success I switch to an egg pattern. Spotting a small group of salmon in a shallow riffle, I roll my fly out into their midst and let it drift downstream. It makes it through without hooking or spooking the salmon. That's the first good sign. A few yards downstream the fly passes over a slight depression in the current. Though I had not seen anything there, a dark shadow separates from a rock and slams my fly. I lift my rod to set the hook, and soon I land a big Dolly Varden. Though I have seen (and even written about) their beautiful colors many times in the past, I never tire of admiring the spangle of orange-red or magenta spots of a Dolly. The noses and jaws of the males in this river look like a kindergarten child who has gotten into theatrical makeup and smeared her lips with bright yellow and orange lipstick. Though I could continue admiring it for a long time, I let the fish swim off. A few minutes later and just a few yards downstream, I land a fat rainbow trout on the same fly. I begin to feel smug, thinking I have found the secret for success for the day. These, however, will be the only trout I catch that morning.

We continue to work our way downstream into the early afternoon. My companions hook a few more rainbows and Dollies, and also continue to accidentally snag the occasional sockeye. Most of the trout manage to spit the hook or break our line, or they simply ignore our flies. As lunchtime approaches, Glen pulls us aside. He has been guiding us to a spot he expects to find some brown bears. It's one of the main reasons he chose this river for our outing. He has already given us a talk on bear safety and etiquette. Having seen several of the big mammals on our flight in, we take those precautions to heart. "We carry everything with us," he'd told us. "No leaving packs on the shore. If a bear decides he wants to come our way, we want to make room for it quickly without leaving anything behind."

I get the impression that these rules weren't so much for our own safety as for the long-term safety of the bears themselves and for any future human visitors to the area. If we left anything edible behind, the bears would come to associate humans with free food, Glen explains. He also notes that pretty much *anything* we leave behind—edible or not—will get chewed on. Even a gas can. After reminding us of these rules, Glen asks us to stay together. The bears don't care that much about us, he explains. We are probably too small and insignificant to mean much to them. They are concerned with each other, and the dynamics of their social hierarchy. We stay together primarily so that the bears have fewer things to pay attention to. If one bear gets spooked or chased by another, and decides to take off up the hill in our direction, it is much easier for it to avoid us if we are single object in a single place instead of four different objects spread out along the hill.

All the reminders and stuff to think about makes me both excited and nervous. We continue on. As we crest the hill and look down upon a new stretch of river, I spot the bears. They are just where Glen had promised. Four of them stand in the river below us, only seventy yards away. It is as close as I have ever intentionally come to a brown bear. It is as close as I have been to four brown bears together intentionally or not. We stop and take a few photos. Glen waits until we are all ready to move together again, and we continue. As we descend toward a little pile of rocks on a bluff overlooking their fishing grounds, two bears lope off up a steep hill. The other two stick around. Glen recognizes the two that stay. "They are here frequently," he tells us. "I don't know the other two that ran off." I'm not sure how he recognizes them, but I trust him. He is calm. The nervous part of my energy subsides, though my heart still thumps with excitement. This is really cool—one of the coolest things I've ever experienced. I continue to take photos and video.

The bears have claimed a wide riffle. To continue upriver between two deeper stretches of water, spawning salmon have to swim through this shallow area. They have no real place to hide and no safe way past. The bear can chase them without having to swim. The larger of the two bears has a prime location. The second bear, slightly smaller and a tinge lighter in color, watches from a distance, looking frustrated. He tries to approach, but the bigger one charges him. The smaller one gets the message and leaves. The big one goes back to fishing. Five or six salmon make the run at one time, shooting upriver with their backs out of the water. I wonder if this is a survival tactic, running the gauntlet in large numbers. If so, it works. So many salmon rushing past at once seems to confuse the bear. It sprints a few yards after one fish, splashing through the shallows, and then sees a different fish out of the corner of its eye, changes its target, and bolts in another direction. The bear comes up empty and the salmon all make it. This goes on for several minutes, like some grand game of tag but with higher stakes. The bear's efforts so far are futile.

Finally, the second bear, unable to watch the ineptitude of his larger counterpart any longer, runs out into the water. Almost instantly the young upstart snaps up a salmon and turns to walk back upriver with dinner in its jaws. The dominant-but-unsuccessful bear isn't having that. It charges the upstart. The whole interaction takes barely the blink of an eye. The smaller bear gives up the fish at once and runs away. The bigger one, content to have gained the salmon, lets the other one escape unpunished. Like a playground bully that has just stolen the little kid's lunch money, it wanders up the grassy slope where it sits down to devour its meal.

With the playground bully now occupied, the smaller bear has the freedom to fish where it wants. Maybe that was its plan all along. It takes it less than a minute to snag another salmon attempting to bolt past. It takes a bite of the fish, doesn't like the bite, and tosses the fish off to the side with a big chunk missing. There are so many sockeye in the river, the bear can afford to be picky. If it bites one with flesh that is already too rotten, it tosses it aside. Though the bear now on the hill is eating the meat, the one in the river is trying just to strip the eggs out of the females. It also likes to play with its food. Both of these habits make for enjoyable watching. I could take photos all day, but after a while I stop and just watch. We pull out our lunches, and for the next hour we sit and enjoy the show. About as we finish our own lunches, the two bears finish theirs. They wander further downriver to the next bend, almost out of sight. It is now safer to be at the water's edge. I take my underwater camera down to the river and video the big school of salmon that have made it past the bears and now wait in a deep pool for the last part of their voyage.

The afternoon is waning. We start back toward the plane. We have a little time to fish on the way, but before long Glen begins to hurry us so that we will make it back to the lodge for dinner. The dinner awaiting is amazing and we are glad we returned. We look at each other's photos, and those of other guests at the lodge, and go to sleep satisfied.

+ + + + + +

A few days later I am back in Katmai National Park for a second time, chasing trout that are chasing sockeye salmon that have migrated up from Bristol Bay following finely tuned senses and instincts to the waters in which they were born. It is the final outing of our week-long stay at the Farm Lodge. Once again Glen is our pilot, but the setting is very different from our previous trip down to Katmai. We are on a small, unnamed river flowing into a much larger lake. It is easy to see and feel that we are at a lower elevation. This is not open tundra. No blueberries grow here. The shore is thickly wooded. The air is warmer and closer. There are also no bears visible, though the thickness of the trees makes us wary of them. This river is deeper and not nearly as clear. The bottom is silt, not gravel and rocks. One thing is the same, however: this river is also full of sockeye. They are schooled up at the mouth of the river. As we move upstream and find a shallower stretch, we see salmon spreading out and claiming their redds.

The same four of us spend the day on only a hundred and fifty yards of river. We begin casting near the mouth where it flows into the lake, but despite the presence of salmon we don't get any hits from trout. We bushwhack up the near shore, find a place to cross where the water doesn't quite reach our armpits, and continue up the opposite bank. We see clear signs that bears have been feeding. Fortunately, Glen is in front leading us. He stops suddenly. I look around for a bear. A half-eaten salmon carcass lies on the ground. Glen isn't looking at the woods or ground, however. He is looking to his right, into the water. "There," he says. "Two thirds of the way across, just off that sandy area." I follow Glen's gaze. At first, I

see what I have seen everyplace else in this river, and nearly every other river we have visited over the past week: several sockeye moving upriver or hovering over the bottom. I look harder, and see what Glen is talking about. A big rainbow trout sits behind a couple salmon on the far side of the current. Within a minute or two Glen spots three more rainbows, and he thinks a couple others are hiding below some bushes upstream, moving in and out of cover. This is the most trout I've seen together in Alaska.

Unlike in the clear, shallow, gravel-bottomed river we had visited a few days earlier, these trout act unaware of, or unperturbed by, our presence. We all begin to cast, each targeting a different trout. Glen fishes with a flesh fly: a pattern tied to imitate a hunk of rotting pink salmon meat that has flaked off a dead fish somewhere upriver and is now drifting downstream. It proves just the right fly, and he is the first to succeed, hooking and landing a rainbow trout easily over twenty inches long. We take a few pictures as he unhooks and releases the fish. Before I can even put my camera away, he lands a second rainbow trout on the same fly.

I still haven't caught a fish, so I sort through my fly box and pull out one of my flesh patterns. I think yet again what the effectiveness of such a fly tells us about this ecosystem—about how much of the nutrients in the water and soil have found their way inland in the form of spawning salmon. I repeat what has become a mantra: salmon are the life of this whole region. Of course, I also realize that this region is the life of the salmon. That is to say, I know just how important these spawning habitats are; the whole ecosystem of the ocean, and all the food we take out of the ocean, depends on places like this. And places like this are becoming fewer. I reflect on how important it is that Katmai National Park and Preserve exists and protects this water.

I also reflect on the fact that not all flesh-pattern flies are equally effective. I reflect on this because my pink flesh pattern fly is smaller and duller and doesn't elicit any strikes. Glen is still catching fish on his—at least until he breaks his line and discovers that the successful fly was the only one of its kind he had with him. While he looks for something similar, I give up on the flesh pattern and change to a big black egg-sucking leech that I created and tied experimentally a few weeks earlier in preparation for this trip. It has a big spherical head of sparkly pink chenille and a tail of black marabou. On my first or second cast, I elicit a strike from the rainbow I had been targeting. It misses my hook, but strikes again on a subsequent cast. I land the fish, release it, and soon hook another.

The rest of the day is like that. We move upstream to a sweeping gravel oxbow, long enough that we can all stand on the inside of the bend and cast without interfering with each other. Some of it is sight-fishing, but we explore a few deep pockets with flies. Over three hours, I land seven of the biggest rainbow trout of my life. The largest is a twenty-seven-inch long torpedo I spotted as a mere shadow lurking *almost* unseen behind a pair of sockeye. There are so many trout here that my fishing companions don't even bother moving upstream. The largest trout sits right in front of a log jam over the deepest part of the pool. It is also the wisest. All of us take turns casting for it, but none of us catch it. Though I'm wary of bears, I leave the others for a few minutes and explore upriver to the next corner. I catch another rainbow up there, and also miss one or two. A sockeye gets annoyed with my fly and snaps at it. Though sockeye don't really eat any more once they begin to spawn, and are thus notoriously difficult to catch fly-fishing, thanks to its aggression I end up fair-hooking the sockeye in the mouth and landing it. It is the first salmon I land on the trip, and also most likely the heaviest fish. I end up fair-hooking one more, a big deep red male with a huge hump and kype. I get a photo of it, in part because I'm proud to have landed it on a 5-weight rod, but mostly because I think it's a kingly-looking fish, and I know how important it is to this river, and how important this river is to it. I know also that the rainbow trout I've been catching wouldn't be nearly so big without these salmon.

Return to Trout Lake Cabin

Chugach National Forest, Kenai Peninsula, October 2017

Late evening light has bathed in gold the few stray clouds that blot the otherwise blue sky. Finally, the chilling wind that has been sweeping across Trout Lake through the late afternoon begins to die down. I gaze out the front window of our USFS cabin. To the south, across the lake, snow has dusted the top of the ridge line. Down the slope, gray rock speckled in white gives way to a mix of rock and lichen, then to grass, moss, and bushes that have already turned tan with the approach of winter. A few scattered scrubby spruce trees form a darker green contrast to the tan and brown. Down close to the shore, the trees grow denser and turn to a thick forest of spruce, poplar, birch, and alder. The spruce are still thickly needled but all the deciduous trees have cast off their summer attire.

When the day began I was still in Anchorage. At 8:00am, after our morning coffee but still before the rising of the mid-October sun, I was driving around the city with my nephews Brad and Michael and my friend Eric, doing a few errands before our three-day trip. The few errands stretched out two hours, and by the time we got onto the Seward Highway and completed the 90-minute drive around the Turnagain Arm of the Cook Inlet, and down to Cooper Landing on the Kenai Peninsula, it was nearly noon. We parked at the trailhead on the southern end of Resurrection Pass, loaded our packs, and started up the trail. A thin layer of ice still coated puddles on the trail. Though the midday sky was blue in every direction, the air was chillier than I'd expected when

I'd planned the trip several months earlier. Michael and Brad both donned hats and gloves, but I heat up quickly when I hike and usually end up sweating like a stainless-steel canteen of ice water on a hot day. I wore only a thin long-sleeve synthetic sweat-wicking tee shirt and a fleece vest.

The trail began near the edge of the famous Kenai River, but gained altitude quickly as it ascended the ridge bounding the Sterling Highway on the north. I was soon sweaty and contemplating removing my vest. The ascent was worthwhile, however. Stunning views of the valley and river, Kenai Lake, and higher snow-covered peaks surrounding the lake, opened up ahead and to our right. The white on the peaks was more than just a speckled dusting. Snow had fallen for real.

As we hiked, we saw several grouse warming in the sun on the ground or in low branches near the edge of the trail. They made little or no effort to avoid us. Here and there high bush cranberries clung tenaciously to branches. The bright red made them hard to miss. The duller red of rose hips also caught my attention. I didn't sample any rose hips—though I've heard one packs more vitamin C than a glass of orange juice—but I plucked a few cranberries for the tart burst of flavor. They were frozen and refreshing. I thought of my son who only eats grapes if they are frozen. The Alaskans I know feel the same about cranberries, opting not to pick them until after the first hard freeze has intensified the flavor.

When the trail reached the top of the ridge, it turned left and north, away from the Kenai River, and up along the rim of a gorge over Juneau Creek. By this time, my nephews had left the two older slower hikers behind. We had gone only a few minutes along the gorge, however, when we found them waiting for us. They'd found a spot for a lunch break with the best views yet of Kenai Lake and the Kenai Mountains. Soon after lunch we came to the waterfalls that are a destination for many day-hikers who start up this trail. For us, it was only about halfway. Above the falls, the trail crossed a bridge over Juneau Creek and climbed a small knoll.

The knoll was liminal. As the trail turned back north we entered a new landscape, leaving behind the big Kenai River valley and the open views off the ridge for a marshy alpine forest that stretched on relatively level for several miles, with rounded peaks looking down from both sides.

The knoll was liminal in another way also. The Kenai River is in many ways a big playground. The road along it is an RV Mecca. Ritzy lodges, private clubs, and guarded vacation homes are tucked away along much of its length. I've heard that on a typical summer day over 1200 boats will float the river. Countless more anglers will wade out from shore, casting for salmon and rainbow trout. Contrary to any idyllic images of wilderness fishing in Alaska, the angling on the Kenai is combat fishing. Near Soldotna the bank erosion from the heavy angling traffic is so bad that boardwalks have been built to provide fishing access, and it is illegal to enter the river except from these boardwalks. In Cooper Landing, both sides of the Sterling Highway are lined with businesses oriented to fishing and rafting: fly and tackle shops, guides, and restaurants and lodging that are mostly seasonal. From June through late August, even the cheap lodging is expensive. In October, when most of the salmon are rotting on the shore or their flesh has drifted out to sea, when most tourists have gone home, when a day on the river is likely to be interrupted by a snow squall, there can still be as many as four hundred boats a day.

But once over this knoll I have entered a new world. This is Chugach National Forest. Not that it is primeval. What Wendell Berry wrote about Kentucky is true even of Alaska: "It is no longer possible to imagine how this country looked in the beginning, before the white people drove their plows into it... The pristine America that the first white man saw is a lost continent, sunk like Atlantis in the sea." We are hiking on a trail. It is not a road. It is not the Sterling Highway. No RVs drive here. No iron plows turn this soil. Yet it is a human mark on the landscape. It impacts erosion, plant life and animal life. The trail has caused gullies.

Mountain bikers and horses as well as hikers have left their marks. Still, the impact is less here. There are no traffic sounds, motorized vehicles, or cell phone towers. There are no fly shops, restaurants, or inns. There is no pavement. The grouse by the trail do not risk getting hit by a car. The pristine continent is lost even in Alaska, but at least in this forest it may be easier to imagine. Maybe what is left might still be preserved from bulldozers, gravel pits, and, most importantly, mining operations. This habitat still remains for the moose, bear, and grouse. Humans come to this national forest to delight in the land. Though we leave some mark, we aren't here to ravage it for resources.

This liminal space, then, was where we left behind the more obvious signs of civilization and entered a space that felt more like wilderness—more like my images of Alaska. I could feel the change. I might have expected a cell phone signal during the first two miles of my hike. Once over this knoll, that no longer seemed a possibility. We kept walking. The trail got wet; marshes to our right drained down toward Juneau Creek, which wandered through the forest to our left.

Finally, we arrived at Trout Lake. Months earlier I reserved this cabin for two nights. I had been here once before in October. Though that previous trip was a week later in the month, it was also twenty degrees warmer. As I came over a small lip in the trail, I stepped into a headwind cutting across Trout Lake. The warmth I had generated on our seven-and-a-half mile hike faded, and the chill caused a shiver on my back. We dumped our packs in the cabin, and while Brad and Michael—at the recommendation of a USFS ranger I had spoken to earlier in the day—set off in the rowboat across Trout Lake to find firewood, I got a fire going in the wood stove with wood left by previous campers. By the time the younger men had returned, and we had cooked our backpacking dinners and purified water, the cabin was noticeably warmer.

Later, I sit enjoying that warmth as I watch the light fade. The tall hill across the lake hides the horizon where the sinking sun colors the afternoon. The sky shines more gold than red, though hints of pink touch the cheeks of clouds like blush. The whole day has been full of beauty and color, from the bright red of little berries to the jagged majestic peaks whose whiteness contrasted so stunningly with the perfect blue of the skies. It is one reason I have come here a second time, carrying food and a sleeping bag, to reflect and write in a primitive wooden cabin beside a lake in the mountains of Alaska in October.

For, if I must tell the truth, I'm not enamored with all aspects of backpacking. Even thirty years ago when my body was less stiff, I never slept especially well in a sleeping bag on a camp pad. Though backpacking meals have improved in the past three decades—and many things taste good in the wilderness after carrying a forty-five-pound pack—they are still inferior to anything my wife cooks. Cleaning up after a meal is harder in the wilderness with no sink. Getting out of my warm sleeping bag tomorrow won't be much fun either. And the biggest thing is that my knees and back are sore. Those are all aspects I endure because of the delight of being in a place like this. Some folks say that the journey is the important thing, and not the destination. When it comes to backpacking, that has never been my opinion. The journey may be enjoyable in and of itself, but the destination definitely motivates the work and sweat. And now I am in my delight. As the sun sets and the sky fades to black, my fellow travelers settle in next to the wood stove with headlamps and Kindles for evening reading. I sit at a table scarred by years of past guests cutting, cooking, and spilling food and drink. At 7:30pm it feels to me more like 10:30pm. Shortly after 8:00pm I give up my work and crawl into my sleeping bag.

✦   ✦   ✦   ✦   ✦   ✦

I have chosen the bed next to the wood stove. During the night, I arise to check on the fire. Though we packed the stove full before going to sleep, we are burning soft wood— mostly dead spruce and old poplar—and by midnight it has dwindled to a few embers. I sit up for half an hour getting the fire stoked and stove reloaded. I take a break from my fire-watching to step outside to look for Northern Lights, and to pay the price of foolishly drinking a mug of hot cocoa before bed. A couple hours later, the fire has died down again and I repeat this process. Later during the night, Eric wanders down from the loft and steps outside to look at stars. He comes back in, and with the aid of his headlamp fills the wood stove a third time.

By 5:45am my hips and shoulders have gotten too sore to lie in my sleeping bag any longer. I can feel that the air has gotten colder. I hatch from my cozy cocoon and check on the fire, and find that it has again burned down to embers. I am up for the day now. I gather the last of the wood we cut last night, and get the fire burning hot. I sit alone by the stove alternately reading, thinking, eating hot oatmeal, and drinking instant coffee. Two hours pass before my cabin-mates arise.

After breakfast, we talk about the day. Michael had planned to hike, but an old ankle injury has resurfaced and he decides to hang out in the cabin instead. We know we will need more wood before long. We have gone through an impressive amount in half a day. Brad opines that we could spend two hours gathering more just to keep warm for one more day. I think of how hard it would have been—and still would be—to homestead and live here. My whole life would be devoted to gathering wood and food for the winter. We talk about the merits of hunting moose and storing it for the winter as opposed to harvesting salmon. I think the variety of being able to eat both would be nice. I'd also want a lot of dried fruit. I'd have to make use of all the summer daylight hours in this northern land, I think.

As the sky lightens, the landscape fades back into view. The mountains and ridges look much the same as yesterday, but the lake is very different this morning. The wind has dropped to the faintest breeze. Only tiny ripples mar the reflection. A low thin fog creeps across the water shrouding it in mystery. I hear fish rising before it is light enough to see them. Eventually I see rings on the water. I think about fishing. I write instead.

◆   ◆   ◆   ◆   ◆   ◆

It is mid-morning. The sun has crept most of the way down the slopes, but the lake still lies in shadow and the fish are still rising. I rig up my fly rod and take the rowboat out onto the water to cast. I have barely had the time to strip line out for a single cast when I see water puddling up around my feet. I guess the problem at once and I lean forward to search for a plug and drain hole. I see the plug. It lies on the bottom of the boat, not in the hole where it belongs. Water is shooting into the drain in the opposite direction it is supposed to flow. I paddle quickly back to shore as more water pours into the boat.

My brother has often commented that Alaska offers many ways for a person to die. My life was not in any serious danger, but I really did not want to spend my day with wet clothes, nor have to hike back down to Cooper Landing wearing drenched hiking boots. I escape the rowboat with only one of my hiking boots getting partly submerged. I sit inside for a short time warming. I think of how much more caution I need out here.

An hour later, mist still clings to the surface of the lake. Brad and I take the row boat out again, this time with the plug in the drain hole. We both have our fly rods. A layer of hard white frost covers the metal seats, and our butts get cold and then wet as our warmth melts the frost. We paddle to where the fish are rising and watch them closely. They are hitting the surface hard, as though chasing some emerging insect. We see no insects, however. Whatever the trout are feeding on are very small—midges, or a tiny variety of mayfly perhaps. Some smaller fish leap completely into the air to grab them. I also see a few bigger noses break the surface. We cast streamer flies into their midst, but the rising fish are interested in insects and not in smaller fish, and they ignore our streamers. We troll around the east end of the lake, and when our butts are too wet from the melted frost we head in. The mist is beautiful.

The cabin is still warm, but we are running out of firewood. We eat an early hot lunch of freeze-dried backpacking food. Eric takes off with a can of bear spray for a hike to the next lake up the trail. Brad takes a nap. Michael and I take the row boat across the lake to get more firewood to last the next twenty-four hours. I bring my fly rod with me. I take off my streamer fly. I have not brought my full fly selection with me on this trip. I sort through what I did bring and select one of the smallest dry flies: an imitation caddis, and not a midge or mayfly. I don't think a picky trout will take it, and I'm proven correct. I make several casts near the shoreline in the lee of a gentle east wind where trout are rising on the calm surface. When it is obvious that the fly won't work, I put my rod down. Michael and I continue to the shoreline to where he found a fallen spruce log the day before.

Forty minutes later we finish loading the boat with wood. We start back across the lake. The wind shifts to the west and blows harder. The trout stop rising. After unloading the wood, I take my fly rod down the trail and spend a little time casting in Juneau Creek and its small tributary flowing out of Trout Lake. I don't have waders, so I'm restricted to fishing from the overgrown shore. I keep my hand on the bear spray and limit my excursion to a stretch of river within sight of the bridge. The stretch does not yield a meal, and I give up and return to the cabin. The wind has kicked up more, yet Michael is still interested in rowing so we head out in the boat again. This time he has the oars, and I sit in the back with my fly rod. I have tied on a pair of streamer flies behind a section of fast sinking leader to get my fly down below the white-capped surface. Michael works hard to bring us westward along the shore into the breeze. Every time his oars cut a crab I get slapped with a spray of cold water. Bundled in fleece and rain paints, with a fleece hat and wool Buff over my neck and ears, I keep my core body temperature from getting chilled. My fingers, however, sticking out the end of fingerless fishing gloves, grow numb. My hands take turns warming in my pockets.

When we get a third of the way up one shore, we cut across the lake to the opposite side, and then we let the boat drift. The wind still moves us quickly enough to keep my fly dragging behind us, but the fly sinks a little deeper. When we approach the cove I feel a strike and set the hook. The fish takes my line down. It does not leap or fight like a rainbow trout, which is what I had caught in this lake on my previous visit. I've read the lake also has lake trout, burbot, whitefish, and grayling. I wonder which I have. After a couple minutes, I pull in a lake trout. Half an hour later, we all sit around the table in the cabin sharing fresh trout with our backpacking dinners. The wind is brisker. The sun, though it won't officially set for a couple more hours, has already dipped behind the hill. In the evening we eat chocolate, read and write, and play cards.

When the dark has fully settled, we step outside to one of those unbelievable clear night skies. There is no light pollution for miles. The stars have bred and multiplied. The Milky Way is creamy smooth. The Big Dipper and the North Star are much higher in the sky than I'm used to seeing in Vermont, while Orion is lower and further south. The brightness and clarity of the stars gives a sense of a universe far vaster than the one I usually dwell in where cell phones expose us to an instant news cycle and the whole world is just a few pushes of a button away.

At 3:30am I arise and rekindle a fire from dying embers. The stars are still brilliant. If it weren't so cold—and if I didn't keep thinking about bears—I'd stay outside the cabin longer and watch them. When I awake at 7:00am, though it is still an hour and a half before dawn, the stars are gone. The sky has clouded over and the wind has kicked up again. I turn on my little set of string lights over my bunk, rekindle the fire yet again, and heat water for coffee and instant oatmeal which I eat by the fire while waiting for the others to rise.

It is too windy to boat or fish. Nobody wants to hike, either. We contemplate leaving, but the consensus is that three more hours at the cabin is greatly preferable to three more hours in the city. So after packing my gear I pull out my iPad. I write for a while, but my eyes are drawn irresistibly to the peak on the far shore. According to the USFS map left in the cabin, the mountain rises to 3940 feet above sea-level, which is 2681 feet above the lake. Even with the late October sun at midday height, shadows stretch down the steep slope almost to the water, etching the ridge in contrasts. Jagged rocky protrusions stick out like the white-tipped waves, making the mountain look even wilder. It would take real work to summit this. I continue to be thankful for the wildness of this place, for the fact that no roads or even any visible trails lead up the slope and no hotels mar its sides. In Vermont, this peak would be in a tie as the eighth highest mountain in the state. So I am disappointed at first that the map gives it no name, nor does it name the 3295-foot peak on the north side of the lake whose top—though still above the timberline—is smoother, less marked by jagged rock, and currently free of snow. Do we name things out of familiarity? Or do we name them only to tame them? I suspect this mountain does have a name, and that those more familiar with this place know it. Perhaps it is good that I leave without knowing it.

My eyes trace the steep slope down to the lake, whose English name at least I know. I think about the fish I found here, and the fish reported to dwell here whose mysteries I have not conquered. In New England, lake trout are generally found only in much bigger lakes. They are the only trout in North America that do not spawn in flowing water—the only truly *lacustrine* trout. The maps indicate that Trout Lake is only two miles long. It is tiny compared to many other lakes I've visited in Alaska: Clark, Skilak,

Kenai, Iliamna, or even Kontrashibuna or Ptarmigan. Though the biting wind roiling up white caps makes it feel bigger than it is, looking out the cabin windows I can see almost its entire body—all but a small cove at the outlet, which I could see if I stood out on the dock. Yet looking at the steepness of the slope dropping down into the water, I have no doubt that the map is correct in claiming the lake is 135 feet deep. Even in the warmer climate of New England that would be deep enough to hold lake trout. Today it feels both deep and wild, and though I would have enjoyed going out and fly-fishing, I am glad to leave here with a deepened sense of the wildness of this beautiful place.

Time to finish loading my backpack. Time to begin a hike out. Time to start wondering when I will be back in this national forest. Time to appreciate the fact that this place exists and is protected, and to hope it remains that way.

Alaska Epilogue:
October in Port Alsworth

Lake Clark National Park and Preserve, October 2017

It's mid-October, but it feels more like mid-November. When I pause too long between casts, ice forms on the guides of my fly rod. Instead of a fishing cap, I have a fleece hat pulled low over my head and a wool Buff over my neck. Although the autumn sun is low in the afternoon sky, I can feel its warmth on my back. I am thankful for it. As much as I enjoyed my stay in the USFS cabin on Trout Lake in the Chugach National Forest two nights earlier, I am thankful that I will sleep tonight in a heated guest apartment, and that I don't have to gather wood and build a fire.

I stand knee deep at the mouth of the Tanalian River where it spills into Lake Clark in the middle of Lake Clark National Park and Preserve, surrounded by jagged mountain peaks and almost surrounded by water. I think back more than two years to my first visit to this river, this village, this national park, when I stood fishing in the same place on an August day less than an hour after landing in Port Alsworth. The mountains look bigger and closer now than they did in August. Maybe it is the lower angle of the sun magnifying the contrasts of shadows, or the snow that bathes the peaks and etches the crevices. It is beautiful. It is cold. I am glad for layers of fleece and Icebreaker merino wool.

Once again, I am trying to learn more Dena'ina place names for this area from Karen E. Evanoff's edited volume *Dena'ina Elnena: A Celebration: Voices of the Dena'ina.*[9] I find it delightful and meaningful that the names in this language are descriptions. I may never learn to pronounce them properly, but the translations into English stick with me. I stand where this "flows into water stream" pours into the "place people gather lake". One thing I noticed about the hills upriver are several giant circular indentations. It looks like a giant or a god dropped some massive bowling balls from the sky. J.R.R.Tolkien or C.S.Lewis would have imagined giants tossing boulders, and named these hills after Old Norse or Old English words for giants, like the Ettinsmoor (in Narnia) or Ettenmoors (in Middle-earth). The Dena'ina called them the *Vahunqishdghuch'i*: the "ones with holes on it."

I have fished this spot several times in the past while staying at the nearby Farm Lodge. I have caught many grayling here— among the largest I have caught in Alaska. They are year-round residents of the Tanalian River. I've caught them at the mouth of the river, and upstream around the big plunge pool below the picturesque Tanalian Falls: the *nudghilen* or "waterfall". Yet grayling are not what first drew me to stay at the Farm Lodge two years ago. The fly-out trips to fish for rainbow trout and Dolly Varden char in Katmai National Park and Preserve and other headwaters of Bristol Bay are what draw most anglers to stay at

---

9 Karen E. Evanoff, Dena'ina Elnena. Except where noted, further place names in this section are from this source.

the lodge, and that was certainly appealing to me. Others come to view and photograph the amazing wildlife and scenery in two nearby national parks and the area north of Lake Iliamna: the caribou roaming the tundra, the salmon-eating brown bears, and the glaciers and volcanic peaks featured in Lake Clark Air's "fire and ice" tours. All of that was appealing to me, and certainly part of the draw.

I also first came to Port Alsworth two years ago because Lake Kontrashibuna holds Arctic char, a close cousin of the Dolly Varden. Even among the numerous species of the cold-water-loving genus *Salvelinus*, Arctic char are especially adapted to and dependent upon frigid northern waters. The circumpolar species is the northernmost freshwater fish in the world. Kontrashibuna is one of the few lakes in Alaska outside the arctic where they can be found near the surface in the summer. It is a still a mystery to me why the Dena'ina people referred to the lake as *Qenighishi Vena*, "boiling lake".[10] Unlike the Dena'ina people who named the lake out of intimate knowledge, I have spent only a half dozen days there in my life; I have experienced only a small portion of its area and a small sampling of its seasons. That is enough time to have become enraptured with its beauty and with the mountains with holes on them, but not nearly enough time to know that water.

I also first came because the national park boundary abuts the site of the proposed Pebble Mine. And I returned to Port Alsworth two years later—in August and again in October—primarily for those same reasons, and because of Glen Alsworth Jr. and the wonderful Farm Lodge hospitality. The grayling fishing

---

10 Lake Clark National Park and Preserve historian John Branson pointed out in a personal correspondence that the Dena'ina place name for Kontrashibuna Lake may also be translated as "lake in which water extends against the mountains," citing work by Albert Wassillie, Priscilla Kari, James Kari, and Andrew Balluta, "Dena'ina place Names In the Lake Clark National Park and Preserve Study Area," appearing in Chapter 7 of *Lake Clark Sociocultural Study: Phase 1*, Linda J. Ellanna, ed., Anchorage: U.S. Department of the Interior, National Park Service, Alaska Region, 1986.

was a pleasant surprise bonus. I would be happy to catch more now. What I am really hoping for, however, is to hook one of the bigger lacustrine or adfluvial trout of Lake Clark: a lake trout or rainbow or even a fat Dolly Varden, though I have read the latter are especially rare in this water.

When I was last here, sockeye salmon congregated by the hundreds at the river mouth, preparing for the final stage of their epic spawning run that had brought them from the salt water of Bristol Bay into this fresh water where they were born: sixty miles up the Kvichak River to Lake Iliamna, forty-five miles across Iliamna and into the swift-flowing Newhalen River, up the Newhalen into Six Mile Lake (*Nundaltin Vena*, the "lake that extends below"), and twenty miles across Lake Clark to the mouth of this river. Watching the bright red sockeye staging in the lake is particularly significant knowing they are the lifeblood of this ecosystem, including its human life. They have been present for as long as humans have inhabited these lands, and for a least a thousand years have been central to that inhabitation.

But summer is over, and the sockeye are essentially spawned out. A few strays may still cling to life, but most have died. If their flesh did not feed some lucky animal and is not decaying on the shore to provide nutrients for plant life, it is drifting back downriver to become food in the aquatic ecosystem. Sockeye flesh from some rivers will drift all the way down to salt water and feed halibut or Alaskan king crabs. As if to remind me of this, a few big sockeyes in various stages of dying or decay lie in shallow water along the gravel shore. A gray jay, its downy wings soft in the afternoon light, lands boldly on the gravel just a few steps from where I stand and pecks at the pink flesh of one dead salmon that has washed onto shore. It flies off with a bit of food in it beak to store under tree bark somewhere for a winter snack when the last of the rotting salmon is gone. A minute later it returns, still unperturbed by my presence and activity.

I return to my own business having to do with fish. I have two rods with me. On one I have tied a fly imitating a golden stonefly nymph, with a little bead imitating a salmon egg a few inches up the line from the nymph in case the grayling or trout are still watching for sockeye eggs drifting down river. On my other rod—the one now in my hand—I've tied on a peach and pink fly intended to imitation a hunk of rotting salmon flesh. Not very appealing to me, but the fact that it is a notoriously good fly this time of year is an indication of how much protein and nutrients these fish have brought up from the ocean into the freshwater ecosystem. Two months earlier, a flesh pattern was the hot fly of the day on a trip to Katmai National Park. There were far more salmon in the river then, however.

I cast the flesh fly for several minutes, letting it drift down the river current and out into the lake where people gather. I hook and release only one small grayling. In an effort to get my fly deeper, down in the water column to a big fish that doesn't want to expend energy swimming in the current, I cast into calmer water. The fly sinks like I want it to, but hangs up on a rock. I have to break it off. Uninterested in taking off my fleece gloves to tie on another fly in the sub-freezing weather, I wade back to shore and switch rods.

Drifting my stonefly nymph through a little pocket on the edge of the swift current, I get into a pod of grayling. Every second or third cast draws a strike. I land a few, but they are all small grayling, under fourteen inches. I move downriver and cast into swifter current and hook two bigger grayling, the kind that put a bend in my 5-wt rod and take me a few minutes to land. After I release the second one—a strong, hard-fighting grayling with light olive sides that shimmer in the emerald water—the sun disappears behind a cloud. The air turns colder. When another fly breaks off, I decide I've had enough fishing for the day.

Before I walk back along the lakeshore, I take out my waterproof pocket-sized camera and click a couple more photos of mountains. I know from maps and previous visits that the inlet directly across Lake Clark is Chulitna Bay. It extends out of sight toward the mountains, where it is fed by the Chulitna River (*Ch'alitnu*, the "flows out river"), which flows out of the proposed Pebble Mine footprint. I think again of the richness of this salmon-dependent ecosystem. Then I turn and walk back toward the hub of Port Alsworth and the warmth of a gas heater.

Later, after dinner, I sit looking out the window at the fading orange and purple of a brilliant sunset at the end of the runway where the ridgeline drops down to the horizon. The sun seems to be making up for the low angle and short duration of its trip across the sky by lingering for an extra-long time just below the horizon. Between the autumnal and vernal equinoxes, twilight lasts a long time here.

Night, however, lasts even longer.

Of Alewives, Salters, and a Heron named Honey

Reflections from Acadia National Park

"Bacchus," said Aslan. "Deliver him from his chains."
"That means the bridge, I expect," thought Lucy. And so it did. Bacchus and his people splashed forward into the shallow water, and a minute later the most curious things began happening. Great, strong trunks of ivy came curling up all the piers of the bridge, growing as quickly as a fire grows, wrapping the stones round, splitting, breaking, separating them. The walls of the bridge turned into hedges gay with hawthorn for a moment and then disappeared as the whole thing with a rush and a rumble collapsed into the swirling water.

–C.S.Lewis, *Prince Caspian*

A Wasabi Subaru and a Lightweight Canoe

Mid-May had come to the Maine seacoast. Forests were alive with color rivaling their more famous autumn foliage. Mixed with the varying evergreen shades of pine, spruce, hemlock, and cedar, the first newborn leaves of aspen and birch glowed more yellow than green, while maples still burned deep red with buds waiting to burst. A few scattered hardwoods had tiny blossoms as white as the wave tips on a windy Echo Lake.

185

Nearing the end of the first week of my three-week stay as artist-in-residence at Acadia National Park, I walked down to a grassy shoreline looking for a good place to launch a canoe for a paddle up a tidal marsh river with my wife. No houses stood in sight. The park's landscapes had largely escaped further development since its founding over a century earlier. Forests crowded the shoreline in all directions, and rose—dark green with soft but vivid yellow-green splotches I knew would fade in a week or two—up the steep slope of the ridge a few miles past the far side of the marsh. Several Canada geese, black and white and tan, paused from searching for delicacies in the bright green grass close to the water, and eyed me cautiously as I approached. A little farther away, I spotted the neck and head of a great blue heron as it waded through taller grass. Its beak might have blended with the sandy brown tops of the grasses, but its long white face and light neck contrasted with the darker red-brown background of the brush behind it which had not yet leafed out.

Over the previous week I had also seen osprey, bald eagles, kingfishers, loons, gulls, and numerous ducks hunting or swimming in various park waters. Yet it was the sight of the heron by the side of an undeveloped Maine river that cycled my thoughts back to how my current journey had really begun some forty-six years earlier. The story unfolding in my visit to Acadia tied back to so many other stories I had been hearing, learning about, and telling in the writing of this book. On this particular river, my thoughts returned—not for the last time—to May of 1972, and that earlier trip to Maine when I also saw heron, osprey, geese, and unfamiliar ducks, and where I first listened to the strange call of an American bittern and the mournful song of a loon. Although I'd never been to Acadia National Park before, when it came to my love of rivers and water, and the inspiration of places wild or almost wild, coming to Mount Desert Island felt like a homecoming.

＊　　＊　　＊　　＊　　＊　　＊

Designers or marketers at Subaru invented some glamorous color-name for the shade our Outback wagon, but my wife Deborah and I forgot it soon after we drove out of the dealer lot. "It's more wasabi mustard than green," Deborah said. The name Wasabi stuck. Two years later, for our thirtieth wedding anniversary gift to each other, we bought a new ultra-light Kevlar canoe we'd been dreaming about for a few years: a fifteen-foot long heron touring canoe made by Wenonah Canoe in Winona, Minnesota. At a mere thirty-eight pounds, it had only half the weight of the ABS plastic canoe we'd been paddling around Vermont the previous quarter of a century. We picked it up at the Contoocook River Canoe Company, a Wenonah dealer in New Hampshire, on our drive from Vermont to Maine at the start of my residency. It took its maiden voyage on a quiet brackish creek on the northeast side of Mount Desert Island, within sight of Acadia's iconic Cadillac mountain—not quite inside the park boundaries, but on a watershed draining its northernmost pond. I think the name *heron* subconsciously attracted me to the canoe model as much as its design, though the design did fit our paddling style. But we don't often refer to the canoe as "the heron". As she had done with Wasabi, Deborah also named the new canoe before it even left the dealer. As we effortlessly lifted it onto the roof of Wasabi—and wondered why we had waited so long to buy a lightweight canoe—the afternoon sunlight shone through the translucent golden Kevlar weave. Deborah commented that it looked like honey in comb. From that day on we would be paddling a heron named Honey. (We would also thereafter refer to the thirtieth anniversary as the "Kevlar anniversary.")

Honey looked good sitting on top of Wasabi as we wandered the roads of Acadia over the next three weeks. It looked even better paddling the park's various lakes, ponds, and tidal rivers. It was the morning of our fifth day when we parked at a dirt pull-off near Bass Harbor Marsh and I walked down to the water and spotted the great blue heron, our canoe's official namesake and the wading icon of marshes, beaver ponds, and quiet rivers. Though this particular river was a tidal marsh—an estuary fed by several small freshwater streams—the shoreline and surrounding forests looked similar to a few stretches of the Allagash Wilderness Waterway where forty-six years earlier a canoeing, fishing, and camping adventure with my father had sparked my imagination. The scene lacked only osprey, brook trout, and the mysterious call of a bittern. Before long, two of those three would make an appearance.

Anadromous Salters and the Streams of Acadia

But now my story is jumping all over the place. Memories have a way of jumbling a narrative. What brought me to this particular water known as Bass Harbor Marsh as part of my artist residency? As a narrative non-fiction writer with an interest in nature, outdoor, and environmental writing, part of my goal was simply to experience the park's many unique and diverse aquatic habitats: to be observant, attentive and curious, to watch and listen, and also to find delight. However, I did have a few topics I came particularly interested in exploring, all of which were related in one way or another to streams and lakes and cold-water ecosystems.

One topic I hoped to write about was the presence of salters on Mount Desert Island. "Salter" is a colloquial term for an anadromous strain of brook trout that move back and forth between salt and fresh water. In comparison with other species of salmonids with greater commercial value, salters have only recently become the object of much scientific study and of conservation efforts. Much is still unknown about them. What is known (and also lamented by many) is that salters (along with numerous other anadromous fish) have disappeared from many waters they inhabited up and down the North Atlantic Coast before European settlers cleared forests and built homes, farms, mills, dams, and roads with bridges and culverts.

Like all brook trout (and nearly all species of salmonids) salters spawn in fresh water: in streams that are small, clean, and cold. In late winter, however, they move down into saltwater, to estuaries and brackish waters where their freshwater streams flow into the ocean. That is to say, *some* brook trout in little coastal streams move down into salt water. Many do not; they stay put in freshwater habitats. Scientists are still unsure what causes only some of these stream trout to migrate to saltwater while others remain content in their shaded sylvan pools. They do know that in late spring, or early summer, the salters migrate back up the streams, and when they do they are larger than their cousins who stayed behind, thanks to the greater abundance of food in the estuarial homes.

Biologists have also discovered that even when the salters move to saltwater, they don't stay put there. They are not like salmon who head out to sea and roam for two or more years before their spawning drive brings them back to their origin streams. Rather, according to Acadia National Park biologist Bruce Connery, the salters move back and forth between freshwater and saltwater despite the metabolic energy it takes to adapt between the two habitats. They swim upstream during the day to avoid the numerous predators in the open spaces of the estuaries, and back down to brackish water at night to feed. Yet their time in food-rich estuaries is enough to change them: to help them grow bigger and fatter than their cousins who stayed upstream, and even to change their appearance. Although they remain identifiable as brook trout, with characteristic bright red and yellow circles on their sides, they can take on a mottled purplish hue, as well as sheens of salmon-like silver. Though the new coloration fades by late summer when they fully abandon the salt water, it is particularly evident in the spring.

This need to move back and forth between the two environments is part of what has made salters so vulnerable to development. Their increasing rarity drew my interest, prompting me to visit some waters where they live. Salters depend not only on cold clear streams like other brook trout, but also on unobstructed passage down to the sea and back. Yet their native range, from Long Island all the way up the coast of Maine, has been developed for centuries. Their little streams have often been dammed right at the edge of saltwater to form ponds, or to power seaside mills before the advent of internal combustion engines. Even streams too small to have been dammed for power, or which avoided being turned into a duck pond for somebody's coastal mansion, have been blocked by culverts in the inevitable spread of the web of coastal highways, local roads, and even driveways. As a result, salters have been extirpated or significantly compromised in many of their historic streams, especially in the southern portions of their range in Long Island, Rhode Island, and Massachusetts. Even along the less-developed Maine coast, their numbers and range have diminished.

The numerous streams flowing out of Acadia National Park have not been immune to this problem. Certainly, the stream-dwelling brook trout have benefited from protection afforded to their habitats by the national park. By and large, their streams have been left to flow through uncut forests with thick riparian buffers. The forest canopies offer shade to keep the waters cool, while the roots protect against streamside erosion that can make a stream too wide and shallow. The forests and undrained marshes also clean the water. Nonetheless, the trout of these Acadian streams—especially the salter populations—have not escaped unscathed. Our species has too often chosen to maximize short-term monetary profit, rather than long-term ecological health. Although it has never been an *ecologically* inexpensive approach, for decades the financially cheap and easy way to put a road over a creek has been to put in a round metal culvert. But culverts degrade habitat in numerous ways. When it comes to salters, the biggest issue is that—like bridges without natural stream bottoms—culverts block or significantly restrict fish migration. That migration is precisely what makes a salter a *salter* and not merely a brook trout that happens to live in a coastal stream.

While the numerous streams *within* the less-developed park are in much better shape than many other coastal streams, most Acadia National Park streams must still cross a strip of developed land outside the park's jurisdiction before reaching the Atlantic. Highways, towns, and private property circle the island almost entirely. The park's boundary reaches the sea along only a few miles of coastline on the southeast and southcentral shoreline. Even there, state highway ME-3 transects the park. Two miles of pristine brook trout habitat is of little use to a salter if the final quarter-mile that dumps into the sea prohibits passage.

OF BRIDGES, REAL AND METAPHORICAL

On a Tuesday afternoon during the second week of my residency, I meet Brian Henkel at the park headquarters on Mount Desert Island. It is midday and I'm dressed for a field trip. I have a bag lunch and multiple cameras in hand as well as my iPhone for recording conversations. The day has turned out to be another unseasonably warm one. Expecting a month of cool, damp, spring weather, I had come to the Maine coast with lots of fleece, sweaters, merino wool shirts and socks, and even long underwear. I need little of it. Even today, wearing long pants and a long shirt, both treated in permethrin to ward off ticks, I am overly warm.

Brian works as a project coordinator for the Wild Acadia initiative, a watershed-based approach to improving degraded ecological conditions and ecological integrity in and around Acadia. The project is a partnership of Acadia National Park, Friends of Acadia, and the Maine Natural History Observatory. Brian's training as a civil engineer with a focus on hydrology, and his fifteen-year background working on surface and groundwater issues, certainly comes in handy. Many of his projects involve bridges and culverts: the movement of water under roads, or roads over water. In particular, they involve replacement or restoration of old bridges to make stream crossings friendly for fish passage. The work of Wild Acadia, however, is not primarily about civil engineering. The building of bridges must be metaphorical as well as literal. To achieve their conservation and restoration goals, Brian must bring together a broad range of stakeholders including other conservation non-profits, local towns, faculty and students from the University of Maine and the College of the Atlantic, and Acadia National Park itself. Within our first fifteen minutes of driving and talking, I am struck by how Brian is simultaneously friendly, passionate about what he does, and knowledgeable— three traits I'm sure are important in bringing together diverse persons and communities.

Together he and I visit Cromwell Brook, a watershed near and dear to him because of both its potential and its problems. The brook gets its start tumbling over a dam out of Tarn Lake. It passes under the entrance road to the *Sieur de Monts* Nature Center, flows through the Great Meadow, then under the famous Loop Road out the park's eastern edge into the busy tourist town of Bar Harbor. After leaving the park it must pass under a road five more times in just a mile-and-a-half journey to the sea.

We start our tour at the lowest bridge where Cromwell Brook passes under ME-3, the major thoroughfare through Bar Harbor and around the eastern half of Mount Desert Island. The bridge is only a few hundred yards upstream of tidewater, near a little town park. It is the sort of place I spent countless enjoyable hours watching my sons play Little League baseball. A few blocks down the road toward the town center sits one branch of a famous local ice cream shop where my wife and I had savored unique gourmet flavors a couple evenings earlier. I'm inclined to think highly of the neighborhood.

At first glance the stream, despite its small size, looks pretty and healthy. The water is clear. Trees line both banks and even at midday the little brook flows beneath a leafy canopy of shade. A breeze blowing off the ocean adds to the feeling of coolness. As we look down into the water, a small fish snatches something off the surface in a little eddy behind a rock. However, the stream flows between an artificially-straightened stream bed armored with vertical stone walls. With its artificial banks, it does not meander as a stream wants to do. The bridge itself, which at a distance looks like it might go over a natural stream crossing, has a concrete bottom. Though better than a round metal culvert, that unnatural flat streambed widens the stream leaving no discernable channel. It is not a friendly place for a little salter to pass, particularly in low water. What would be better, Brian explains—short of replacing the entire bridge—is to cut a narrow channel out of the existing concrete bottom to offer a path with passable depth even in low flow conditions.

Still, salters have managed to inhabit the stream. We drive a short distance out of town, working upstream over two more bridge-crossings. In terms of stream ecology, these next bridges are in much better shape, and I learn why. Both have recently been replaced with natural stream bottoms—one in 2013 and one in 2017. They offer good cover and a natural channel. I wonder why more bridges over rivers and streams weren't built that way in the first place.

Brian parks the car at a dirt pull-off above that third bridge, and it takes me a moment to realize this is the confluence of two streams: Cromwell Brook and Kebo Brook. Here is where things get really bad. What appears to be a continuation upstream of Crowell turns out to be Kebo. Cromwell flows in from the side through a long narrow metal culvert angling underneath the road. It ends with a slight plunge into a pool where it dumps muddy water. At the confluence just below the culvert pool, the contrast between the silty Cromwell water coming through the pipe and the clearer water of Kebo is obvious in the seam where the two run alongside one another down a short riffle before fully mingling. A second longer culvert runs under the road just two-tenths of a mile up Cromwell. It would take a miracle for any trout to migrate through these gauntlets.

And yet, as I stand in the stream taking a photo of the mess, Brian calls out to me in a whisper-shout, making urgent hand entreaties to come his way. Intrigued, I climb up the bank. He leads me ten yards upstream. In the shadows on the near side of Kebo Brook, he points out a trout finning in the current, looking upstream for a meal to float her way. The fish looks to be at least ten inches long, and as we stand quietly looking at it through a gap in the trees, Brian announces with confidence that it is a salter. I ask him what—other than our proximity to the ocean—makes him think so. It's the size of the fish, he tells me. He references biologist Bruce Connery, who has assured him that wild trout in such a tiny stream never get that big without spending time in saltwater. Even a five-inch trout is big for a little Mount Desert Island stream.

I admire Kebo Brook for a moment. I admire the trout. I'm glad that any trout surviving passage this far up from the sea has the choice to follow Kebo rather than Cromwell. Yet even Kebo, though it has nothing like those two culverts on Cromwell, has problems. A trout continuing its migration upstream to spawning habitat in the park must cross a golf course, including passage through an artificial pond as well as open stretches with no canopy. That salters have still managed to survive in the Cromwell-Kebo watershed speaks of the tremendous potential of these streams, and helps explain why Brian is passionate about the opportunities to restore them by fixing the concrete-bottomed bridges, and replacing the old culverts—or even slightly rerouting a portion of road and maybe tying the two streams together further upstream. It's a dream project that could have tremendous benefit to anadromous trout.

A short way up the road, we enter the park and stop to gaze up Cromwell Brook across the Great Meadow by the Loop Road bridge. This meadow is another of the park's iconic scenes, and I can see why. It is beautiful. Even before I study the beaver dam just a stone's throw upstream, my eyes are drawn across the marsh grass, undulating in a soft breeze, toward the ridgeline running from Dorr Mountain to Kebo Mountain. It is painted in millions of tiny dots of numerous shades of green, yellow, red, and white like a flowery Claude Monet scene. It is such a pristine landscape, I think. The wild wetland must be a big reason why clean water can flow down Cromwell Brook.

Or so I imagine. Yet I'm also standing on top of a third culvert only two tenths of a mile above the second one. And even as we stand there, two park techs busily remove a beaver dam from below the footbridge just downstream of the Loop Road. So much for allowing the stream to exist in a wild state. That alone doesn't fully shatter my illusion that this is natural—not until Brian informs me that early developers of the area dug ditches in an attempt to drain this marsh. They thought marshes were a useless part of a landscape, and wanted to replace Great Meadow with a working orchard. Fortunately, the meadow was never wholly destroyed and the orchard never planted. Still, the drainage ditches remain, and likely prevent the Great Meadow from holding the amount of water it ought to hold, and thus also hinder it from fully doing its natural job of cleaning and protecting against downstream floods. Brian also dreams of one day filling those ditches to allow the meadow to return to something more resembling its natural state.

As we continue our tour, we talk more about the challenging and sometimes conflicting goals of preserving the park's cultural heritage—which includes, for example, the famous carriage roads as well as numerous stone bridges crossing little streams—as well as preserving or restoring ecological health to the park's streams, meadows, wetlands, and forests. "Bridging cultural authenticity with ecological integrity" is the phrase Brian uses repeatedly to describe his work with Wild Acadia. When we drive further up toward the sources of Cromwell Brook, and come to the edge of a famous garden, Brian shows an example of how both goals can sometimes be met with careful work: the project replaced an old gravel footpath with a new wooden path on stilts. While the old path degraded the water, and was repeatedly washed out by spring floods flowing down steep slopes, the new raised path follows the same historic route, yet it barely impedes the natural movement of water underneath.

I learn also that despite all the damage done to the watershed, cold spring water abounds above the meadow, and the upstream portion of Cromwell still holds native brook trout. This population has been aided by yet another bridge replacement on the *Sieur de Monts* entry road restoring a natural stream crossing. Perhaps only three long culverts—and maybe a concrete bridge bottom—stand in the way of salters returning to Cromwell Brook. Or, rather, such work would provide a way for Cromwell's remaining native trout that still hold the salter genes and instincts to find their way down to the sea.

THE GIFT OF GLACIERS

Meanwhile, I content myself with catching a few stocked brook trout from the park's numerous lakes and ponds. Over our first nine days, Deborah and I manage to get our new canoe onto nine different water bodies. Two were saltwater marshes or estuaries, and the third—though labeled on one map as a stream—was a little lagoon with three tributary streams. The rest of our paddles were on freshwater lakes and ponds. Before my three weeks finished, we would paddle even more waters, and also return to a couple favorites, including Bass Harbor Marsh where this oft-interrupted story began and will eventually return.

As I consider these lakes and ponds, I am struck first by the incredible amount of freshwater on Mount Desert Island caused and then left by the carving and then receding of glaciers. And I am struck second by their diversity and unique beauty. Islands and peninsulas are not typically known for an abundance of freshwater. On the Schoodic side of Acadia, just a couple miles away by gull-flight, not a single freshwater lake is to be found. Only a handful of tiny streams, some barely more than seasonal trickles, show up on the map, often flowing out of bogs too small to be named or mapped. Unless you look closely for those streams as you drive the one-way loop around Schoodic Head, you won't see them. Yet Mount Desert Island boasts twenty-eight water bodies fitting the Maine definition of a "great pond"—a natural inland water body of more than ten acres—as well as numerous smaller beaver ponds. And connecting these bodies to one another or to the ocean, or flowing out of wetlands and down to the sea, is an even greater number of little streams. Yet, though you can drive from the parking lot of any one of these ponds to any other in less than an hour—not counting delays for summer tourist traffic—

they are as different from each other as the freshwater streams that flow into an estuary are from the saltwater brought in by the tides.

On the east side of the island, we paddled Honey around the lengths of Eagle Lake (the park's second largest), Jordan Pond (the fifth largest), and Bubble Pond. Tests of Eagle Lake show it is clean enough to provide unfiltered drinking water for a nearby town, and Jordan is purported to have the clearest water in the state of Maine with a bottom visible at forty-six feet of depth. At one point while paddling at a swift pace down the west shore of Jordan thanks to a brisk tailwind, Deborah let out a panicked shout. "Rock!" Not wanting to gouge our new canoe, I veered hard right, and we passed by the rock without damage. The rock turned out to be about three feet below the surface—ten times deeper than any obstacle we had to worry about. The water clarity combined with the distortion cause by the waves had made it look *so* much closer.

Bubble Pond, like Jordan and Eagle, also sits between steep ridgelines in the shadows of Cadillac, Pemetic, and Penobscot Mountains. Bubble had more the feel of mountain tarn than a coastal pond. As we made our way upwind along the steeper eastern shore, we admired the ambitious and opportunist birch trees growing among massive boulders strewn along the shoreline. The contrast of gray rock, white trees, and the newborn yellow-green leaves was stunning. "It looks like a giant rock garden," Deborah said. Thinking of the Narnia and Middle-earth stories, I thought perhaps a giant's rock garden.

By contrast, Upper and Lower Breakneck Ponds—which lie a short enough walk north of Eagle Lake that it took us only twenty minutes to wheel our canoe in along the carriage road for an afternoon paddle—seemed like a different world. Their relatively flat shorelines, shallow silty bottoms, and marshy edges gave the sense I was paddling a large beaver pond rather than a named lake. That sense was amplified when I reached the far end and saw a beaver dam across the outlet and a large beaver house nearby. As we sat there, a beaver swam across the cove and disappeared into the house. And just a hop, skip, and jump east of the two Breakneck Ponds—though in a different watershed—another series of ponds are even more like beaver ponds and less like Eagle Lake. Indeed, before emerging to a confluence with Duck Brook, Halfmoon Pond drains into Witch Hole Pond through a pair of ponds identified on the map precisely as that: Beaver Ponds.

Deborah and I wheeled our canoe into Witch Hole for a sunset paddle one evening. Like most boggy waters we paddled including Northeast Creek through Fresh Meadow, it was dark and rich in tannin, more the color of tea than the tall glass of spring water that was Jordan Pond. I would have been surprised if it offered one tenth the visibility of Jordan. A pair of beavers made an appearance at dusk to entertain us, and a brook trout consented to strike the fly I paused to cast along the eastern shore near the outlet. Though nearly identical in size, the difference between Bubble Pond and Witch Hole couldn't have been more striking—except that I managed to find brook trout in both waters.

While in the smaller marshier ponds we caught sight of a few beavers, in the bigger lakes loons made frequent appearances. We never got out onto Long Pond on the west side of the park—which at close to nine-hundred acres is the biggest lake on the island—but we did manage to paddle the length of Echo Lake, another cold, deep lake west of Somes Sound. In the space of less than an hour, our journey took us from the lake's southwest corner and a steep narrow valley where the towering Beech Cliff plunged to water's edge, to a relatively flat northern shoreline where—unless we turned and looked over our shoulders—we didn't feel like we were in the mountains at all.

As we continued our circuit around Echo Lake and paddled back southward toward the car, I glanced up to see an eagle soar above Beech Cliff and out over the water. Almost at once, one of the loons we had recently passed began to cry out in an anguished call both more frantic and more prolonged than Deborah's warning about the rock. The cry went on for several minutes, and soon the loons at the far end gave an answering call that reverberated off the cliffs reminding us of the lake's name. I'm sure the loons were responding to the presence of the eagle overhead.

THE RESTORATION OF ALEWIVES

Their discomfort also reminded me of what I had recently learned spending a day with Park biologist Bruce Connery. On a Friday at the start of Memorial Day weekend, I spent a day with Bruce Connery, a National Park Service biologist working in Acadia. The plan, after spending time talking in his office at park headquarters, was to go on a field trip to three alewife spawning streams further down the coast where collaborative work had been done to restore fish passage. We were joining two folks from the Maine Coast Heritage Foundation, another from the Somes-Meynell Wildlife Sanctuary, an NOAA engineer, and some of Bruce's summer staff. These projects offered potential models for similar sorts of projects on Mount Desert Island—work that would take place outside the park, but with ramifications to the greater marine ecosystems as well as a potential positive impact on freshwaters within the park.

Though my own experience over the past few years writing about trout and salmon had made me more aware of Acadia's brook trout, salters are not the only anadromous fish that historically have made importance use of Mount Desert Island. Alewives (also known as river herring) and rainbow smelt also move from salt water to freshwater to spawn, while American eels have a catadromous lifecycle, beginning life in the ocean, moving into freshwater as adults, and then returning to the saltwater to spawn. Together, all the fish that spend time in both salt and freshwater are known as diadromous.

Among these, alewives are of particular interest. While brook trout have always held an important place in my own life, alewives are ecologically and economically far more important than salters. These fish, typically only about ten inches long, are food for *everything* up and down the northern Atlantic coast from North Carolina to the Saint Lawrence Gulf—from bigger fish like striped bass and cod, to the numerous sea and shore birds I enjoyed on my paddles around the various marshes. They are a key link between the zooplankton they consume and piscivores farther up the food chain. Some researchers have attributed some of the collapse of Atlantic cod, and their failure to recover, to the precipitous decline of a primary food source: alewives.

And this little forage fish not only provides food for much of the marine life in the Gulf of Maine; when they spawn they bring the nutrients gained from years in the ocean into freshwater rivers, streams, and lakes. The abundance of eggs they lay in ponds, as well as the 25% or more of the fish that die during spawning, all add nutrients to freshwater ecosystems, while the alewife fry are an important food fish for freshwater species like lake trout. Even terrestrial plants benefit as predators carry alewife carcasses onto land to rot, or defecate the remains of their meals onto the soil. Alewives are even believed to be an indirect but important link in the hoped-for restoration of Atlantic salmon. Huge schools of alewives used to spawn up some of the same rivers as the salmon at the same time the previous year's salmon fry headed downstream to the ocean underneath them. The abundant alewives provided an important cover to shield little salmon from predators. When the alewives disappeared from the rivers, then predators such as cormorants and gulls could focus on salmon fry.

Once again, my time in Acadia and the stories that emerged were linking back to other threads and stories running through this book, including stories taking place at the opposite side of the continent. Alewives and other herring are to north Atlantic ecosystems what salmon are to the north Pacific. Remove them, and everything collapses.

Which, indeed, is what has happened over the past nearly two centuries. Although by the middle of the 19th century, the negative impact on salmon and alewives of migration-blocking dams was already being addressed by state legislations, dams and roads continued to be built. As the number of rivers with viable alewife runs decreased, harvest pressure on remaining rivers grew. One 1953 Department of the Interior bulletin on "Fishes of the Gulf of Maine" states that 16,400,000 alewives were taken in New England in 1898, weighing a total of about 8,800,000 pounds.[1] Two years earlier, 5,832,900 alewives were reported taken from rivers and streams on the coast of Maine. Fifty years later, the catch in Maine had dropped to one third. And by the end of the 20th century, the fish had nearly vanished from many Maine rivers once holding historic runs. Only a handful of famous runs remained.

At the start of the day, Bruce shared an interesting insight with me. In the past few decades, bald eagles have made a remarkable comeback on the east coast. The comeback has been so successful that some residents and visitors to Maine now want to reduce the number of bald eagles. Eagles have been preying on the young of many other much-loved coastal birds like blue heron and loons, causing a significant population decline. As a lover of loons and heron, I'm sympathetic. But I'm also struck again by human arrogance and short-sightedness. I think of bounties put on native

1 Henry B. Bigelow and William C. Schroeder, "Fishes of the Gulf of Maine", Fishery Bulletin of the Fish and Wildlife Service Volume *U.S. Department of the Interior: Fish and Wildlife Service* 53:74 (1953) http://www.gma.org/fogm/ Pomolobus_pseudoharengus.htm, accessed May 26, 2018.

Dolly Varden trout in Alaska last century at the initiative of the salmon industry because it was believed that trout consumption of salmon eggs or young salmon had a detrimental impact on salmon populations. Or I think of the historical efforts to get rid of wolves in order to increase populations of elk in the Rockies, or caribou in Alaska. Even in Maine, there is resistance to restoring alewives in some rivers, not because of the costs of bridge or culvert repair to restore migration, but because of a fear that alewives in a pond will hurt the recreational bass fishery. I wonder how I might be blind to my own selfish desires to have "nature" fit my whims, and ways those desires have impacted me.

Natural systems are very good at tuning themselves, and retuning throughout continual change—particularly when the change happens at natural scales, and not the sudden time scales caused by human tinkering with ecosystems. In the case of the decline of herons and loons, Bruce pointed out that the real culprits are not eagles, but the factors that caused the decline of alewives, or have slowed their recovery. Bald eagles are fish eaters. Even as recently as the 1980s, Bruce spoke of one raptor specialist who reported that approximately 50% of the diet of a Maine-coast eagle was fish, which in May and early June meant easily accessible alewives in their spawning streams. As if to illustrate that point, when our field trip arrived at one of the streams where alewives were spawning, we learned that four eagles had been feasting streamside on alewives the past several days. The remnants of their meals were visible in the decaying half-eaten fish on the shore. Because of the decline of alewives, however, today only 15% of a coastal bald eagle diet is fish.

I'm excited, therefore, to tag along on the trip to visit some recent migration-restoration projects. At the first location, the problem had been a restricted stream flow and steep gradient caused by a highway bridge. The second two projects involved revisions to migration-blocking dams. In all three cases, a series of weirs had been built from natural rock to create a passable stream. All three projects appeared wildly successful. Spawning alewives filled each river when we visited. In some pools, fish swam so thick I couldn't see the bottom of the stream only a foot or two deep. One encouraging aspect of the projects, and similar projects on Mount Desert Island, was the number of organizations that collaborated, including federal government agencies (National Park Service, and the NOAA), national conservation groups like Trout Unlimited, regional conservation groups like the Maine Coast Heritage Trust and the Somes-Meynell Wildlife Sanctuary, and town governments.

Bruce had also spoken of similar projects that had already taken place in Acadia National Park and Mount Desert Island within the past decade. Working with a U.S. Fish and Wildlife biologist and stream passage engineer, between 2006 and 2010 they completed geomorphology research and basic engineering plans for a number of important fish passage projects. When the American Recovery and Reinvestment Act was passed in 2009, it opened up an opportunity for funding. Since the research and design had already been done, Bruce was able to move quickly on the funds and in 2010 and 2011 they completed five projects impacting Cromwell Brook, a tributary of Stanley Brook, two branches of Hunters Brook, and Storm Beach Brook. Since then, with help from the NOAA, they have been able to complete eight more projects to reclaim crossings and improve migration and stream habitat. Among the additional beneficiaries were the small cold-water tributaries to Bass Harbor Marsh.

STALKING SALTERS BY THE SEASHORE

One morning after sitting on a wharf watching the dawn break over a quiet Bar Harbor at low tide, smelling the sea, and listening to lobstermen load bait into their boat—possibly alewives, a favored lobster bait—my wife and I drove to Hunters Beach Cove and the confluence of Hunters Brook with the Gulf of Maine. There we ate a picnic breakfast, and enjoyed the sunrise a second time as light slowly crept down the rock on the west side of the cove. Then, while my wife sat on a log and read, I wandered upstream with my six-foot six-inch three-weight L.L.Bean fly rod. It's a small rod I use mostly for fishing tiny mountain streams overhung with alders, and not a rod one would think of using to catch an ocean-going fish. And Hunters Brook *is* a tiny mountain stream, flowing off the southwestern slope of Cadillac Mountain and the southeastern slope of Pemetic, through a thickly wooded narrow valley. It also happens to be a mountain stream in which one can catch a trout while listening to lobster boats. Though it does have to pass under ME-3 at the recently restored crossing, Hunters Brook benefits from being one of only a few on Mount Desert Island to flow from its source to the sea without leaving park protection.

There is little about the outlet of Hunters Brook that looks like an estuary. At the edge of the beach, where the woods meet the rocky coast, the stream ends in a pool thirty yards long and four or five yards wide. The upper end of the pool sits in the cool shade. A small grassy meadow, full of wildflowers and poison ivy, adorns the shore at the lower end where the pool is open to the sky. There the stream leaves the pool, disappears beneath rocks, then reappears to trickle down the beach to saltwater ten feet lower in elevation. No real stream exists for a trout to swim down or up. Even if a trout managed to reach the ocean, it would not have found an estuary; Hunter Brooks' little current of freshwater is immediately overwhelmed by the vastness of the sea and the crashing of incoming waves. I guessed a single ocean swell held more saltwater than the volume of freshwater flowing out of the stream in several hours. But then I looked at the seaweed sitting on the rocks at the outlet, and I realized that the pool itself was

the estuary. At higher tides, the incoming waves break into the pool, and salt and freshwater intermingle.

I spent an hour exploring up into the woods. I caught one little trout, and saw a few more. I had dressed warmly for a chilly dawn, but the day had broken unseasonably warm and I was sweaty when I returned to the beach to join my wife. I felt a little disappointed not to have seen any brook trout I could be *sure* were salters—though a hint of mottled purple suggested that one I caught had spent time in saltwater. As we started back up the path to the car, however, I caught sight of a fish rising for insects in a little pocket behind a fallen log on the far side of the pool, right where the stream left the trees. Though I'd been hoping for salters, I'd not taken many casts in the estuarial pool simply because from the trail on a high bank I'd looked over the clear shallow water quite carefully—or so I'd thought—and not seen anything. Now I put my rod back together and went back down with a little dry fly that might pass as one of the mosquitoes buzzing around. A minute later I gently held a little salter in my wet hands. I caught and released one more before departing.

The three trout I caught that morning at Hunters Brook were beneficiaries of the work that had been done upstream to make it possible for them to get to their spawning habitat. So too, I suppose was the kingfisher that might someday make a meal out of that little salter. I thought back on the projects I had visited to help restore alewife migrations, and the ones Bruce and his partners at the Maine Coast Heritage Trust, the Somes-Meynell Sanctuary, and the NOAA hoped to do at Seal Cove Pond. Collectively, those alewives will provide forage for more creatures than just a few kingfishers. For the most part, the streams up which alewives migrate are different than those of salters. Alewives spawn in freshwater ponds, like Somes Pond. The streams are just paths—or, in the case of alewives, congested highways—to get from ocean to pond, and back again. Alewives can't handle some of the higher-gradient streams trout spawn up. For these two reasons, many streams where salters spawn are of no use to alewives. On the other hand, trout need water that is colder than that of many alewife streams. Still, the problem is one shared among these two, and many other diadromous species: dams and culverts blocking migration around Mount Desert Island, and up and down the New England coast.

Bass Harbor Marsh, and the Restoration of Narnia

Those stories—the near-mythical salter brook trout I had heard about for many years but had never seen, the spawning alewives and their importance to the marine, freshwater, and even terrestrial ecosystems, the efforts to protect and restore both these and other diadromous species by restoring their migration streams, and the experience of New England's only national park—had flowed together in a confluence. So there we were paddling Honey up Bass Harbor Marsh trying to reach the top of a tidal water where five cold streams flowed together to form a brackish estuary, and where kingfishers and osprey hunted, and where I would make acquaintance with a salter. It was perhaps the most work I'd done in a long time in order to catch a fish less than seven inches long

It also proved to be a beautiful paddle. In the wide marshy expanse at the start, we could see the slopes of Bernard Mountain, Great Notch, and Mansell Mountain, the sources of the cold streams that fed this estuary. Though at first we could hear trucks passing on ME-102, the traffic noise soon died out. As with our previous canoe trips in Acadia, we had the water to ourselves—at least with respect to human boaters. At the recommendation of somebody at the Hulls Cove Visitor Center I'd timed our paddle to start a couple hours before high tide so that we might ride the incoming tide, and to be sure we'd have enough water to navigate the shallow marsh. The advice proved moot. The ME-102 bridge over the outlet of the marsh had narrowed the stream flow so much that—like Northeast Creek which we paddled on our first day on Mount Desert Island, which had also been artificially narrowed by a concrete bridge—Bass Harbor Marsh never fully drained. As I would later learn from Brian Henkel, the water level fluctuated only about eighteen inches despite Gulf of Maine tides that are among the highest in the world. Not until near the peak of the tide does water in Bass Harbor rise enough to push through the bridge into the marsh. The good news was that even at the lowest point in the draining of the marsh, we had enough water (though just barely) to paddle. The bad news was that no incoming tide pushed us upstream, and we had to battle a wind.

In our first couple days in the park, we had already paddled deep lakes, small lily-pad filled ponds, and one other tidal marsh. This water was unique. For the first half of the paddle, the marsh stood open and windy. Even beyond the wide river, more grass nearly doubled its width. Ducks, spooked by our paddling, rose up and disappeared into those grasses, presumably landing in some hidden pool or slough. I guessed that particularly high tides—perhaps at full moons—flooded those grasses.

Slowly, though, as we worked upstream the wood drew closer on both sides. The river channel narrowed and deepened. We could dip our paddles into the water without hitting the mud. The wind made only a gentle sough. An osprey left a roost at our approach and moved upstream. More ducks fled, and I felt guilty to be the cause of their wasted energy. A second osprey soared overhead. Kingfishers moved along the shoreline, chattering noisily.

As we moved further up and further in, the river began to bend more sharply, winding in oxbows so tight I could easily toss a rock across to a next bend that we would have to paddle ten times as far to reach by canoe. From time to time we paused as my wife patiently allowed me to cast flies imitating little forage fish to deep undercut banks. Nothing struck my fly. Still the river narrowed, and the trees grew closer. Our view of the distant mountains shrunk. The wind faded altogether. When the river was barely wider than our new canoe is long we reached the end of our voyage. A beaver had built a dam across what was now not much of a river but just a stream.

No more than two years after the Allagash trip had spurred my love of wilderness and rivers with the mysterious calls of bitterns and loons, my imagination was nourished in yet another way: my mother introduced me to the Narnia stories. C.S.Lewis spoke to my nature imagination through my literary imagination. Talking animals and talking trees and even sentient rivers pointed me to a world full of enchantment, where humans lived in harmony with nature as opposed to exploitation. Peter, Susan, Edmund and Lucy have not been together in Narnia more than a few hours in *The Lion, the Witch and the Wardrobe* before they see their first beaver dam, and are welcomed into the beaver home by the memorable Mr. and Mrs. Beaver. It's hard for me to see a beaver dam and not think of that scene, just as it is hard for me to use the phrase "further up" without it becoming the "further up and further in" of *The Last Battle*, the final book in *The Chronicles of Narnia*. It's hard for me to paddle a marsh like Bass Harbor and not think of Puddleglum, the brave and morose eel-eating Marsh-wiggle from *The Silver Chair*. Puddleglum, I think, would be appreciative of efforts to protect and restore diadromous American eels.

Reaching this dam, however, meant we had reached the end of our voyage. There wouldn't be any further in or further up. *Was it also the end of tidal water?*

Though this beaver dam marked the end of our paddle, it also suggested the likelihood of finding a trout. Of course, a trout trapped above the beaver dam, not free to migrate downstream, would not be a salter. Still, I love beaver dams. They play a different role in Lewis' world than the artifices of human construction. The former are *part* of nature. The latter are often meant to *tame* nature. When I co-wrote my book *Narnia and the Fields of Arbol: the Environmental Vision of C.S.Lewis* with David O'Hara, Dave got to write the chapter exploring *Prince Caspian*. So, while both our names are on all the chapters, I quote from his words describing a scene when Aslan comes to free a river.

> Consider several of the steps taken by Aslan and the Old Narnians when they restore Narnia and rescue it from its oppression. One of the first acts in this restoration is the tearing down of the bridge of Beruna. Aslan himself orders this. "Deliver him from his chains," he tells demigod Bacchus, which Lucy correctly understands to mean the deliverance of the river from the bridge. This act is both symbolic and practical. It is symbolic because it is a man-made edifice (like a dam) that gives the Telmarine humans more power over nature; with a bridge, they don't have to cross at a ford and thus are not at the whims of the river and its water levels. When the bridge is destroyed, people may cross only in harmony with the water. The destruction is also symbolic because it is done by the forces of nature, namely huge trunks of ivy—although with their work sped up considerably by the power of Bacchus so that it takes a matter of a few moments rather than decades or centuries.[2]

I think of the negative impact of dams and culverts, and also of bridges—especially when poorly made with little consideration for the rivers or streams they cross. I wonder if this Narnian bridge was like that. I love the picture of Bacchus, at the command

---

2 Matthew Dickerson and David O'Hara, *Narnia and the Fields of Arbol: the Environmental Vision of C.S.Lewis* (Lexington: University Press of Kentucky), 2009, pp.57-58.

of Aslan, using the power of nature itself to free the river from human construction meant to tame it.

At the beaver dam, we pulled our canoe out of the water and ate a picnic lunch in the grass. Then I wandered upstream. I had gone barely a dozen steps when I saw a "T" ahead of me, with streams flowing in from opposite sides. Though I'd not been here before, I recognized the scene from maps and satellite photos. This spot had been my destination from the start, and I had reached it. I looked into the water wondering if I might be able to spot some trout and get underwater photos with my GoPro. The water, however, was too deep and dark with tannins. I could not see the bottom, nor could I see any fish. So I pulled out my fly rod as an alternate method of enticing a fish in for a photo. I walked a short distance upstream and took a few casts, still with the little fly imitating a bait fish. A trout chased my fly, but missed. It chased it again and missed again. Then it wised up and ignored my offering.

A moment later my wife called me back. A trout was rising right above the beaver dam where we'd eaten our picnic lunch by the canoe. I tied on a dry fly imitating a little mayfly and laid it against the far bank where the trout had risen. A minute later I gently held in my hand a little brightly-colored brook trout, no more than seven inches long. It had the silver sheen and purple blotches of a salter. Or was that only my imagination? I was fishing above the beaver dam in freshwater, not saltwater. I fished a little longer up one of the tributaries, where I found yet another beaver dam, bigger and newer. I saw a few more trout, and spent a wary hour trying to entice them, but they proved even warier. I landed only one more small brook trout.

As I walked back down to the canoe and to my wife who sat reading, I realized that patches of soft dirt I'd walked through an hour earlier now lay under water. The tide had come in and the water had risen. The little beaver pond now looked even darker, not just with tannins but stirred up with silt. I glanced at the dam. When we'd arrived, it had sat above water level, causing a drop of about a foot to the outlet. Now tidewater had risen right over the top of the dam. Bits of seaweed rolled around in the water. The incoming ocean had reached us. The entire little beaver pond I had been fishing, and where I had caught two trout, was now saltwater: an estuary. The trout I had caught were, indeed, salters.

Half an hour later we paddled back down the marsh. In theory we were riding the outgoing tide, but again thanks to the bridge, the minimal change in water level made any current barely noticeable. As we loaded Honey back onto Wasabi, I thought again about dams, bridges, and culverts, as I would continue to do for the next couple weeks of my residency roaming the lakes and ponds, hiking and biking trails, and even the loop roads of Acadia.

I thought of how nature ultimately rose up and tore down the Bridge of Beruna in *Prince Caspian*—though with a speed accelerated many times by the power of Bacchus. Tearing down all the bridges and dams across the United States is not a practical nor even desirable option, of course. But continuing to remove a few where possible, and making the effort to repair or replace other bridges and culverts, is vital—as is making significant changes in how we build them. That will require more metaphorical bridge-building, and valuing long-term ecological health (that impacts us all) rather than short-term economic profit (that benefits a few). And that principle goes far behind just bridges and culverts.

As with the Bridge at Beruna in Prince Caspian, I think that if the human race doesn't do something, maybe nature itself will—with the blessing of Aslan himself.

Epilogue

On the Restoration of Wild Brook Trout, and Non-Federal Lands

———

Late morning on a crisp June day, almost two years before my residency at Acadia, I arrived on foot at Baker Pond with my wife Deborah, my brother Ted, my sister-in-law Susie, and our eighty-pound black lab Coda. We walked along the shore beneath a canopy of spruce and fir. The scent of the woods, decaying spruce needles padding the floor, the mix of conifers and deciduous trees, the blending of steep ridges and rounded hills, and especially the tea-stained tint of slightly acidic water reminded me of childhood visits to the Allagash Wilderness Waterway a few hours north. I half expected to hear the *galloot* of a bittern, or see a prehistoric-looking great blue heron sail silently overhead. The sparse understory allowed glimpses of rounded hills on the far shore where dark conifers gave way to the lighter greens of mixed deciduous trees, then back again to dark green farther up the slope. Brisk wind stirred the treetops and rippled the water, but the pond was too small and protected for whitecaps.

Although it was a three-hour drive north of Mount Desert Island, the property around Baker Pond would connect to my time at Acadia National Park in two important ways. One was via waterway, a connection an anadromous salmon would appreciate.

Baker Pond is a headwater of the Penobscot River, some 120 river-miles upstream from where the Penobscot River flows into Penobscot Bay, very close to two alewife restoration projects I would visit while at Acadia. Small beaver ponds in the hills feed Baker Brook which flows through Baker Pond and out the other side, down into Mountain Brook Pond, which flows out through Mountain Brook into the West Branch of the Pleasant at a confluence a short walk upriver from the Appalachian Mountain Club's Little Lyford Lodge where Ted, Susie, Deborah and I were staying.

As the West Branch continues south, it gathers more waters from brooks all over the AMC property. Five miles downriver, it plunges into the canyon known as Gulf Hagas, then on into Silver Lake. Downstream of Silver Lake, it becomes the Pleasant River, which flows into the Piscataquis River, a major tributary of the Penobscot River, the largest watershed in the state of Maine. The West Branch of the Pleasant once had a run of Atlantic salmon, but the building of countless dams on the Penobscot and Piscataquis killed the run, as it did on so many other rivers in New England.

Alhough Atlantic salmon have long been gone from most of their historic range, recent projects to remove the Great Works and Veazie Dams along the Penobscot, and revise the Howland Dam on the Piscataquis, have helped improve access to over 2000 miles of water for the endangered salmon, as well as for alewife and other anadromous fish. The projects have, in theory, made it possible for salmon to once again make it all the way to Gulf Hagas. I wonder if that will ever happen. I hope it does.

Above Gulf Hagas, the West Branch is strictly wild native brook trout water. Like the little streams on Mount Desert Island, the brooks on the AMC property have also benefited from restoration work involving old bridges and culverts, which is another connection between the properties as least with respect to the essays in this collection.

✦　　✦　　✦　　✦　　✦　　✦

The trip to Baker Pond was not strenuous, though it did have several components that made it feel more adventurous. Our day began at Little Lyford Lodge, an historic wilderness lodge dating back to 1874, and one of three AMC lodges on their 66,000-acre property in the old Katahdin Ironworks district of the 100-Mile Wilderness. After Ted and I took a dawn fishing excursion to one of many beaver ponds scattered around the property—and gained first-hand evidence that it was loaded with small wild brook trout—we returned to the lodge to join our wives for a hearty breakfast. The four of us then loaded our dog, lunch, fishing gear, and borrowed AMC paddles and life jackets into the car and drove down old gravel lumber roads to the trailhead.

Only a few hundred yards into the woods from the trailhead, we came to Mountain Brook Pond and spotted the AMC canoes locked to the trees by the shore. Mountain Brook Pond is slightly larger than Baker Pond, our final destination, and offered similar views of rounded hills topped by stands of dark evergreens. Once we got Coda settled into the canoe—and not threatening to spill us—we took the next half an hour to paddle leisurely around, exploring the shallow lily-padded cove on the marshy eastern side near the mouth of Baker Brook. Deborah kept an eye out for moose, but saw none. Eventually we pulled the canoes onto shore opposite where we put in to begin our mile-long hike following the contour of Baker Brook up a gradual ascent to Baker Pond.

Part of the hike took us along a section of old lumber road that the AMC had recently retired in their Aldo Leopold-like conservation efforts to restore ecological health of a property once ravaged by mining and forestry. Learning more about that effort, and seeing it firsthand, was part of what had brought me there. The previous evening, AMC land manager Steve Tatco and programs manager Casey Mealey had taken me out on a short tour. The 66,000-acre property is split over two watersheds. The smaller northwest portion includes tributaries that feed the Roach River, a well-known fly-fishing-only catch-and-release trophy brook trout and landlocked salmon stream flowing west into Moosehead Lake. Medawisla Lodge sits near the outlet of Second Roach Pond, offering a good base for fishing the trophy section of Roach River and exploring the headwater ponds and little streams. The larger southeastern portion contains all the headwaters of the West Branch of the Pleasant, a watershed that may prove important to the recovery of salmon downstream, though I had come more to learn about the restoration of brook trout habitat.

One of the AMC's goals for the property is to protect the riparian corridors of the Roach and West Pleasant rivers, and restore habitats not just for fish, but for everything dependent on aquatic life. Though the management plan still allows sustainable forestry in places, 24,000 acres are completely protected from lumbering or motorized vehicle use. By 2016 when I first visited, forty of one hundred and twenty miles of inherited gravel lumber roads had been retired—"put to bed" as Steve called it—and numerous old metal culverts had been removed or replaced. Learning about these provided an introduction to the projects I would visit two years later in Acadia. In addition to restricting fish passage up important spawning tributaries, the culverts also caused flooding, siltation, and warming of water. On sections of retired road, the culverts had been removed altogether to restore natural stream flow. Where roads still needed to cross, however, they had to be replaced with bridges or bottomless culverts with natural, unrestricted stream bottoms. The typical cost of one replacement was $25,000. The work had been done in collaboration with the Natural Resource Conservation Services of the USDA (which provided both engineering services and cost-share) and the Maine Department of Inland Fisheries and Wildlife, with grant support or partnership from that Nature Conservancy, Orvis, Sweet Water Trust, Trout Unlimited, and Patagonia. More than eighteen miles of new upstream brook trout habitat, including important spawning water, has been opened up as a result.

On our evening tour, Steve and Casey showed me a couple places where culverts had been replaced. Standing on the bank and looking down into the water, we had spotted little brook trout finning in the current or darting into the shadows at the appearance of our silhouettes. They also pointed out trails that led to some active beaver ponds—secrets Ted and I made use of—as well as suggesting our excursion to Baker Pond.

＋　　＋　　＋　　＋　　＋　　＋

A short distance up the shore of Baker Pond, we came to a shaded picnic table. Several classic green Old Town Discovery canoes with the AMC logo lay cabled together to a nearby tree as they had down at Mountain Brook Pond. After a drink and snack, Ted and I rigged up our fly rods. We dialed in the AMC combination, unlocked the canoes, and carried two to the shore. For the second time that day, Deborah and I enticed Coda into our canoe, and we followed Ted and Susie out onto the water so that Ted and I could cast flies for wild Maine brook trout while our wives generously paddled us about.

Once on the water, Deborah, Coda, and I made a quick exploration up a narrow channel where Baker Brook flowed in. Though deep enough for a canoe, it was barely wide enough to paddle. The water was still, and the bottom silty. If there were trout there, we spooked them before I caught a glimpse. We backed out and headed into the open water.

I had lent my nine-foot 5-wt rod to Ted whose fly-fishing gear was still in storage from his recent move back to Maine from Alaska. I fished with a little 3-weight rod, which proved hard to cast in the wind. Out of laziness I started with the caddis imitation already tied on from the morning's beaver pond excursion. I took a few casts into the calm water in the lee of the shore. A small trout came up, looked disdainfully at the fly, and turned away. The wind caught our canoe and pushed us out. I decided it was not a good day to fish a dry fly. Ted was drifting a heavy black leech pattern down deep, hoping to entice bigger trout up from below. The strategy seemed reasonable. As I searched my box for something similar, my fly line fluttered downwind and landed my caddisfly on the surface. Before I had a chance to swap flies, a brook trout slammed it. I pulled the fish in next to the canoe and admired its beauty. It stretched only a little more than the length of my wrist to the tip of my middle finger. No trophy, but it was bigger than anything I'd caught that morning in the beaver pond. I knew also that it was a wild native brook trout, almost certainly free of the genes of hatchery-raised fish. Here, in this pond I now paddled— in the fish I held briefly under water before I gently released it— was some of the past and the future of Appalachian brook trout.

For the next hour, Ted and I had steady action casting from our canoes. I landed at least a dozen trout on my caddis fly, all around the same size. When we got tired of fighting the wind from the canoe—and our wives tired of paddling us around, and Coda got bored and threatened to capsize us—we moved to a large flat boulder on the edge of some deep water. There Ted and I spent another hour casting, landing another eight or nine fish between us.

✦   ✦   ✦   ✦   ✦   ✦

At times, I couldn't help but wonder what my brother thought of the experience, casting for fish that could almost lie in the palm of my hand. Although we had grown up fishing together for brook trout in small Maine streams thirty-five years earlier, he had just spent the past eight years living and working in Anchorage. He'd been fighting Alaskan salmon and trophy-sized Kenai River rainbow and Dolly Varden which could have swallowed whole the little Baker Pond brook trout. Yet he took the same delight I did in the beauty of the place, and of the fish, and knowledge of the restored hope for the wildness of both.

As evidence of his delight, after dinner I had no trouble persuading him to join me for one more excursion. Though we were approaching the peak of mosquito-hour, we hiked ten minutes into another beaver pond, larger and older-looking than the one we'd fished in the morning. The hill across the pond still shone bright green in late evening light, but tall white pines towered over us and over the spruce near the shoreline, leaving us in shadows. In the dusk the water looked almost black—not pollution-black or oily black or muddy black, but a black suggesting mysterious hidden depths: black from tannins and a bottom covered in years of decaying organic matter; black from the darkening sky. The bleached skeletons of dead trees, likely killed years ago by the dam-induced flooding, added to the feeling of mystery, and to the promise of a big trout lurking under a log.

Other than standing atop the beaver dam, it would have been impossible to fly fish from the shore. Thankfully, the AMC had another canoe locked up there. We slid it down into the water, and paddled out. And we caught fish. The brook trout were fat, numerous, and hungry. They rose for imitation mosquitoes and caddis flies. They swirled out from beneath logs and snapped at black wooly bugger leeches. It was the best action of the day. As dusk settled, it got even better. For the last fifteen minutes of daylight, fish rose all around us. Any reasonable cast to a rising fish elicited a strike. Though we hooked a few smaller trout, many were close to a foot long and had backs so dark green they looked black in contrast to their impossibly bright red spots.

It was hard to quit. A kingfisher was working the same water. Ducks paddled around, keeping a safe distance. A beaver made an appearance and checked us out. The mosquitoes checked us out also, but though we were glad for our insect repellent attire it was far from the worst infestation I've fished in. I'd thought the morning beaver pond looked great. This, however, was far and away the best *Castor canadensis* water impoundment I'd ever fished.

Before our departure the following morning, Susie and Deborah took a long walk with Coda along the shoes of Little Lyford Pond while Ted and I took one more outing with our fly rods down to the river. On the AMC property near its headwaters, the West Pleasant is a small river—too small to float a canoe on. It has a mix of long slow pools, undercut banks, and shallow riffle. Big boulders stick up every few yards. Near the lodge it was not much more than three rod-lengths across, ranging from shin to knee deep in the riffs, and waist deep in a few pools. It is shaded by a thick canopy and often straddled by high banks, alders, or thick brush. When we arrived at the end of a long June day, the water temperature had been only 50°F.

Unlike the windy ponds where I felt underpowered, the river was perfect for my L.L. Bean 6'6" 3-wt fly rod. A few mayflies were coming off the water. I've read that Maine has more than a hundred and sixty known species of mayfly. The actual number is likely at least a hundred and eighty. There was a typical smörgåsbord of varieties present on the West Branch, but no single species that could constitute a hatch, and no signs of rising fish. A few caddis were coming up also, and so I tried a fly imitating one of them. It succeeded in fooling a few trout as I worked my way downstream back to the cabin, delighting in the beauty of the place, the presence of wild fish, and knowledge of the work being done to protect them.

At mid-morning we had to pack up our car and begin a long drive back to Vermont. That 2016 summer trip, however, would be only the first of four to this AMC property over the next twenty months. I would return with my family for two winter lodge-to-lodge cross-country ski trips making use of eighty miles of groomed woodland trails, and September of the following year I would return with my brother to visit the Roach River watershed.

+   +   +   +   +   +

As I finished this final essay of *The Voices of Rivers*, I spent some more time looking at maps of the AMC property. I want to return there and explore more. Just as the alewives of the Gulf of Maine depend on spawning habitats like Somes Pond, or the restoration projects I visited near Penobscot, I know that the trophy brook trout in Moosehead Lake, Maine's largest freshwater body, depend on a few high-quality spawning streams like the Roach River, which in turn depends in part on the protection of its headwaters up in AMC lands. I'd like to return to the Roach River in late September. I'd like to get down into Gulf Hagas some time, too. I could spend a whole month, or even a whole summer, exploring the hike-in mountain ponds. Whether I return there or not, however, I'm delighted to know the place exists, and that so much effort continues to be poured into conservation. I want to support that effort.

Most of the essays in this book have been set in national parks and national forests. I didn't set out with that goal. However, I did want to write about places that are wild or almost wild or returning to wildness, and especially about rivers in those places. I am drawn to rivers as I am also to wild places. And, as it turns out, most of the remaining wild and protected places in our country are on public lands: in national parks, wildlife refuges, and in national forests also, especially portions managed as wilderness.

So that is where I ended up spending my time. And the more time I spent in those places, the more I became convinced of their importance as places of protection and preservation. Not the least of the reasons is the importance of protecting the waters that flow through and out of those places of wildness and wilderness. Though the system is not perfect, our national parks, preserves and wildlife refuges, and in most cases our national forests, do that superbly well—and in a way nobody else can.

This chapter on the Appalachian Mountain Club property was the exception. The 100-mile Wilderness property at the Old Katahdin Ironworks is a notable and in many ways exemplary conservation and preservation effort of a private group—or, rather, a collaboration of many private groups, also working alongside state and federal groups. Like the management of some public lands, it hasn't been perfect. A couple years before my first visit, an AMC project on a headwater pond of the Roach River resulted in a small disaster. Contractors constructing a new dam did not have a failsafe in place on the water pump generator needed to keep a minimum flow out of the pond and into the Roach River. When the generator went down, a portion of the river dried up for half of a hot summer day. A generation of salmon and trout fry upriver from First Roach Pond died. Though the fault could be pinned on the contractor, the AMC accepted some of the responsibility for having failed to monitor the project closely enough. That failure, however, was one of process and not intention. The project ultimately provided the ability to *improve* year-round water flow through sections of the stream that could get overly warm and low on hot dry summers by impounding more water in the spring when flow was high and releasing it gradually over the summer. Nonetheless, the blunder raised the ire of numerous anglers.

That misstep aside, however, the AMC management of the property has resulted in a tremendous improvement in habitat not only for native brook trout, but for all wildlife—while keeping the property open for recreational use and in places for sustainable and economically viable forestry. As already noted, the protected headwaters of the West Pleasant could prove vital for the return of salmon in years to come.

I have no problem with the sort of work that the AMC is doing on their 100-Mile Wilderness property. I am encouraged by it, and by their small-footprint wilderness lodges, which operate off the grid. I think the ecological benefits are tremendous. We could use more projects like this. I hope for more. Every time I hear about a similar project—a local land trust or conservancy that acquires land to protect a wetland or watershed, or a project supported by Trout Unlimited—I get excited. They are an important *part* of the solution. But only a part.

The shortcoming of the project is not in its goals or approaches, but in scale. The AMC property spans 66,000 acres. It's a vast area compared to my house lot. It has days' worth of hiking and cross-country skiing trails, and enough lakes and ponds and miles of stream for months of exploration. Yet that is only enough to protect the upper headwaters of one small tributary of a tributary of the Penobscot watershed, which—though the largest in Maine and second largest in New England—is but one of many rivers in the state, the region, the country. Compare that with even a large state park in Alaska. Chugach State Park has roughly half a million acres while Kachemak Bay State Park—managed as wilderness—has 400,000 acres. Lake Clark National Park and Preserve covers 4,000,000 acres. Granted that those are all in the vast landscape of Alaska. But even Glacier National Park in Montana covers roughly a million acres, with a total of three million counting adjoining national forests. The scale is smaller in New England. Acadia National Park, at 50,000 acres, is smaller than the AMC property. But the Green Mountain National Forest across the street from my house spans 400,000 acres. The White Mountain National Forest, which crosses from

New Hampshire into Maine, is almost 800,000 acres. It would take more than twelve AMC properties to equal just the White Mountain National Forest in size. As I hinted at earlier in my essays on Glacier National Park, those national parks and forests are the scales needed for conservation efforts in this country to protect not just little streams, but whole ecosystems and rivers and populations.

Is that sort of scale of conservation possible in the private sector where economics so easily pushes owners to extract value?

✦   ✦   ✦   ✦   ✦   ✦

More than two decades ago, my father's family gathered for a reunion in southwestern Colorado at a cabin owned by his sister on the shores of Vallecito Reservoir. I have three lasting memories of the trip. One is of the car ride down to Vallecito and back from Longmont, Colorado with Ted and his family in their rumble-seat station wagon. On the six-and-a-half hour drive down, we stopped for a night at a motel in the mountains. Ted and I got up the next morning and fished for an hour and a half at the nearby Arkansas River, which was running high with spring snow melt. I caught a half dozen trout casting in the little eddies against the shoreline where the fish were taking shelter from the high water. On the way back, however, we not only had a long backtrack and detour when an eighteen-wheeler jackknifed causing a closure of a narrow highway, but two of the three kids in the car got the stomach bug.

My second memory is of getting hooked in the lip by my brother as we stood on opposite pontoons of our aunt's boat casting for rising cutthroat at the mouth of the Los Pinos River where it flows into a cove on Vallecito. It is the only time I have ever been seriously hooked by a fly. Ted was casting a #14 olive elk-hair caddis and apparently tried to change the direction of his forward cast in the midst of his back cast. The result was a sort of whip-like motion of his fly line, redirecting it around my cheek where I stood on my pontoon. I had about a second or so of anticipation knowing what was about to happen, but not enough time to do anything except yell twice—once in a failed warning and once in response to the penetration of the fly into my lower lip. Most likely, it all just came out as a single loud yell. After going back to the reunion cabin and showing my new lip piercing and corresponding adornment to my wife, I had to drive forty-five minutes down to the Durango hospital to have the barbed fly removed. That experience is one of the memories that prompts me to crimp the barbs off my flies for the sake of the lips of any fish I might catch.

My third memory is of heading out to do some river fishing with Ted on the Los Pinos upriver from the reservoir. We drove for miles along Colorado 501 looking for any access to the river, but were blocked by a steady line of fences and strongly worded "No Trespass" postings alongside signs to places like *Wilderness Trails Ranch* and *Ranch Teelawuket*. Growing up in the East where rivers and streams are considered public right-of-way as long as you stay within the river bank, I was not used to western water rights where somebody who owns both banks of a river can claim the river bottom also, and even rights to some of the water in the river. I got the bitter taste of that then. Though we were surrounded by the San Juan National Forest, the little corridor along the river was a plot of old private land within the forest. The owners had claim to the river, and they did not allow anglers.

Knowing that the road led to a public trailhead into the national forest, we pressed on all the way to the end—all the while looking longingly to our right at a gorgeous river valley inaccessible to us. We arrived at the trailhead on the San Juan National Forest, glad finally to have reached public access to the river, only to read a sign at the parking lot that there was no public access to the Los Pinos for another three miles. With only a couple hours to fish before we were expected back for dinner, and having already used time puttering along looking for a place to fish, we didn't have time to hike another several miles. We gave up and drove back to the cabin in defeat without having wet a line.

About two hundred miles north of Vallecito, near Colorado's border with Utah, sits the High Lonesome Ranch. I first learned of this ranch in June of 2017 while serving as artist-in-residence at Glacier National Park. I was reading Chris Dombrowski's fascinating and beautifully written book, *Body of Water: A Sage, a Seeker, and the World's Most Alluring Fish*. My friend Phil Brodersen had given me the book, along with a loan of his RainSong carbon fiber guitar, so I would have access to music and literature during my month-long mostly-alone stay in a cabin. The book at first glance may be an odd place to learn about a ranch in Colorado. *Body of Water* takes place in the bonefishing community in the East End of Grand Bahama. Yet it is about fly-fishing only in the sense that Norman Maclean's *A River Runs Through It* is about fly-fishing. It turned out to be a very appropriate read for a stay at Glacier, and not only because Dombrowski had worked as fly-fishing guide in Montana.

I mentioned the problem of scale: private lands devoted to conservation don't exist at the same scale as national parks and forests. *Or do they?* High Lonesome Ranch near Grand Junction is a guest ranch that portrays itself as being devoted to a land stewardship ethic in the model of Aldo Leopold. At roughly a quarter million acres, it is big enough to be the 12th largest national park in the United States. I had also never heard of it until 2017. Dombrowski gives some of the history of ranch. To create the ranch, CEO and president Paul Vahldiek purchased several privately-owned properties adjoining Bureau of Land Management lands until the BLM lands were surrounded and no longer accessible—in other words, until the public lands ceased to be usable as *public* lands. As to how a private group could purchase so much property, Dombrowski notes that the High Lonesome Ranch owners are "some of the wealthiest people in America" having invested some ten million dollars each.[3] This may be one of the reasons I'd never heard of the ranch.

As I learned more, I found myself sharing some of the skepticism Dombrowski expresses regarding "a land ethic that bastions large chunks of public land away from the public."[4] My thoughts flashed back to my family reunion some twenty-five years ago and my drive along the Los Pinos River in our failed attempt to find any place we could cast—a failure I have since repeated in other western states.

Yet there are reasons to be hopeful about a property of this size with any serious commitment to conservation. The fact that Vahldiek is a board member of Trout Unlimited's Coldwater Conservation Fund certainly makes me more inclined to think highly of him. Plus, the BLM lands he was able to take away from public use are a very different thing than our national parks or even national forests. Unlike Glacier National Park, or the Popo Agie Wilderness area in the Shoshone National Forests, or any other of the numerous national parks and forests I've visited in the past decade, BLM lands are not managed as wilderness or conservation lands by any stretch of the imagination. Indeed, I've often been critical of the management and exploitation of BLM lands over the past two or three decades, since I've been old enough to pay attention to news stories. As for other concerns about the privatization of so much land, *Body of Water* raises an important point.

---

3 Chris Dombrowski, *Body of Water*, (Minneapolis: Milkweed Editions, 2016), pp. 149, 159.
4 Dombrowski, p.150.

The truth here, like every important truth, is complicated. If Paul Vahldiek hadn't purchased the lands that comprise the [High Lonesome Ranch], much of the government-owned tracts would likely remain cattle-hammered, mine-shaft-shunted disgraces to land management; the truth is that Vahldiek has largely proven that for wide-scale conservation to truly take root in contemporary Western states, it must lead to some economic benefit; further, much of Vahldiek's private land purchases were from older ranchers whose own descendants either couldn't afford the inheritance taxes on the land, or might have quickly parceled up the ranches for resale; what's more, if Vahldiek hadn't kicked them off, Shell and Chevron would likely be wreaking a fracking havoc on the ecosystem and its watershed.[5]

As I wrote this final essay, I pondered contacting the ranch and trying to arrange a visit before the publication of this book. My schedule, and the schedule for this book, probably would have prohibited it anyway, but my real hesitancy was more a matter of personal integrity—an issue of my own vulnerabilities. At the cost of several thousand dollars the ranch charges for a visit of a few days, the option of a paid trip was not in my budget. One look at the website makes it clear that the ranch caters to a very wealthy clientele. Their quarter million acres of wilderness is not being conserved for *everybody*. On the off-chance they had invited me for a free stay, I certainly would have loved the trip, the property, the experience, and especially the fishing or hunting or whatever I did there. It sounds exactly like the sort of thing I'd want to be a part of if I had an extra ten million dollars to invest. I'd be lying if I said I've never dreamed of owning a large stretch of private trout stream. I'd certainly want to do all within my power to protect the ecological health of the watershed and to make sure that the water

5 Dombrowski, p.153.

flowing out of my property into the next property remained clean and cold. But I'd be continuing to lie if I claimed that I wouldn't consider posting at least a few favorite stretches of river to have to myself. How easy it would be to praise the High Lonesome Ranch, if suddenly I was one of the elite few with access to its lands, even if only for brief while? How much more difficult to write anything objective about the possibility of important large-scale conservation in private hands?

Again, I think of Dombrowski's comment about the High Lonesome Ranch's claims:

> It all sounds wonderful, and who doesn't love Leopold, but I reckon my reservations would be tempered if I were on a high lonesome of my own, a real bender, oblivious to the fact that the 'future generations' [to benefit from the conservation] are most certainly the relations of those who can afford to frequent such a colossally expensive place; and if I didn't know that the powers that be at the [High Lonesome Ranch] could at any time, if they so wish, begin the parcel-by-parcel sale of the property, or develop it to their own specifications.[6]

Though I am glad that the current owners of High Lonesome Ranch profess a concern for the restoration and preservation of the property, and at least for the time I'm intrigued by the possibility of a private stewardship model of that scale seeking to preserve wilderness, it is the final comment above from Dombrowski that perhaps most gets at my fears of entrusting the important task of conservation to a private organization like High Lonesome Ranch—a property owned by a small number of very wealthy investors who all have financial stakes. It is a concern I don't have to the same extent for a non-profit outdoor and conservation organization like Appalachian Mountain Club.

---

6 Dombrowski, p.152.

It is a concern we also should not have with national parks, forests, and wildlife refuges. They provide both the scale we need for conservation in this country if we are to have clean water and clean earth and large mammals living on the continent in years to come, and the protection from being sold off or developed parcel-by-parcel at the whims of the owner.

Or do they? The irony, as I write these final few pages, is that the current administration in Washington has just passed a new tax plan and issued presidential orders that collectively call for the parceling off of public lands for exploitation. Does this book end with a cliff hanger—like the final episode of the season of some popular television series? In a year, when this is finally in print, what will we see? How much damage will have been done, and how difficult will it be to undo that damage? Have I just written a hymn of praise to the great wild lands and rivers? Or have I written a eulogy? I hope and pray it is not a eulogy.

ABOUT THE AUTHOR

Matthew Dickerson was a June 2017 artist-in-residence at Glacier National Park and a May 2018 artist-in-residence at Acadia National Park. He is the author of several works of fiction and creative non-fiction, as well as literary explorations of mythopoeic literature with a particular focus on environmental aspects of the writings of J.R.R.Tolkien and C.S.Lewis.

His previous narrative non-fiction nature writing includes several books about rivers and the trout that dwell in them: *Downstream: Reflections on Brook Trout, Fly Fishing, and the Waters of Appalachia* (2014), *Trout in the Desert: on Fly Fishing, Human Habits, and the Cold Waters of the Arid Southwest* (2015), and *A Tale of Three Rivers: of Wooly Buggers, Bowling Balls, Cigarette Butts, and the Future of Appalachian Brook Trout* (2018). His most recent novel is a work of medieval historical fiction titled *The Rood and the Torc* (2014), set in 7th-Century Europe and inspired by a fragment of the medieval poem Beowulf. He is also the co-author of *Ents, Elves, and Eriador: the Environmental Vision of J.R.R.Tolkien* (2006), *Narnia and the Fields of Arbol: the Environmental Vision of C.S.Lewis* (2009), and *From Homer to Harry Potter: a Handbook of Myth and Fantasy* (2006).

Dickerson has also written essays for several periodicals ranging from literal journals to fly fishing magazines, including: *Written River, Image, The Other Journal, Middlebury Magazine, Books and Culture, Creation Care, Eastern Fly Fishing,* and *The Drake.* He is a professor at Middlebury College in Vermont where he has had affiliations with the Computer Science Department, Environmental Studies Program, Writing Program, and the New England Young Writers Conference at Bread Loaf.

Visit him at
www.matthewdickerson.net and *www.troutdownstream.net*

WAYFARER

BASED IN THE PIONEER VALLEY, MASS.

At Wayfarer Books we believe poetry is the language of the earth. We believe words—shaped like rivers through wild places—can change the shape of the world. We publish poets and writers and renegades who stand outside of mainstream culture—poets, essayists, and storytellers whose work might withstand the scrutiny of crows and coyotes, those who are cryptic and floral, the crepuscular, and the queer-at-heart. We are more than just a publisher but a community of writers. Our mission is to produce books that can serve as a compass and map to all wayfarers through wild terrain.

wayfarerbooks.org

www.ingramcontent.com/pod-product-compliance
Lightning Source LLC
Chambersburg PA
CBHW021715120626
46545CB00004B/1566